Edited by Robert Hedin & Gary Holthaus

The Great Land

Reflections on Alaska

The University of Arizona Press / Tucson & London

The University of Arizona Press
Copyright © 1994
The Arizona Board of Regents
All rights reserved

♾ This book is printed on acid-free, archival-quality paper.
Manufactured in the United States of America

99 98 97 96 95 94   6 5 4 3 2 1

Library of Congress Cataloging-in-Publication Data

The Great land : reflections on Alaska / edited by Robert Hedin and
Gary Holthaus.
    p. cm.
    ISBN 0-8165-1417-8 (acid-free paper). —
    ISBN 0-8165-1437-2 (pbk.: acid-free paper)
    1. Alaska—Civilization.   2. Alaska—Description and travel.
  3. Alaska—Tours. I. Hedin, Robert, 1949–   . II. Holthaus, Gary
H., 1932– .
    F904.5.G74   1994   93-43506
    917.9804'5—dc20   CIP

British Cataloguing-in-Publication Data
A catalogue record for this book is available from the British Library.

Contents

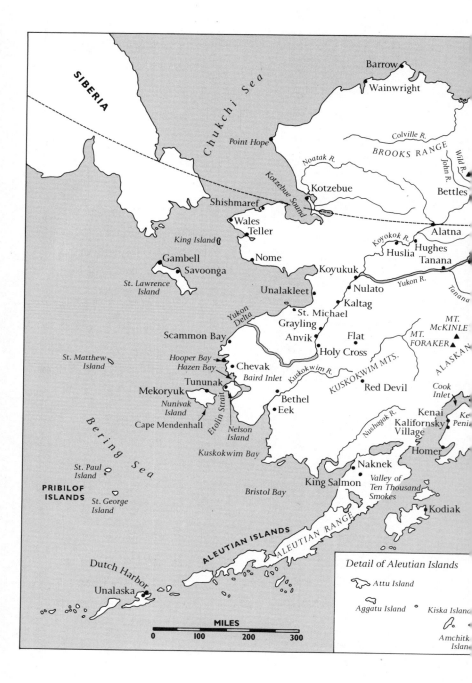

SIBERIA

Chukchi Sea

Barrow
Wainwright

Point Hope

Colville R.

BROOKS RANGE

Noatak R.

Wild R.
John R.

Kotzebue Sound

Kotzebue

Bettles

Shishmaref

Wales
Teller

Alatna

Koyokok R.

Hughes
Huslia
Tanana

King Island

Nome

Gambell
Savoonga

Koyukuk

St. Lawrence
Island

Unalakleet

Nulato

Yukon R.

Tanana

Kaltag

Yukon
Delta

St. Michael
Grayling
Anvik

Flat

MT.
McKINLE
MT.
FORAKER ▲

Scammon Bay

Holy Cross

ALASKAN

St. Matthew
Island

Hooper Bay
Hazen Bay

Chevak

Baird Inlet

Kuskokwim R.

KUSKOKWIM MTS.

Red Devil

Cook
Inlet

Tununak

Mekoryuk

Nunivak
Island

Cape Mendenhall

Etolin Strait

Bethel
Eek

Nelson
Island

Nushagak R.

Kenai

Ke
Peni

Kalifornsky
Village

Homer

Bering Sea

Kuskokwim Bay

Naknek

St. Paul
Island

King Salmon

Valley of
Ten Thousand
Smokes

PRIBILOF
ISLANDS

St. George
Island

Bristol Bay

Kodiak

ALEUTIAN ISLANDS

ALEUTIAN RANGE

Detail of Aleutian Islands

Dutch Harbor

Attu Island

Unalaska

Aggatu Island   Kiska Island

MILES

0   100   200   300

Amchitk
Islan

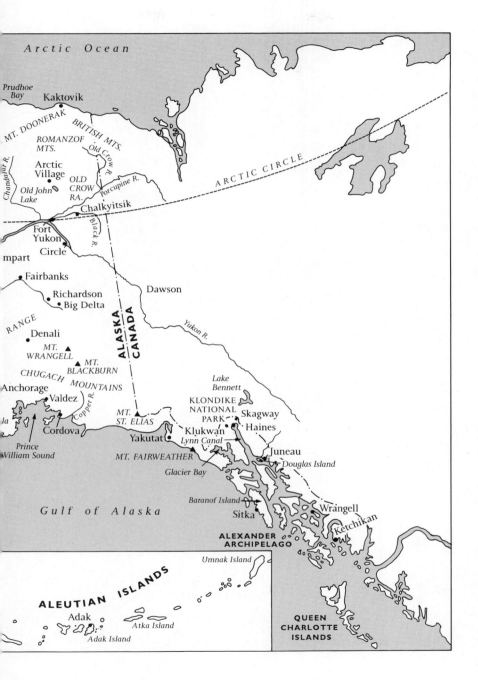

Arctic Ocean

Prudhoe
Bay
Kaktovik

MT. DOONERAK
BRITISH MTS.
ROMANZOF
MTS.
Old Crow R.

Arctic
Village
OLD
CROW
RA.
Old John
Lake
Porcupine R.

Chandalar R.

ARCTIC CIRCLE

Chalkyitsik

Fort
Yukon
Circle
Rampart

Black R.

Fairbanks

Richardson
Big Delta

Dawson

RANGE

Denali

MT.
WRANGELL

MT.
BLACKBURN

CHUGACH
MOUNTAINS

Anchorage
Valdez

Cordova

Copper R.

MT.
ST. ELIAS

Yakutat

ALASKA
CANADA

Yukon R.

Lake
Bennett

KLONDIKE
NATIONAL
PARK
Klukwan

Skagway
Haines

Lynn Canal

Prince
William Sound

MT. FAIRWEATHER

Glacier Bay

Juneau
Douglas Island

Baranof Island

Sitka

Wrangell

Ketchikan

Gulf of Alaska

ALEXANDER
ARCHIPELAGO

Umnak Island

ALEUTIAN ISLANDS

Adak
Atka Island

Adak Island

QUEEN
CHARLOTTE
ISLANDS

Introduction

In the selections that follow, the writers invite you into the book as if you were their guest, a guest in the state of Alaska, about to become acquainted with some of its people and places. You'll find some writers in these pages whom you didn't meet in our first volume. They will show you some events, people, and wildlife that you might not see otherwise, share their experience in this place, and talk about why it means so much to them.

Alaska is too big for anyone to show you everything, either on a tour or in a book. No one in Alaska, not even the oldest sourdough, knows it all. These writers can only offer bits and pieces, the incidents that have impressed or touched them enough to make them stop and put something down on paper. In this introduction we try to put these bits into a fuller context, to offer some additional views of the Great Land and the stories about it that do not appear elsewhere.

Though Alaska is one of the most recent entrants in the family of states that comprise the Union, in its human history it is the oldest, for the earliest settlers of the Lower 48 lived here first, crossing a land bridge from Siberia perhaps 25,000 years ago during the second stage of the Wisconsin glaciation. So the vantage point for our view of Alaska is from the perspective of great age, and some of the writers here represent cultures far older than any in the Western tradition we know so well.

We begin in Southeast Alaska, a great panhandle the size of Florida that usurps the coast of Northern British Columbia: a place of mountain slopes, green timbered or clear-cut; of fog-shrouded islands; of abandoned fox farms standing in the rain; and of cedar totems leaning into their age and the wind along deserted beaches or hidden among the Sitka spruce. The totems are symbols of ancient and sometimes resurgent cultures, many of whose people—the Tlingit, Haida, and Tsimshian—still live in villages with names like Hoonah, Angoon, Klukwan and Metlakatla. Noted for their totem poles, they are the creators of a marvelous abstract art that is really a carefully coded system of designs that people within the complex mix of clans, phratries, and families understand.

All the ineffable mystery of the past, the whole of human history, resides in these Southeastern clouds and mountains, and some sodden dawns in this country are like the earliest dawns in the formation of the earth. Here the great mystery of the past can be lost in the darkness of rain, as the great flukes of the humpback whales are lost in their soundings in the Inside Passage, for the music of Southeast Alaska is rain, always rain, falling softly on the dark spruce canopy above the devil's club. "The grace of this soft rain," writes Seferis about Greece. Here it is equally soft and far more abundant: 160 inches a year in Ketchikan, 330 inches on Montague Island, and 400 inches on some forested mountain heights.

Carolyn Servid, one of the guides to Southeast you will find in this book, will take you in a skiff to see whales bubble-net feeding in the deep waters off Sitka. In a beautifully evocative essay, she ponders our human role, and the whales', and the meaning of awe in this coastal world. John Hildebrand will take you aboard the *Alpha Helix*, a research vessel, as its scientists look at the sea otter feeding grounds in the Alexander Archipelago, working their way south from Sitka and then patrolling back. Hildebrand takes us close to a large grizzly while running a rubber raft along the shore of a small estuary. Only whales, a humpback cow and her calf, could upstage such a fierce creature, and they do, inspiring a kind of awe similar to that experienced by Servid.

The music of Southeast includes the honky-tonk music of the tourist bars in Juneau, where the capital city politicians now conduct their after-hours business. John Dos Passos will take us from there on the ferry around Douglas Island and up Lynn Canal until we are far back in time, "entering the Ice Age," Dos Passos says. Here the music is enhanced by the silence of glaciers and ice fields.

At Skagway, John Burroughs takes us over White Pass, the treacherous ascent that defeated so many miners on their way to the goldfields. Then he brings us back down into Glacier Bay, where "huge masses of ice had recently toppled over . . . but while I stayed not a pebble moved, all was silence and inertia." It is but a short trip from Skagway to Haines, site of an old military post, and up the road to Klukwan, an ancient Tlingit Indian village and the home of Jennie Thlunaut, one of the last great Chilkat Indian weavers. In our selection she welcomes a handful of younger women who have come to her to learn the secrets of weaving the Chilkat blanket. Her joy in knowing that an ancient tradition will not die with her is apparent, even in her native Tlingit language. Nora Dauenhauer, who translates Thlunaut's greeting, is a Tlingit Indian woman whose own roots go back for millennia in this land and who now serves her people by collecting, editing, and translating the traditional oratory, history, and tales of her people, working hard to keep the Tlingit language alive.

Farther north, past mountains that rise directly from the sea, past a glacier that is, by itself, bigger than Rhode Island, tucked away in a majestic fjord, lie Valdez, the pipeline terminal for the world, and Cordova, where a favorite story has to do with a man whose wife left him and who, upon hearing her decision, grabbed a chain saw, went outside, and proceeded to cut the house in two because "She, by God, isn't getting any more'n her half of anything." Years ago, Cordovans protested the location of the pipeline terminal at Valdez, and her fishermen sued to stop its construction for fear a tanker spill would destroy the salmon fishery. Now, John Keeble writes that they are wrestling again with their fears, realized by the rip in the side of the Exxon *Valdez*. But that disaster for fish has meant huge profits for some people who worked on the cleanup of Prince William Sound, and Keeble shows us a community haunted by ambivalence about oil, fish, and fast money, and wondering what it all means for the future.

At the center of the great coastal curve of Alaska from Ketchikan to Dutch Harbor lies the Kenai Peninsula, and the little towns with Native Athapaskan or Russian names: Kenai, Soldotna, Ninilchik. The Kenai Peninsula brings a person in contact with America's Russian past. The blue onion domes of chapels and churches do not seem out of place here but probe the gray sky as if perfectly at home. In the mouth of the Kenai River there are beluga whales, and in the early fall snow geese descend on the flats like a blizzard. The Kenai Peninsula long was home to the Kenaitze Indians, members of Dena'ina Athapaskans. Here Peter

Kalifornsky worked at his writing until the summer of 1993, not only writing down the traditional stories of his people but also doing his own creative work in his people's traditional language. He was one of the last speakers of Kenaitze, and the only one who was also literate. One can learn the nature of the country here from the Kenaitze place-names that Kalifornsky uses to describe the trapping route he followed as a young man, and by reading between the lines one can discern the changes in the society and the landscape as well: "Our people trapped in these areas until after World War II, when the animals began to disappear." Other works in this book reflect similar changes on the land, the same tensions that have been introduced into the culture as a result of growth and development, and Richard Nelson echoes the importance of names in a more northern portion of the state.

To get to the Aleutians from Kenai, we can fly past Iliamna and Redoubt, two active volcanoes, over Kodiak, once the home of Alexander Baranov and now a fishing town on the island of the same name. From Kodiak we cross the Alaska Peninsula and enter Bristol Bay, heart of the world's largest red salmon spawning grounds. Five species of salmon swim up the Bay, reds coming in far greater numbers than the rest, swimming up spawning rivers with names like Egekik, Nushagak, Naknek, and Kvichak.

In Bristol Bay we sense that we are on the edge: the edge of the continent, the edge of the world's tree line, the edge of permafrost and tundra, the edge of American culture, the edge of the use of English as the common primary language. We are entering the homeland and source of two major language families whose speakers now range from Alaska to Greenland and south to the Apache and Navajo settlements in the Southwest. One of these is Eskimo-Aleut, the other is Na-Dene, the language of the Athapaskan Indians wherever they are found. The other two genetically isolated languages, spoken in Southeast Alaska, Haida and Tsimshian, bring to twenty the number of distinct languages spoken by indigenous people here. Each of the languages is as different from the rest as Swedish is from French, and Aleut is as different from Athapaskan as Swedish or French are from the Semitic tongues.

On out the Aleutian chain, storm center for North America, we move among fogbound islands lost in the wind and rain. Here Aleut hunters used to take whales in frail one-man kayaks and two-man bidarkas. The

Aleuts were perhaps the most settled indigenous people in all Alaska. They had everything they needed for their diet: sea mammals, fish, clams, mussels, and eggs. For clothing they had elaborate parkas made of bird skins, and raincoats sewn from the intestines of seals, sea lions, and walrus. They lived in semiunderground dwellings called barabaras, and made the finest grass baskets ever devised by human hands. The Aleuts also had a system of health care, including surgery, and an intimate knowledge of the internal organs of the human anatomy, gained by analogy from their observation of sea mammals. These treeless islands are beset throughout the seasons by squalls, snow or rain, and high winds.

Perhaps one of the most astute and systematic observers of the Aleut people was Father Ivan Veniaminov, a Russian Orthodox priest who arrived at Unalaska in the summer of 1824. A tireless worker, Veniaminov traveled extensively throughout the islands and then down to Sitka and as far south as California. He was the first person to keep a daily record of the Aleutian weather. Some of his observations of Aleut traditions are reprinted from his journals, which were not translated in full until Lydia Black and R. H. Geoghegen completed the task in 1984.

From the Aleutians we move just north to another Aleut outpost, the Pribilof Islands, home of the fur seal and site of America's little-recognized penal colony. Aleut families were held on the island at the will of a white administrator, like indentured servants with no escape, to secure the harvest of seals for the government-controlled fur trade. Libby Beaman, daughter of a prominent Washington, D.C., family, was the first non-Native American woman to reside in the Pribilofs for any length of time. She sketched, wrote in her journal, and toured the island to witness the harvest or watch the seals, the sea birds, and the clouds that were her constant companions. Her encounters with the land and its wildlife, as revealed in our selection from her diaries, had unsettling moments.

From the Pribilofs we'll go back to the mainland, to the lower end of the Kuskokwim River, running west and a little south from up in central Alaska near Mt. McKinley. Along the upper reaches of this river, Athapaskan Indians live in little villages like Nikolai. But the river moves inexorably out of the foothills, down out of the timber that provides the logs for homes, through Aniak, where the Yup'ik Eskimos begin, to the tundra town of Bethel, where some wag once put two signs on either side of a couple of scraggly spruce trees less than three feet tall. The first sign said, "Entering Bethel National Forest," and ten yards away the second read, "Leaving Bethel National Forest." At the mouths of the Kuskokwim and Yukon rivers is the broad delta where we have come from the Pribilofs. We could say, echoing Seferis again, "The land absorbs us." The Lower Kuskokwim School District is the size of Ohio. Here the music is of birds, incredible numbers of ducks and geese, gulls and cormorants, murres and arctic terns—a springtime full of feathers and down caught in the nests of the tundra and marsh grasses and the sounds of wings and calls. Under it all, from 20,000 years of history, comes the sound of Yup'ik Eskimo drums made of walrus gut stretched over a circular wooden frame and beaten with a slender wand. Here are people still celebrating the great occasions of their lives with music and dance and song. Carolyn Kremers shows us life in a delta village, Tununak. She takes us into the qasgiq, the heart of Tununak, and lets us see the singing and dancing that take place there. "The traditions and the power of Yup'ik music lay deep in Tununak people's souls," she says rightly.

Along the coast north of the delta we find still another culture and climate, with the weather changing, finally becoming more like that stereotype of ice and snow everyone imagines when they think of Alaska. The language changes too, from Yup'ik to Inupiaq Eskimo, and Unalakleet represents the border area for all those changes, a little village, not by Alaskan standards but by most—800 or so people perched on the edge of the Bering Sea. Nome is just a little farther north. From Nome, Paul Tiulana, a young King Island Eskimo, was drafted into the U.S. Army in World War II. War was foreign to his Eskimo experience. "We did not understand what was wrong, why countries were fighting each other," he recounts. "A lot of times people would say, 'What the heck are they doing, fighting each other, killing people? They cannot eat human beings. They should come here to Alaska and hunt some animals.'" As he tells his story, we catch glimpses of the confusion and the changes that were in the air for all Eskimo people at the time.

The challenge of living in Nome is documented by Sally Carrighar, known for her nature writing and her biological research. Here too we get a sense of being on the edge of the continent as she shows us around town: "Each of the lighted homes we passed meant more to the owners, I thought, than homes do in most places. Beginning at about fifteen degrees below zero, the hot air from the stovepipes vaporizes and for some reason is luminous. In the usual winter wind from the north, the white plumes level down: 'The smoke is lying on the roofs,' people say of those nights. And the little houses of Nome are close and neighborly under this cover of driven and shining mist, which flows away into the night, over the icy width of the Bering Sea."

Lest we begin to think this country is too pretty or that the winter night is more romantic than in other climes, John Muir will lead us over to St. Lawrence Island, off the coast west of Nome. He arrived after a "starving time," in what he calls "The villages of the dead." Any romance we may have felt is quickly replaced by a sense of how close arctic life is to the edge—in this case, to the edge of extinction.

Just north of Nome we cross the Arctic Circle to Kotzebue, and beyond "Kotz" to Point Hope. In these coastal villages the men still win status and appreciation in the community for their prowess in traditional skills. Straight-backed men of all ages still dance the traditional dances with great pride in their own strength and history, but in Point Hope especially they are honored for their ability to hunt whales. Barrow, northernmost point on the North American continent, belongs in this region too, and here Eskimo people continue to depend, as they have for thousands of years, upon sea mammals and fish as their primary food source, moving upriver from their coastal villages in the summer to catch fish for themselves and their dogs, and returning to the coast in the spring to hunt whales as soon as the migrations and the open leads in the sea ice permit.

All through this land, people call themselves Inuit, The People, and they never lived in igloos, as most people think; that was a Canadian, Central Eskimo habitation. Geographically the largest local government unit in the world, the North Slope Borough, has its offices here. Richard Nelson, a nature writer and anthropologist, meditates on the meaning of names he learned while living with the Inuit along this northern coast. The place-names are as "vital as a map" when he travels crosscountry. But they have meanings even more profound than the sense of location they offer, and if the names are ever lost or forgotten, Nelson says, "the earth would be diminished as a consequence."

South of the Arctic Slope we come into a region of mountains, the famous Brooks Range. Caribou cross the Brooks and move through Arctic Village, traversing from interior Eskimo country to Qwich'in Athapaskan territory. Lois Crisler describes their passage in an indelible picture of thousands of animals on the move. Perhaps only down among the caribou on the Alaska Peninsula or among wildebeest on the African plains can we still see so many animals moving at once.

From Crisler's location in the Brooks Range we turn east in a great arc through Arctic Village to Chalkyitsik on the Black River, the home of Belle Herbert. One of the editors reports meeting Belle Herbert in Chalkyitsik when she was estimated to be about 124 years old. She was sewing beads on a tiny parka she was making for her great-granddaughter, her knobby hands working the needle through the tough fur as if driven by the memory of strength. She was quite deaf, and the translator would put a question into Qwich'in so that her daughter could understand. Her daughter would then lean down and, putting her mouth to her mother's ear, shout the question loudly. Belle would nod and begin to talk, telling us how the white men came to the Yukon. With Belle, as with Peter Kalifornsky and Jennie Thlunaut, we have presented the text in a bilingual format. Belle's translators, Bill Pfisterer and Katherine Peter, made numerous arduous trips, winter and summer, to talk with Belle and record her stories. He translated them with line breaks to match her own pauses for breath or endings in an effort to provide some sense of the rhythms and patterns of her language. The English translation tries to match that rhythm as well. The result is a remarkable piece of work that makes Belle, now deceased, seem present to all.

Down the Black from Chalkyitsik lies Fort Yukon, an ungainly mix of Athapaskan and white cultures, where most residents still subsist on the local flora and fauna. It is also an outpost of the University of Alaska, tied to the Fairbanks campus by satellite communication. Some people come here because it's the last real town before they can find a place in the woods. Edward Hoagland has chronicled the journey of some of these escapists. They are important, for they act out fantasies many have harbored at one time or another. Hoagland describes his own experience there as well.

From clear up on the Canadian side, down the Yukon through the Fort, Athapaskan Indians inhabit the land. Formerly nomadic hunters of caribou and moose, these Athapaskans tended to be highly individualistic, traveling in family-sized groups that followed a subsistence lifeway that included hunting in the fall, trapping in the winter, and fishing and berry picking in the summer.

Down all the great rivers of interior Alaska we can move too, through Athapaskan country all the way, along the prepotent Yukon, the Beaver, the Porcupine, the Tanana, the Nenana. Fairbanks sits along the banks of the Chena River as a crazy amalgamation of pop American absurd and frontier effrontery and tenacity. It is also the jumping-off place for construction workers, trappers, miners, and oil-patch junkies heading for the bush or the North Slope. It is the home of the main campus of the University of Alaska.

Outside of Fairbanks, on the Richardson Highway, John Haines also made his home for twenty-five years. He tells us what it means to leave a place that has meant so much hardship, in which one has invested oneself so profoundly, and which has returned such dividends. He does not leave with the expectation that all will be well with this hard land, and one senses both resignation and relief at his going; he does not want to witness the end of a wilderness, and a life, he has cherished.

There were others along this route, characters famous in American history and myth. Wyatt Earp, of Tombstone fame, came to Alaska with his wife. Josephine Sarah Marcus Earp made three separate journeys to Alaska with Wyatt and reported them in a book. Here she takes us through events along the Yukon, at Rampart, and at St. Michael as she and her husband find their way, inevitably it seems, to the goldfields. Her record of life in the rough-cut frontier towns rings true.

Finally, Tom Kizzia takes us to the end of our journey, back down at the mouth of the Yukon, in the delta near where Carolyn Kremers taught school for a time. But Kizzia has another interest in this country, among the swans and the fish and the people who still must harvest the bounty of the land in order to live. He shows us still another facet of Alaskan life, and when we have read him, we feel as he did, as if we are "walking home with something tugging at my fist—the heart of the tundra, a living thing. Qavlunaq."

So this is Alaska, as best we can show you. The accounts in this book describe not only a land of extensive and peculiar geography but also a place where time is warped and anomalies abound, a place where T. S. Eliot's notion of time past and time future being contained in time present is a fact of daily experience. Subsistence hunters still roam the arctic tundra, and their drums and dances still mark a life that contrasts starkly with the arrival of a 727 with passengers and mail. In eighty years Alaska has gone from explorers with white-rimed beards to the most sophisticated satellite communications in the country. Just twenty-five years ago, long-retired B-17 bombers from World War II were still mapping portions of the state, and only twenty years ago battered Constellations, which had been the overseas flagships taking off from Boston's Logan Field in 1961, were making their last runs to Kodiak Island. The prehistoric, the merely out of date, and the technology of the future are all mixed together in Alaska. Time is so compressed that even in Anchorage, where everyone is a newcomer, there are people still living who can remember when the first oil-boom Texan came to town.

Through Alaska, 25,000 years ago, the first migrants came, moving on down the ice-free valleys of Alaska through what is now Canada and on into the Southwest and Mexico. Some of those early sojourners moved back north and settled in a great arc in the Yukon Territory of Canada and interior Alaska. These became the Athapaskans. The Eskimos arrived later and settled along the coast, except for a small enclave of inland hunters of caribou. Another group moved south and settled along the Aleutian chain. Over the course of thousands of years, they became Aleuts and developed a language and life of their own.

The land base that has sustained these Native Alaskans for thousands of years has been gradually eroding under the incursions of outsiders. The Alaska Native Claims Settlement Act of 1971 was designed to protect Native interests in the land and provide some compensation for land taken without reimbursement. Under the act, thirteen regional corporations were established to reflect the cultural divisions of Native peoples. Now, nearly twenty-five years into the implementation of the act, it appears that its effect may be much different from its intent, and the Native population, which comprises more than 16 percent of the state's total population, faces difficult decisions that will affect the political, economic, and social future of all Alaskans. Alaska represents one of the final scenes in a five-hundred-year drama of western European expansion and exploration in the new world. The travels of Vespucci, Columbus, Shelikov, and Baranov seem very recent in its light.

Despite the old reports of Alaska's oil wealth, we have known for a number of years that oil revenues would begin to decline as production fell off in the late 1980s and the 1990s, but the loss of revenue has been greatly exacerbated by the drop in world oil prices in recent years. For a time, oil prices here were so low that one Alaska red salmon was worth more than a barrel of oil, and one tanner crab was worth five barrels. This revenue decline has affected every sector of Alaskan life. In 1987 Alaska was the only state to record declines in both employment and earnings. By February 1, 1989, Laborers Union Local 341 could show only one in ten of its members as employed. The difficulties the economy poses to the society as a whole can be measured in the increase in the number of suicides and cases of child abuse. Always an abusive community for children, Anchorage in 1989 turned away forty-five families every weekend who needed the temporary respite offered by a twenty-four-hour crisis nursery. Suicide had become so common that newspapers no longer noted it for fear it would cause a further increase in a rate that was already of epidemic proportions.

The state faces many other complex issues, most of which cannot be resolved by money alone and some of which are so complicated by geographic or cultural barriers — or by human frailty, ignorance, or sheer cussedness — that they may never be resolved. The place of indigenous people in our society is only one such question. The place of education, including higher education, in the funding priorities of the legislature is another.

For many Native Alaskans, poverty is still routine. For others, the sense of loss that stems from dramatic cultural trauma, the breakdown of family life, the collapse of the organizing principles of community and of social control, the loss of language, and the depletion of hunting and fishing resources has meant a loss of direction, a sense of failure, helplessness, and ennui. The symptoms of this loss are easy to see: a high suicide rate, widespread alcoholism, assault, manslaughter, rape, child neglect, and anti-white racism are among the negative aspects of village life. As an Athapaskan man remarked recently about his village, "I can only think of three people out of about seventy-five who died a natural death in the last few years."

Now, in the midst of this turmoil, many villagers are turning again to their elders, the people who remember some of the old ways. The positive aspects of village life—the tenacity of traditional values even under the onslaught of our educational system, an appreciation for extended family ties, a close bond with the land and an appreciation of its value beyond its ability to produce fish and game or oil and gold—enable some of our people to find new nourishment from these old sources. Generations now in middle age missed much of what the elders had to teach because they grew up in white schools where the elders' wisdom was often denigrated or suppressed, and because the boarding schools they attended were located far from home. For many Natives, nine months of each childhood year were spent away from the elders during the time when they might have learned the value systems they now hope to re-establish. Many feel that such learning is not only important for themselves but absolutely essential for their children. What will our children do? they ask. How will they know what they need to know? How will they live without knowing these things?

Yet the misunderstanding of non-Natives complicates everything. Few whites have the freedom to travel to villages, many are poor observers when they do travel, most have little understanding of issues Native people deal with every day, and few have any idea of the cultural heritage or ethnography of the various Native peoples in the state. This lack of understanding is due in part to the fact that they are new. They come to Alaska as part of a highly mobile federal force employed by the Federal Aviation Administration, the Weather Bureau, the Bureau of Land Management, the Bureau of Indian Affairs, or another agency, or they are employed by a multinational corporation that shuffles employees through an international series of job sites. Most of these are here for a two-year tour. They have little time to comprehend the nuances of public issues or Native concerns. Often they are sympathetic to indigenous populations and are eager to obtain information about them, but they have neither the time nor the means to obtain it from reliable sources.

Alaskans are a long way from the rest of the country, and their speech reflects their sense of distance and alienation. They talk about "going Outside," or to "the Lower 48," or even of "going to America." Despite this feeling of distance, they are connected, and they recognize the connections every time they think about their circumstances.

All of this is to say that Alaska is oxymoronic and paradoxical. Internal conflicts assail Alaskans on every side. What is true for one place is false for another; no single statement will hold for the whole state. The place is so big that one might be led to think that many things would operate independently. A tragedy in Kotzebue is as distant from Anchorage as a tragedy in Cleveland is from Baltimore. But Alaska is one place with distinctive regions, not many distinct places. Further, the chances are great that, unlike Cleveland and Baltimore, a number of people in Anchorage are apt to be well acquainted with the victim of tragedy in Kotzebue.

Alaskans are one people; in a special way, what affects anyone affects everyone. But they are also divided, and the divisions run deep. Some of them—the ancient gulf between Eskimo and Athapaskan, for instance —are older than all of Western history as we traditionally conceive it. Other serious divisions separate "outsiders" from residents, urbanites from villagers, developers from environmentalists, newcomers from old-timers or sourdoughs. Because Alaskans are so few in number, it might seem easy to heal the breaches; instead, the small population amplifies them. They are more painful to bear. The support system for the bridges that Alaskans need to build are not yet in place.

Alaskans are one people living in a great house. But few of its rooms are finished, and the furnishings are spartan. They run into one another at every turn, but when they meet, they do not know what to say across the cultural barriers, or how to act. If they speak, they are often misunderstood. They retreat into silence, or clichés, or false, ingratiating rhetoric, hoping to hide their fear, hostility, or confusion. Tensions run high, tempers flare. They worry about racial violence and about matters more immediate: How can we stop the physical violence Alaskans inflict on one another at such a great rate? How can we exert more control over our own destiny, with Washington so far away in miles and understanding? They love their surroundings, are thrilled and challenged by them, but Alaska is a hard place to live, hard and cold and sharp. All the corners are jagged, the surfaces splintered, the edges honed and stropped. Alaskans have to be careful how they move. They fret over how to allocate the space they have, and how to put it to proper use. Some seem to want it all developed and paved; they would paint obscenities on the walls. Others seek to preserve it; they would make it a museum, a static display without a future, frozen in the present. Some wish to make everything here exactly as it was in the place they despised and left. As Wright Morris has said, "Publicly we create and promote the very civilization we privately reject." Others seem to come only in order to make preparations to leave again, to make their fortune and get out. Their greed infects the state's commerce, and occasionally its politics and educational system.

Everyone in the state is an immigrant, ancient or recent, but many seem bent on barring the gate to everyone else (now that they are here) to keep newcomers from spoiling the place they have already begun to spoil themselves. To paraphrase Morris, it is little wonder that the Alaskan mind sometimes wonders where it is going and what, indeed, it is to be an Alaskan.

We hope that as you visit the parts of Alaska the writers show you here, you will come to a richer understanding of the complexities of the Great Land and its peoples.

Gary Holthaus
Robert Hedin

The Great Land

CAROLYN SERVID

Carolyn Servid was born in Vengurla, India, and was educated at Evergreen State College and Claremont Graduate School. Before venturing to Alaska in 1980, she taught in the community college system in Seattle, Washington. Presently living in Sitka, she directs the Island Institute, an arts and humanities organization dealing with social and cultural issues.

Soundings

Whales again—at sunrise on a frigid November morning. Humpback.
A lone one this time. Its steamy shot of air bursts from the water into
apricot light. The dark back with pointed dorsal fin breaks the surface, curves slightly into colored air, then sinks into water. The world
that holds this morning has been caught by winter. High snowy ridges
across the bay whet their edges on the cold. Below, frosted hemlock
and huckleberry trim the forest, and patchy ice rises on the tide. I stand
at the window, uneasily anticipating the bitter chill outside. It seems
to have slowed everything within its reach, sent blood and sap deep,
leaving stillness and silence. But there is a second spout. The whale's
hot breath, spangled with light, lingers in the cold air as its back rises
again and disappears. In another few seconds, a third spout. Through
binoculars now I can see the whale's blowhole, follow the line of its
back as it rises once more, arching higher this time, the peak of its
dorsal fin crowning the arc that continues until the thick wedge of tail
raises the whale's flukes to finish the curve. They slip gracefully below
the surface in the dive that takes the whale deep. In these few minutes
of the whale's surfacing, the icy fist of the morning has lost its grip.
Here is a massive blood-hot life, holding its own, steaming into the
cold, a welcome demonstration of the pervasive balance, the tension
that holds the world. Warmed by this reminder, I am braced against the
sharp edge of winter.

Humpback whales frequent this area enough that they often move
through my days. When I came here eight years ago, I didn't realize
I would be living in a sphere which overlapped so consistently with
theirs. Whales had existed in a remote realm of mystery I assumed
would always withhold its clues from me. Now I find the rhythms of

their surfacing familiar — the series of blows before the deep dive, the easy rise and fall of the back, the arc that brings the show of flukes. Becoming accustomed to the whales' presence has been paradoxical, for it has meant getting used to the extraordinary. In time, I've found this paradox turning on itself and becoming another: the marvel of these animals has not diminished with familiarity. In fact, what I know of the whales is merely an outline of their movements, but the points where that line intersects my world are points where delight gives way to reverence, points that resonate with wonder. The whales' presence stays with me long after they've gone. The extended line of their black bodies breaks air with specific form. The light glinting off their backs is branding. Their flukes have imprinted a shadow on my mind and their explosive breaths echo in my ear. The sheer mass of body and the strength with which they move are difficult to comprehend since they surface intermittently from a world not readily available to my eyes. But witnessing the breach of a whale, seeing it propel itself all the way out of the water and fly into the air, watching the upheaval as its forty tons hit water again, I am struck silent by a kind of power that will never be mine to understand. The wake of that whale's splash washes my memory still.

Rumors that humpbacks were in the area prompted some friends and me to arrange a chartered whale-watching trip my first winter in Alaska. There was no guarantee we would see whales, but we couldn't pass up a chance none of us had known. In our minds, these were spiritual creatures that transcended the natural world. They held the essence of something we didn't know how to name, but wanted to believe in. They were the key, perhaps, to one of life's great secrets. Encountering them was a dream almost too magnificent to come true.

The day of our trip brought cold wind and rain. The cabin of the boat was littered with boots, sweaters, rain gear, cameras, and binoculars. We headed north to the bay where whales had been sighted and, almost as soon as we entered the bay, began to see spouts: first two, then another pair and another. We greeted them with whoops of excitement, amazed that our dreams were materializing before our eyes. Our skipper was the only calm one among us. An experienced whale watcher, he was keenly aware of their sensitivity to intrusion and approached them cautiously, running the boat's engine at a slow idle, trying to let them know we were there but meant no harm. The whales seemed to pay little attention and allowed us to get close enough to see that they were feeding. Their surfacing was accompanied by a flurry of birds—eagles, gulls, murres, goldeneyes, grebes—all attracted by whatever feed was in the area. As if this were not enough, there were sea lions and otters close by. This testimony to the abundance of life in these waters intoxicated us. We sang to the whales, hugged each other, laughed at our giddiness, and eventually chattered ourselves to silence as we watched show after show of spouts and backs, flippers and flukes.

Looking back, I recall significant pauses that punctuated the whirl of exhilaration that day, interruptions caused by a simple but profound realization. The whales were not what we had thought. They certainly were magnificent, but not transcendent. They moved in the same water we did, edged the same shoreline and rocks. Their breaths, warm like ours, steamed into the same cold air. Our proximity to them forced us to recognize not some spiritual essence unique to them but rather the systematic grace of intricate relationships that are the very foundation of our mutual existence, of the natural world. It is this race that we, as human beings, can choose to acknowledge, or not, to give it the reverence it is due, or not. Sometimes, however, it is not a matter of choice. Sometimes, we simply see—then swallow our inadequate words and hold that moment in our hearts.

It is seven o'clock on a summer morning. The sun has been up for hours and my eyes have to adjust to full daylight as I reach over to turn off the alarm. No sooner does the ringing stop than I hear the explosion. My mind flips through the possibilities, and in seconds I know it is whales. I am instantly wide awake at the window, watching three dark hulks sinking below the water's surface. They are closer to shore than I have ever seen them, just beyond some rocks that are fifty yards from the beach. The whales have been feeding in the bay for the past few days. From the way they surfaced—all three at once—and from the show of heads rather than backs or flukes, I assume they are indulging again. The moment my eyes lose them to the water, I find bathrobe and slippers and my way downstairs to the porch outside.

The water is a sheet of glass, mirroring the light of the morning. The air is cool. If there are sounds, I don't hear them. My attention is fixed on that spot just beyond the rocks. The conditions are perfect for watching what I know is to come. I stand silent, arms crossed for a bit of warmth, determined to be a witness. I don't have to wait more than a few minutes before the bubbles begin to ripple the surface. They start at a fixed point and move clockwise in an arc, first away from shore and then back toward me in a continuing line around to the point where they began. The circle completes itself, and in seconds the water explodes in what appears to be mass confusion: the gaping mouths, warty heads, thrashing flippers, and spouting blowholes of three forty-foot whales. A rush of noise echoes through the bay. Here on the porch there are only the silent exclamations my heart pounds to my brain.

What I am witnessing is not confusion at all but the final movement in an intricate dance humpback whales sometimes engage in when they feed. The technique is called bubble-net feeding. Diagrams I have seen of it show a whale diving down to get under a school of krill or small fish, then blowing bubbles as it swims gradually upward in a spiral. The rising bubbles eventually form a cylindrical net around the krill or fish, effectively herding them into a confined area. The whale then lunges to the surface inside the circumference of that cylinder, mouth open, engulfing everything in its way. These are not toothed whales; instead they have long tapered plates of baleen hanging from their top jaws, arranged like teeth on a comb. The baleen is pliable when wet and frayed along one edge. The hundreds of plates along each side of the mouth act like a sieve, trapping food and letting water pour back out into the ocean. As the whales swallow their latest catch, they loll about at the surface for a few moments, as though relishing the enormous bite. Then comes the series of spouts and arching backs that precedes the deep dive that will let them begin the process again.

The long fluid motion of this act of eating performed by a single whale is one I can visualize because the concept is one I am able to grasp. What is intriguing is how and why whales take part in the process together. What relationship do they have to each other? Is this group feeding activity a cooperative effort? If so, how do the whales delegate roles in the performance? Which whale or whales blow the bubbles? How do they position themselves so as to get the completed motion, the timing just right? The questions surface like so many bubbles of the unknown, trapping me in the realm of the human. I can only marvel at the elegant form given to such a fundamental act of living, at its precision and efficacy, at the intelligence that conceived of it.

As I get accustomed to the company of whales, I realize they are re-defining the parameters of my world. Thinking of myself in relationship to them helps me understand proportion, focuses my attention on the connections we each have to the continuum of nature. The whales have shown me what it means to live in an animate world, one in which process and motion are constants, rendering things to life. This is not a new sensibility but a long-forgotten one stirred back into being. The movement of whales through my days has reawakened me to the form and detail of living things: not only the distinct line that is humpback but also the specific flowering of huckleberry, the particularity of winter wren song, the quality of air in season. Otherness. That which is outside myself. To know my place in the arrangement is to foster a sense of kinship, to know deep regard for the exquisite relationships that hold the natural world. I would that this knowledge was an inherent sense, as necessary as food, as easy as breathing. It comes not so naturally, but feels that essential. It comes more easily if I can leave myself open to wonder.

On a mild June afternoon I set out in an aluminum canoe to try to catch up with a lone humpback whale. This canoe has been modified for rowing, a small advantage in the effort to keep up with this powerful swimmer. The whale has been bubble-net feeding, grazing widely throughout the bay. I pursue it out of a simple desire for closeness, proximity. I want nothing between us but air and water and the bottom of my boat. I want the noise of its sharp breaths fresh in my ears. I want to see the specific blackness of its skin, watch the water pour off its flukes as they rise. I want a true sense of its size. Without binoculars, I want to discern the swell of its blowhole, note the pattern of white markings on the underside of its tail when it dives. I want to make out the ring of bubbles that will mark its presence, hold my breath while I wait for the whale to appear.

The day is calm, the conditions just right for rowing. A steady stroke of the oars moves the canoe swiftly over the water. I head toward the vicinity where the whale last surfaced, having no clue where it will come up again. Nearing some islands half a mile from shore, I pause to adjust the oars. As soon as I stop rowing, my attention is alerted to a

resonant tone permeating the whole area around me. It is like the ringing of crystal, a pure single note vibrating in my ears. I glance about
quickly, trying to discern where it is coming from. Turning to look
behind me, I notice the curving line of bubbles marking the water's
surface several hundred feet away. As the bubbles move around in their
circle, the ringing continues. I barely have time to make a connection
between the two when the circle of bubbles is completed and the ringing stops. I am stunned. Not only do these whales feed with a flourish
of form, but they add music to this performance! I am so taken by the
idea that the whale's lunge to the surface startles me. I can only stare
as it lounges about, swallowing its mouthful of food. The questions
begin to flood my mind while the whale rights itself, blows a few sharp
breaths, and sounds with a show of flukes.

Once I am free to move again, I ease back into the rhythm of rowing
and head in the same direction the whale seemed to be going when it
went down. With each stroke of the oars, my imagination pulls at the
truth about the whale's song. Why and how? Why didn't I hear it from
the porch that morning? I can't help asking the questions, and having
no answers only fuels my urge to encounter the whale as completely
and directly as I can. I want its presence lodged firmly in my mind.
I want a constant reminder that this whale is an integral part of the
world. I want to keep myself open to wonder.

I have rowed some distance now and have seen no sign of the whale.
Any assumption of where it will surface would simply be a guess, so
I decide to stop rowing, drift and wait for the next rising. I am in the
middle of a wide channel, a mile or more from either shore. The canoe
seems especially small in this expanse of water, but there is no wind,
and swells from the ocean beyond are small and gradual. The freedom
of wide-open air is welcome and I feel safe. I scan the distance of this
watery stretch for signs of the whale. There are none. The only apparent
motion is that of a few gulls riding the air. I notice some larger boats a
long way off and think perhaps the whale is theirs to watch now, that
it has moved on. But then the ringing begins. It seems to be coming
directly up through the bottom of the canoe. My eyes dart around the
immediate area and find the bubble ring forming on the starboard side
only thirty feet away. In the few seconds I have, my mind races through
the possibilities. I can quickly get out of the way or I can stay put. I am

fairly confident the whale won't come up underneath me, but its lunge to the surface could generate waves that would catch the canoe sideways. I have a life-vest on, but there is no flotation in the canoe and no boat close by to pluck me out of the water if I go in. I know how cold the water is, but I may never have a chance to be this close to a whale again.

I stay where I am. The whale's song fills me. My heart pounds out its own rhythmic accompaniment and I am not afraid. I watch the circle of bubbles define itself. In its center the water boils with fish, their silver backs flashing in the light. They are driven into a frenzy by their ringing captivity, trying without a chance to escape. The bubbles complete the circle, the ringing stops, and in a matter of moments I am looking directly into the enormous mouth of the whale, pink and fleshy and spotted with gray. The dark tunnel of its throat extends into the water. Its accordion jaw balloons out to hold everything it took in on its way up, and water begins to pour from its baleen plates. The slap of a warty flipper keeps it at the surface, where it rolls about lazily. If it is aware of my presence, it is unconcerned and matter-of-factly goes about its routine. I watch it blow and surface twice, see and hear the air burst from its blowhole, run my eyes over its back gleaming in summer light. It blows a third time, arches its body sharply and raises its flukes in the grand motion of the deep dive. White underneath, bordered in black, they slide silently into the water.

I sit motionless a moment, then reach forward with the oars and realize my whole body is trembling. The day has been filled. I steady myself with each stroke and head home.

It is winter and the whales are back again. Each time they appear I am struck by the mark they leave on my days—the awareness of an order that elicits my regard, the swell of a reverent delight. I return home late one night after an evening with friends. Before going into the house, I walk to the edge of the porch for a few minutes with the darkness. The sky is black and speckled with stars, the air still and cold. Out of the silence, the sound: whales blowing. I linger, wishing I could stay the hours, but leave them to the night, imagining their black forms in the darkness, their sleek, wet backs lit by the stars.

JOHN HILDEBRAND

John Hildebrand was born in 1949 in Royal Oak, Michigan, and attended the University of Michigan and the University of Alaska in Fairbanks, where he also taught for several years. Mr. Hildebrand is the author of *Reading the River: A Voyage Down the Yukon*, which received the 1988 Friends of American Writers Award. His articles and short stories appear in *Outside, Sports Illustrated, Harrowsmith*, and the *Missouri Review*. He has been teaching at the University of Wisconsin—Eau Claire since 1977.

Beyond Whales

We came down the outer coast of Baranof Island at night in eight-foot seas. With no stabilizers, nothing to counter the swells rolling off the Gulf of Alaska, the ship pitched and wallowed through the darkness. Next morning, though, the horizon was restored, my cabin strangely calmed. I stepped onto the balustraded deck to find the ship anchored at the end of a long, fjordlike arm of Whale Bay, surrounded by lush green mountains rising into the clouds. Descending the companionway, I found the captain of the research vessel *Alpha Helix* in the mess room, weary from his watch but brightening over coffee as he spoke of whales blowing at the entrance to the bay.

All day we sheltered out of the storm until evening, when the sea calmed enough so we could cross the bay in a rubber boat to explore its other arm. We passed hanging valleys filled with snow and the long, ropey strands of waterfalls—half a dozen in one cirque—gushing down from the clouds. The arm was eighty fathoms deep and steeply canted, its banks dense and jungly, a dream forest out of Rousseau. It ended, miles from the sea, in an estuary stream that poured out of a crack in the forest. We watched a brown bear grazing beside the stream, tearing up wild celery roots and chewing them like cud. One of our party, a wildlife photographer, wanted to move closer for a better shot. "You can never get close enough," she said, although we seemed plenty close to me. The tide was in, so we tilted back the outboard and rowed up the cobbled streambed until the bear rose and, pushing a massive shoulder through the greenery, disappeared.

Now we were heading back to the ship. At the mouth of the bay I braced for oncoming rollers but the storm had left behind only gentle swells and a long, pearly twilight. The *Alpha Helix* was visible in the distance. I had just taken the walkie-talkie from its waterproof bag to radio our imminent return when the photographer pointed at two quick white puffs of vapor rising off the horizon like exclamation points. Changing course, we raced toward the geysers until we could see a pair of black hillocks beneath them, curving purposefully through the water. Humpback whales, a cow and calf judging from their size. Humpbacks are the "singing" whales with pleated mouths full of baleen and long, oarlike flippers.

There is an etiquette to whale watching, a threshold of distance beyond which lies harassment, and we were close to crossing it. But a whale spout is a terrific come-on, like a searchlight above a grand opening, the whale's great size itself a form of magnanimity. Despite their having been hunted for millennia by men in small boats, probably in this very bay (100,000 whales were killed in Alaskan waters in the 1870s alone), we drew closer, as if to enlarge ourselves, trusting that among whales good intentions count for something.

The next time the whales blew, we heard the blast from the blowhole and felt the cool mist of their breath on our cheeks. A smell like rancid seaweed hung in the air. Then the whales sounded, diving vertically with a characteristic upstroke of the tail. A beautiful and emblematic sight—immense horizontal flukes planing off the water and upending in a gesture as meaningful and final as a wave of the hand.

Afterward, rocking silently in the boat, I experienced a kind of tunnel vision, as if I had been looking through the photographer's telephoto lens, everything cropped away but the whale's flukes. Now my field of vision was widening again to encompass the surrounding bay, the dome of sky, and our own strangely exultant faces.

When the whales surfaced again, they were far away, heading for the open sea. In the middle distance were the lights of our ship. We ran open-throttle toward them, anxious to tell what we had seen. In the excitement, the brown bear had been forgotten, upstaged by a larger, seemingly more benign creature.

"Whales!" exclaimed the photographer. "How are you going to top that?"

Whales, however, were incidental to this cruise. The scientists aboard the *Alpha Helix* were conducting a survey of sea otter feeding grounds in the Alexander Archipelago of Southeast Alaska. Sea otters are a "keystone species," which is to say an animal that, by its feeding and activities, can modify the nature of the community in which it lives. Yet two days out of Sitka we still hadn't spotted any sea otters. Mostly we had seen what sea otters eat: clams and sea urchins brought up by the divers in green net bags.

"We chase stores," said John Oliver, chief scientist aboard. "We know where the otter fronts are. We know where they're moving. Nobody's ever gotten in front of them to see what happens when they come into an area. We're getting in front of them just enough to see what happens when they move in and trash a place."

In the wake of the Exxon Valdez, there was a certain irony in speaking of sea otters as trashing anything. Dead sea otters mired in oily goo, jaws caught in a fatal rictus—trashed, so to speak—had become the quasi-official measure of the oil spill. But on the outer coast of Baranof Island, the spill seemed only a distant rumor of war. Prevailing currents had carried the oil slick westward from the grounded tanker and away from the Alexander Archipelago. The cruise plan of the *Alpha Helix* called for us to steam south to Dixon Entrance, not to document atrocities in Prince William Sound. But the spill had forced many sea otters to migrate to new territories, presenting an opportunity to examine the effects of otter predation on previously undisturbed areas. We would be looking chiefly at their prey, marine invertebrates, creatures so small and arcane as to call into question where their lives even fit into the big picture.

The red Zodiac was the newest and fastest of the four small boats aboard the *Alpha Helix*. The only indication of John Oliver's rank as chief scientist on this cruise was that nobody else asked for the red boat. Oliver would ride figurehead in its prow, one knee on the rubber tube, hands clasped behind his back except when he'd indicate a change in direction with a short chopping motion of his arm. We briefly crossed open coast, past wave-battered shoreline, scaring up gulls, until Oliver signalled us into a hidden bay on Beauchamp Island. Surfing on an incoming roller, we rode the wave through a gap in the rocks until they opened up into a cove, smooth and green in its depths.

Oliver spit into his mask and adjusted it so that the hood of his dry suit overlapped the top, leaving only an oval of exposed skin around his mouth. Then he tumbled backward off the boat. Another diver followed, and I watched them disappear into a trail of bubbles.

These were "bounce" dives, a quick reconnaissance of likely areas for clams or urchins. The dives would be marked on a map so that follow-up studies could be done in the future if sea otters moved into the area. Looking over the side, I could see, at a depth of twenty feet, what appeared to be rows of cabbage heads growing in sand. It was an urchin barrens, barren of almost everything, that is, except sea urchins, which had grazed the algae and kelp down to bare sand and rock.

A few minutes later, Oliver "hallooed" from the far side of the cove, and I ran the Zodiac over to pick him up. He was holding a large fuchsia-colored sea urchin that resembled a hedgehog curled into a ball (urchin is French for hedgehog). Placing the urchin in a white collecting bucket, I hauled Oliver aboard and grabbed my waterproof notebook to take dictation as Oliver spit the words out.

"White sand bottom to fifty feet. Urchin barrens. Some sea pins. Sea cucumbers, some saxidomus siphons, starfish—"

He was interrupted by the other diver, who surfaced holding an enormous *pycnopedia helianthoides*, or sunflower starfish. It was mottled blue and gray with more than twenty arms, and it felt like wet papier-mâché. Before tossing the starfish back into the sea, Oliver placed it on his head and posed briefly as the Statue of Liberty.

In the evening the scientists divided into groups to catalogue their data. One group classified species of clams in the dry lab; another entered dive logs into the two computers aboard. I joined a semicircle of people who sat beneath floodlights on the afterdeck, cutting open sea urchins. There was nothing rhapsodic about this aspect of field biology except that it was the real work of the voyage. By comparing the size and weight of these sea urchins with those in areas containing sea otters, the scientists hoped to learn about the effects of otter predation on prey communities. When otters move into an area, they decimate the sea urchins, which feed on kelp. The result is a kelp forest, an environment more suitable for fish but not for shellfish. The implications of such research are important for places like the California coast, where a transplanted sea otter population is frequently at odds with people who catch shellfish and vulnerable to offshore oil development.

The urchins were piled in several white plastic buckets. They were red or purple, globular, and covered with articulating spines. They looked like something to hang on a Christmas tree. As echinoderms, like star-fish and sand dollars, sea urchins are marked by radial symmetry, their shells banded in swirls like Byzantine domes. Only the scratching of spines against the sides of the buckets reminded us that the urchins were alive.

Selecting a sea urchin, our leader, a doctoral student, would measure its width, weigh it, then split the shell with a diver's knife, letting the seawater drain out as if she were cracking an egg. Inside were orange fingers of roe (which taste like egg yolk), a watery gut, and an intricate, five-toothed jaw assembly called Aristotle's Lantern, used for grazing on kelp. After weighing the roe and guts on a tabular hanging scale, I'd call out the numbers and then throw the whole mess over the side.

Someone had placed a boom box on the hatch cover. While The Best of James Brown blasted from the speakers, we shucked sea urchins at a rate even otters might find appalling. One of the crew, a droopy-pants character who billed himself as the Fishin' Magician, was jigging a line over the railing. Pretty soon he had something on that bent his fishing rod in a parabola. A few of us stopped shucking urchins long enough to watch him winch a large red snapper over the railing. Workman-like, the crewman yanked the hook out of the fish's jaw, baited up, and resumed jigging. By now we were all watching. The snapper was still alive, saucer-eyes bulging, air bladder ballooning out of its mouth from having been brought up from forty fathoms. Even the boom box couldn't drown out the awful flap of fish against deck.

"Why don't you put that fish out of its misery?" one of the grad students shouted. "Don't you know it's cruel to let something die like that?"

The crewman did a slow about-face. If he was intimidated by this circle of intent, questioning faces, people with advanced degrees, he didn't show it.

"Look who's talking. You guys just killed, what, a hundred sea urchins? At least I'm going to eat my fish."

Nobody had an answer for that, so the Fishin' Magician resumed fishing.

These days it's hard to know where one's sympathies should begin in regard to animals. "The question is not Can they reason, nor Can they talk," Jeremy Bentham wrote a century ago, "but, Can they *suffer?*" Who knows what suffering means to an animal lacking a central nervous system? As a litmus test for where our loyalties for living organisms should begin, the capacity for suffering is as limited and anthropocentrically weighted as the ability to maintain eye contact. Bentham might as well have said, Can they *evoke* our sympathy? As far as echinoderms go, I don't think so. Still, under the floodlights, my hands, stained a deep purple from shell pigment, suddenly looked bloodstained. As the feverish voice of James Brown launched into "I Break Out in a Cold Sweat," I couldn't help thinking of the next sea urchin.

On the third day of the voyage, the ship anchored in Aats Bay on Coronation Island. The photographer, her husband, and I took the grey Zodiac around the bay to look for sea otters, which were supposed to be in this area. The luxuriant brown kelp forests were a good indicator, as well as the fact that the few sea urchins the divers had found were small, living as fugitives in crevices under rocks, subsisting on drift algae.

A fog was burning off the water as we passed rafts of pigeon guillemots and pelagic cormorants. The first otters we saw turned out to be spotted seals arrayed like sunbathers on the rocks. They seemed naked and vulnerable and reluctant to return to the sea. Rounding the point to Alikula Bay, we finally spotted a sea otter, a female with a pup riding on her chest. She had a blunt, yellowish head, more catlike and cleverlooking than a seal's, and she never let the gap close between us. She whistled, and eight more otters popped up from a kelp bed where they'd been snoozing. Without taking their eyes off us, they moved away, backpeddling so that they appeared to walk on water.

It's easy to see why people find sea otters so appealing. They look like furry handpuppets and obviously enjoy themselves. The history of their exploitation and near extinction is a familiar tale of human greed. It was the projected profits in sea otter skins that prompted the United States to purchase Alaska in 1864, and the knowledge that the species was fast being depleted made the Russians eager to sell. It's difficult to understand how people could have hunted sea otters so ruthlessly. For one thing, they had to get past those eyes.

After several days without sighting a whale, the photographer's husband, a cartoonist, was growing listless. To entertain himself, he drew a cartoon strip on the mess room blackboard entitled "What We Saw Today." There was a cartoon sea otter in a Mexican sombrero—"Otter Fajitas"—and a humpback whale breaching under John Oliver's Zodiac.

"I'd be curious to know," said the cartoonist, "what you end up writing about. The whales were interesting, but otherwise this trip has been pretty dry-clams and bugs. What's the good of all this research? Frankly, who cares?"

The "bugs" were in fact nit-sized crustaceans called amphipods. Kathy Conlan, biologist from the Canadian Museum of Nature, spent most of her time in the ship's dry lab, looking at them through a microscope. There are an estimated 25,000 species of amphipods in the world, only a third of which have been identified. Those on land are commonly called beach hoppers; those in the sea are called scuds. The names are hardly promising.

She collected scuds with a bait trap lowered to the bottom and attached to a buoy. The trap was nothing but a screened funnel attached to a plastic jar baited with a dead herring. After an hour she'd pull the trap up to find a nest of amphipods and nothing left of the herring but a fine comb of bones.

"Look at this," Kathy said. "Here's a female with a brood pouch of fifteen."

She was studying *Dulichia rhabdoplastis*, a species of amphipod that lives commensally on the spines of red sea urchins. Fastening a strand of detritus that trails off from the spine tip, it feeds on particles of plankton that float past. The sea urchin is the whole world to *Dulichia rhabdoplastis*, and it holds on for dear life.

Looking into the microscope, I felt like I was free-falling several rungs down the food chain. The spine of the sea urchin was magnified to the scale of a redwood, and balancing on it was a lobsterlike creature with outsized claws and glowing, iridescent eyes. Hunched over her brood of young, mama amphipod moved with a hideous swaying motion. There is nothing spiritual in these lives, nothing exultant; they are simply grist for larger animals from sea urchins to whales. Diving off Coronation Island, the divers had discovered gouges in the soft mud of the sea floor made by gray whales feeding on amphipods.

"This one's a male," said Kathy, moving the specimen jar slightly until a larger amphipod hovered into view. "You can tell it's a male because its claws are larger. They're not only used to defend territories but to grasp a mate as well. You can see he's holding a female under his thorax. They'll mate when the female molts. It's very exciting to watch!"

I climbed the stairs to the wheelhouse, which was dark except for the luminous green dials of radar and electronic navigation devices steering us through the night. We had left Coronation Island and were passing south of the lighthouse at Cape Decision (a flash every five seconds) toward Iphigenia Bay. The bay had been named by a nineteenth-century British naval officer to commemorate bad weather and his knowledge of the classics.

In Greek mythology Iphigenia was the eldest daughter of Agamemnon and the first victim of the Trojan War. On the eve of battle, Agamemnon's fleet lay stormbound. A soothsayer explained the problem: the goddess Artemis had been offended because one of Agamemnon's men had killed a sacred animal in the goddess's sacred grove. (In some accounts the sacred beast is a stag, in others a pregnant hare.) To appease Artemis and get underway, Agamemnon reluctantly agreed to sacrifice his daughter.

If Hollywood ever gets around to making "The Sacrifice of Iphigenia," Alaska would be the sacred grove, an Exxon official could play Agamemnon, and the part of the sacred beast would be a toss-up between a sea otter and a whale. Few creatures engage our emotions as intensely or elicit such outrage when threatened. Both are marine mammals that have come back from the verge of extinction to become flagships of the environmental movement. Both have attracted the kind of merchandising once reserved for dead rock stars: t-shirts, limited-edition commemorative coins, and, in the case of humpbacks, record albums and hints of spiritual powers. If an animal is a keystone species, does that necessarily give it more spiritual significance?

The strategy of promoting highly visible species in order to protect entire ecosystems has been a successful one. It's been easier to rally around Save the Whales than Save the Oceans even when the oceans clearly need saving. But such a star system presents a distorted view of life on earth. Most of the species on this planet do not have backbones. And it's the unruly masses at the bottom of the food chain that support the big, glamorous mammals at the top, not the other way around. Clams and sea urchins can get along perfectly well without sea otters, but the reverse is not true. We've separated questions of animal rights from those of habitat as though the two weren't interconnected, as though the ocean itself weren't a living organism. There is a kind of fatalism in all this, in narrowing our focus to a few large mammals while smaller, inconspicuous creatures, like the snail darter, slip toward the abyss. It's as if we perceive the ark to be shrinking and believe that if only a few species can be saved from extinction, they ought to be the sentient, warm-blooded ones, the ones that remind us of ourselves. But the others, the smaller creatures we'd just as soon jettison, *are* the ark.

Head down, bent over, I made my way along the black whale beach of Thorne Island. It was a hot day. My orange float coat and rain pants lay in a heap on the beach. In the lagoon behind me, a scientist sunned himself aboard the Boston whaler, playing Irish tunes on a pennywhistle.

Every so often I stooped to overturn a moist chunk of rock and flailed after the beach hoppers that skittered out from underneath and stuffed them into a plastic collecting bag. I had promised Kathy Conlon to look for terrestrial amphipods to add to her collection. I was chasing their stories, pretending to care, as she did, about the differences among species. But in truth, their skittering reminded me of cockroaches and past apartments I'd just as soon forget.

Moving up the beach, I found the bleached skull and ribs of a Sitka deer scattered among the luxuriant beach grass. Here was a mystery: What had killed the deer? Where was the rest of the skeleton? What was the story here? The poignancy of any skull is, of course, entirely a matter of how closely it resembles one's own. All morning I'd been walking on a boneyard of clam and cockle shells, a charnel house of ectoskeletons, unmoved because I could not imagine lives to inhabit them or stories for how they ended. Picking up the deer skull, I arranged it totemlike upon a rock, eye sockets facing out to sea.

The tide was ebbing. I waded out in my fireman's boots to a rocky tide pool to see the lines of zonation, patterns of color on the rocks where one species' sphere of influence ends and another's begins. Starfish, which prey on mussels, were the keystone species here, the head honchos. Clinging to the face of the rock like mountain climbers, they limit the downward expansion of mussels, while the height of tide limits their own upward mobility.

A friend of mine who loves tide pools cannot bring herself to climb over them because of all the small lives there, almost indistinguishable from the rocks to which they adhere. It would be like walking, she says, on people's heads. But I am no such saint and go clambering over the acorn barnacles and mussels. We all live in one tide pool or other, and by the same harsh dynamics. We may not chase after whales in small boats, harpoon in hand, without the sheer weight of our lives being felt, and we must learn to place our feet more carefully.

Starfish aside, I was for the moment the headman here, the keystone species. Small crabs scuttled over the rocks to hide in crevices, fleeing my approach as if I were the biggest thing in the world, as big as a whale. Not one of them paused to wonder whether my intentions were good.

JOHN DOS PASSOS

John Dos Passos was born in Chicago, Illinois, in 1896 and until his death in 1970 pursued a highly prolific literary career. He was a member of the American Academy of Arts and Letters, the American Academy of Arts and Sciences, the Authors League, and many other honorary societies. His honors and awards included three Guggenheim fellowships, the National Institute of Arts and Letters Gold Medal Award for fiction, and the Antonio Feltrinelli Prize from the Italian Academia Nazionale dei Lincei for narrative innovation. He is best known for *Manhattan Transfer, U.S.A., 42nd Parallel, 1919,* and *The Big Money.*

Entering the Ice Age

Next morning the wind swings into the north, and the sky clears. By the time the ferry leaves the Juneau dock, the sun is breaking through. We have to backtrack, rounding Douglas Island, vague and cloud-veiled, to the southwest. More big brown bears there than any other place in the world. After we swing around a steep, rocky point, the Lynn Canal stretches ahead into the bright north. The ruffled water is a dense jade green. To the right of us, Shelter Island, which I couldn't see for the mist the day before, stands out shaggy with dark-green, pointed spruces. On the mainland beyond, a few small white houses, dotted along the road from Tee Harbor into Juneau, shine like cubes of sugar. Above them the gray mass of Mendenhall Glacier, striped with ice green, rises to the broad, white shoulders of its snowfields. An S-shaped streak shows up dark down the middle, where the torrent runs off from the melting ice.

Now, to the left, the Chilkat Range piles up as far as you can see, peak after jagged peak with snowfields and glaciers draped between. Snow bright, ice gray, rock charcoal-dark. To the right the rising ranges are the Kakunau Mountains. As the channel narrows into the north, snow mountains rise higher and whiter on either side.

There is an unearthly brilliance about the day. Sky of a robin's-egg blue. Jade water. Clouds suffused with rosy amber. Snow cones glisten. Foaming waterfalls catch the sun. Peaks parade past like circus performers in their glittering finery.

Marine life, the man said. Yes, indeed. Porpoises roll near the ship. Blackfish surface. Whales spout in the distance. Some creature shows a great shining fluke as it sounds right off the bow.

We are entering the Ice Age. Here glaciers still carve out the valleys. With your own eyes you can detect the piling up of moraines. The streams that gush, gray with rock flour, from under the ice, wind and wander over plains of broken stones. Some day they may dig themselves beds and become rivers. Now they are mere torrents that flood the land in the spring thaw. Water pours from sievelike cliffs. The grinding weight of the ice and the rush of thawed water toward the sea is fashioning these gorges. Escarpments stand up raw and new. Between snowfields, seamed and splintered by frost and storm, rock ridges strain toward the sky. It is a land in agonies of creation.

JENNIE THLUNAUT

Jennie Thlunaut was born in 1890 in the Chilkat area of Alaska. Surrounded all her life with Tlingit art, some of which is currently world famous, she spent nearly three quarters of a century working as a Chilkat weaver. In 1984 she received a Governor's Award for the Arts, and in 1986 she was one of twelve American artists selected to receive a National Heritage Fellowship Award from the National Endowment for the Arts. She participated in the Alaska Native Sisterhood and also taught at the Chilkat Weaving Workshop at Raven House in Haines, Alaska, in 1985, which she inaugurated with her Welcome Speech to apprentice weavers. Jennie Thlunaut died in 1986. The speech was transcribed and translated by Nora Dauenhauer.

Welcome Speech

Ax̱ tuwáa sigóo
yee éen at kax̱waneegí
ax̱ sisdees.
Ax̱ toowú yak'éi,
aaa,
hóoch'i gaawú
yaa kunax̱laséin
(x̱at yeeytéen)
aax̱ yá gaaw
yee tuwaá sigóo yeeysakoowú
yá aan x̱at kawdudlix̱edli át.
Tléil yaa ux̱shagé.
Ax̱ tuwaá sigóo goot ḵaach wuskoowú.
Aaa, shux'áanáx̱
ax̱ tláa,
Sitgeedáx̱ áwé,
ax̱ éeshch uwasháa
Tlákw.aandéi.
Ax' áwé ḵux̱dzitee.
Ax̱ aat hás jeedáx̱ atwuskú áyá.
Yá gaaw
yá blanket
ax̱ éesh dlaak'
yéi dusáagun
Deinḵul.át.
Du jeedáx̱ atwuskú áyá
ax̱ jee yéi wootee.

29

Tlél aan ḵukin x̱at x̱'eiti.
Ax̱ tuwáa sigóo
ax̱ x̱ooni ḵáach wuskoowú.
Ha yá gaaw
gunalchéesh.
Yéi yoo yee kayasheik ax̱ x̱ándéi.
Aaa,
aadéi shtugáa x̱at ditee.
Áyá ax̱ Aanḵáawooch aan x̱at kawlix̱étl
yá yéi jiné.
Aaa,
yá gaaw ḵu.aa,
tlél ch'a koogéiyi.
Ch'a yéi x̱at gusagenk'idáx̱
ax̱ chachi
áa x̱at shukawajeis' ax̱ tláa,
ḵa ax̱ éesh;
Wednesday ḵa Sunday
yaa x̱at jigatánch cháchdei.
Aax̱ yá gaaw
yá aan x̱at kawdudlix̱etli át.
Gunalchéesh,
yee tuwáa sagoowú.
Ha gu.aal kwshé
Dikaanḵáawux' yan tuytán x'wan,
aa yan nax̱yidlaaḵ.
Aaa Yáat'aa
dei du ée at x̱alatóowun.
Haa yá gaaw áwé
gunalchéesh yei ax̱ toowú yatee,
ax̱ x̱ándei yéi yee kasheigí.
Aaa, Dikaanḵáawu éex̱ ḵwá g̱ayisg̱áax̱
yanax̱ yidlaag̱í
yá akáx̱ haat ḵayeeytini át.
Yéi áwé ax̱ tundátaani yatee yáa yagiyee,
aadéi sh tugáa x̱at ditee.
Aaa, ax̱ g̱aawú uwayáa yaa kunayach'i yáx̱ yatee.

Shux'áanáx̱
1901
áwé ax̱ tláa
ax̱ éeshch áwé akaa ḵoowaḵéi.
Ax̱ tlaak'w yéi duwasáakw,
Saantáas'.
Áwe
yéi wé dulgeis'ín:
fifty dollars
one blanket.
Yéi áwé x̱'alatseenín.
A jeet awatée
wé fifty dollars ax̱ tláak'w jeet.
Aag̱áa áwé ax̱ tláa ee awlitúw.
1901.
Tlél yeedadi yáx̱.
Shaax̱'sáani
át luwugooḵ ch'áakw.
Gwál ch'a x̱át giwé yéi x̱at wuduswáat.
"Haagú!"
Any time you start it.
"Haagú!"
Áyá du déix̱'i ḵanúkch.
I am watching what they're doing.
1908 áwé woonaa ax̱ tláa.
Aag̱áa áwé yan akawsinéi yóot'aa yáx̱,
black and yellow.
All mine.
Ax̱ éeshch
ax̱ jeet uwatée.
Dei ḵwa x̱ashigóok.
I know how to weave.
Aanáx̱ áwé
ax̱ léelk'w
ax̱ éesh du tláa
hooch áwé
shux̱'áanáx̱ ax̱ ée awlitúw.

1908,
Porcupine gold mine-ix' tle all summer áwé
yan ka<u>x</u>wsinéi,
tléix' <u>k</u>utaan.
Yawdi.aa wéit'át; it's a slow job.
A<u>x</u>oo aa yú lingít
two years <u>x</u>'áak aksané.
Aa yei gaxyisatéen aadéi lich'éeyagu yé.
Aa<u>x</u> yan néi
yéi áwé
wududzigéy fifty dollars.
Déi<u>x</u>,
I got two twenty
and one ten,
gold.
Aa<u>g</u>áa áwé
shux'áaná<u>x</u> a<u>x</u> <u>x</u>án.aa
"take good care of that money.
Don't use it."
Yéi wooyáat' aa<u>g</u>áa
a<u>x</u> jee yéi wooteeyi yé,
wé naaxein yeidí.
Aaa, yáa yeedadi <u>k</u>áawu dáanaa yaa ayakanadlá<u>k</u>.
They spend it right away.
Ha yéi sh kadulneek á yahaayí <u>k</u>udzitee dáanaa.
Sh tóon yoo diteek <u>k</u>óodá<u>x</u>
I áyáa ayaduneiyí.
Ách áwé
tsu <u>x</u>wahooní
a<u>x</u> naaxeiní
I keep the money for two, three months
or four months.
Ách áwé yeedát tlél <u>k</u>'anashgidei<u>x</u> <u>x</u>at ustée.
Aaa,
A<u>x</u> éesh hás,
a<u>x</u> aat hás jeedá<u>x</u>
atwuskú áwé.

Ách áwé ayaa awuxaanéi.

Ha yá gaaw ku.aa ax tundatáani ax x'agáax'i yéi yatee,

ch'a aadooch sá yan gadlaagí

yáa yéi daaxane át.

Kanay.aakw yee Aankaawoox' yan tuytán

aa yanax yidlaagí.

Yéi áwé

áwé aadéi yoo kawaneiyi yé wé naaxein.

Tlákw.aannáx áwé kuwdzitee.

Gaanaxteidí yóo

s duwasáakw ax éesh hás.

Hásch áwé s aawasháa

Tsimshian woman.

Yéi áwé

du saayí tlél du káx xat seix'aakw.

Yei áwé wduwasáa

Hayuwáas Tláa.

I remember the name.

Hayuwáas Tláa jeedáx atwuskú áwé

first in Tlákw.aan.

Kux has akawsikéi

we naaxein.

Ch'u yeedát áwoo á.

They got it.

Martha Willard got it,

that blanket.

First blanket from a Tsimshian.

Áwé kux has akawsikéi.

Ch'as ax aat hásx siteeyi áach áwé

has awshigóok.

Yaax' áwé s du kaani yán ee s awlituw, yá uhaan.

Yanwaa Sháa ee s awlitúw.

Ach áwé yéi duwasáakw

Jilkáat Blanket.

Tlél tsu Sitka,

tlél tsu Hoonah,

tlél tsu goox' sá yéi daaduné.

Only Tlákw.aan.
That's why they call it Jilḵáat Blanket.
Ha yéi áwé yee tóo yéi kgwatée.
I don't know why they lost the art
wé Tsimshian ḵu.aa.
Tlél yeedát
I don't see
somebody make it like that.
Aaa
yá gaaw ḵu.aa aẖ toowu yak'éi,
yee tuwaa wusgóowu.
Aẖ ẖagáax'i yéi yatee ch'a aadóoch sá yawudlaagi.
Aaa
yéi áwé.

I would like
to tell you something,
my sisters.
I am happy,
yes,
I am coming close
to my final hour
(you can see my condition)
that at this time
you want to learn
this weaving I was blessed with.
I don't want to keep it to myself.
I want someone else to learn.
Yes, to begin with,
my father married
my mother,
who was from Sitka,
and they moved to Klukwan.
I was born there.
This is the art of my paternal aunts.

My father's sister
at the time
of that blanket
was called
Deinkul.at.
This is the art from her
that was passed to my hands.
I'm not stingy.
I would like
someone like me to learn it.
Now, at this time,
thank you.
You have experienced hardships to be with me
for this work.
Yes,
I'm grateful for this.
God gave his blessing to me
for this work.
Yes,
and I want to tell you now
none of this was by accident.
From when I was little
my mother
and my father instructed me
on where my church was;
Wednesday and Sunday
she would take me by the hand to church.
From that time to this
I have been blessed with this weaving.
Thank you
for wanting it.
My hope is
you will have faith in God,
that you will learn.
Yes,
I have been teaching her already.
Now, at this time,

I feel thankful
that you have experienced hardships to be with me.
Ask our Lord above
to learn
what you came for.
This is how I feel today, I'm grateful for this.
Yes, my time seems to be getting short.
In the beginning,
in 1901,
my father paid
for my mother's instruction.
My maternal aunt was named
Saantáas'.
Then,
they used to pay this much for it:
fifty dollars`
for one blanket.
This was the dollar value.
He gave
the fifty dollars to my aunt.
This was when she taught my mother.
1901.
It wasn't like now.
The young girls
didn't run around long ago.
Maybe it was only me that was raised this way.
"Come here!" they'd say,
every time they began weaving.
"Come here!"
I would sit behind her.
I'd watch what they were doing.
My mother died in 1908.
This is when she finished weaving it, like that one,
black and yellow.
All mine.
My father
gave it to me.

I already knew how to weave.
I knew how to weave.
After this
my grandmother,
my father's mother,
was the one
who first taught it to me.
In 1908,
at Porcupine gold mine I weaved all summer
and finished it
in one summer.
Those things take time; it's slow work.
It takes some people
two years to weave one.
Now you'll all see how slow it is.
When it was finished
it was bought
for this much: fifty dollars.
Two,
I got two twenties
and one ten,
gold pieces.
This is when
my first husband said to me,
"Take good care of the money.
Don't spend it."
I kept the money
for a long time then,
the money from the naaxein.
Yes, people of today, as soon as they make the money
they spend it right away.
Well, they say money has a spirit.
You can offend it
if you don't respect it.
That's why
when I sold
my naaxein

I kept the money for two, three,
or four months.
This is why I'm not a poor person.
Yes,
this art
is from my fathers
and my paternal aunts.
Because of this I respect it.
And now at this time my thoughts are, my prayers are,
that someone master
the things that I do.
Try to concentrate on your Lord
so that you'll master it.
This is the way
it happened with the naaxein.
It came through Klukwan.
My fathers are called
Gaanaxteidí.
They were the ones who married
the Tsimshian woman.
This is why
I don't forget her name.
Her name was
Hayuwáas Tláa.
I remember the name.
This is art from Hayuwáas Tláa
first done in Klukwan.
They unraveled
the naaxein.
It's still there now.
They have it.
Martha Willard has
that blanket.
The first blanket from a Tsimshian.
They unraveled it.
Only those who were my paternal aunts
learned it.

Then they taught it to their sisters-in-law, to us.
They taught it to the Yaanwaa Sháa.
That is why it's called
Chilkat Blanket.
It wasn't made in Sitka,
or Hoonah,
or anywhere else.
Only in Klukwan.
That is why it's called Chilkat Blanket.
This is what you will keep in mind.
I don't know why the Tsimshians
lost the art.
I don't see
anyone now
making them like that.
Yes,
but now I feel good
that you have wanted to do it.
My prayer is that someone learn it.
Yes,
that is how I feel.

JOHN BURROUGHS

Born in 1837, John Burroughs grew up on a farm near Roxbury, New York. Along with Henry David Thoreau and Ralph Waldo Emerson, he is often credited with helping to establish the "nature essay" as a serious literary genre. The author of numerous books including *Notes on Walt Whitman: Poet and Person*, *Birds and Poets*, *Locusts and Wild Honey*, *The Breath of Life*, and *Accepting the Universe*, Mr. Burroughs journeyed to Alaska as part of the famous 1899 Harriman Expedition. He died in 1921.

FROM *Narrative of the Expedition*

Lynn Canal and Skagway

All the afternoon we steamed up Lynn Canal over broad, placid waters, shut in by dark smooth-based mountains that end in bare serrated peaks. Glaciers became more and more numerous; one on our right hung high on the brink of a sheer, naked precipice, as if drawing back from the fearful plunge. But plunge it did not and probably never will.

We were soon in sight of a much larger glacier, the Davidson, on our left. It flows out of a deep gorge and almost reaches the inlet. Seen from afar it suggests the side view of a huge white foot with its toe pressing a dark line of forest into the sea.

Before sunset we reached Skagway and landed at the long, high pier (the tides here are sixteen or eighteen feet). The pier was swarming with people. Such a gathering and such curiosity and alertness we had not before seen. Hotel runners flourished their cards and called out the names of their various hostelries before we had touched the dock. Boys greeted us with shouts and comments; women and girls, some of them in bicycle suits, pushed to the front and gazed intently at the strangers. All seemed to be expecting something, friends or news, or some sensational occurrence. No sooner had we touched than the boys swarmed in upon us like ants and began to explore the ship, and were as promptly swept ashore again. Skagway is barely two years old. Born of the gold fever, it is still feverish and excitable. It is on a broad delta of land made by the Skagway River between the mountains, and, it seems to me, is likely at any time by a great flood in the river to be swept into the sea. It began at the stump and probably is still the stumpiest town in the country. Many of the houses stand upon stumps; there are stumps in nearly every dooryard, but the people already speak of the "early times," three years ago.

On the steep, bushy mountain-side near the wharf I heard the melodious note of my first Alaska hermit thrush. It was sweet and pleasing, but not so prolonged and powerful as the song of our hermit.

White Pass

The next day the officials of the Yukon and White Pass Railroad took our party on an excursion to the top of the famous White Pass, twenty-one miles distant. The grade up the mountain is in places over two hundred feet to the mile, and in making the ascent the train climbs about twenty-nine hundred feet. After the road leaves Skagway River its course is along the face of precipitous granite peaks and domes, with long loops around the heads of gorges and chasms; occasionally on trestles over yawning gulfs, but for the most part on a shelf of rock blasted out of the side of the mountain. The train stopped from time to time and allowed us to walk ahead and come face to face with the scene. The terrible and the sublime were on every hand. It was as appalling to look up as to look down; chaos and death below us, impending avalanches of hanging rocks above us. How elemental and cataclysmal it all looked! I felt as if I were seeing for the first time the real granite ribs of the earth; they had been cut into and slivered, and there was no mistake about them. All I had seen before were but scales and warts on the surface by comparison; here were the primal rocks that held the planet together, sweeping up into the clouds and plunging down into the abyss. Over against us on the other side of the chasm we caught glimpses here and there of the "Dead Horse Trail." Among the spruces and along the rocky terraces are said to have perished several thousand horses on this terrible trail. The poor beasts became so weak from lack of food that they slipped on the steep places and plunged over the precipices in sheer desperation, and thus ended their misery.

On the summit we found typical March weather: snow, ice, water, mud, slush, fog, and chill. The fog prevented us from getting a view down toward the Klondike country, six hundred miles away. The British flag and the Stars and Stripes were floating side by side on the provisional boundary line between Alaska and British Columbia, and several Canadian police were on duty there. Even in this bleak spot we found birds nesting or preparing to nest: the pipit, the golden-crowned sparrow, and the rosy finch. The vegetation was mostly moss and lichens and low stunted spruce, the latter so flattened by the snow that one could walk over them.

In keeping with the snow and desolation and general dissolution was the group of hasty, ragged canvas buildings and tents at the railroad terminus, the larger ones belonging to the company, the others for the accommodation of traveling gold-seekers. In one of the larger tents a really good dinner was served our party, through the courtesy of the railroad officials. We saw on the trail a few gold-seekers with their heavy packs; they paused and looked up wistfully at our train.

In ascending the Pass we met a small party of naturalists from the U.S. Biological Survey on their way to the Yukon, the entire length of which they intended traversing in a small boat. We stopped long enough to visit their tent and take a hasty look at the interesting collection of birds and mammals they had already secured here. They have since returned and published a report on the results of their labors.

At the time of our visit the railroad terminus was at the summit of the pass, from which point passengers bound for the Klondike were transported to Lake Bennett by sleighs. The deep snow was melting so rapidly and slumping so badly that the sled-loads of people and grain we saw depart for the Upper Yukon were, we were told, the last to go through before the completion of the railroad to Bennett.

The next day found us in Glacier Bay on our way to the Muir Glacier. Our course was up an arm of the sea, dotted with masses of floating ice, till in the distance we saw the great glacier itself. Its front looked gray and dim there twenty miles away, but in the background the mountains that feed it lifted up vast masses of snow in the afternoon sun. At five o'clock we dropped anchor about two miles from its front, in eighty fathoms of water, abreast of the little cabin on the east shore built by John Muir some years ago. Not till after repeated soundings did we find bottom within reach of our anchor cables. Could the inlet have been emptied of its water for a moment, we should have seen before us a palisade of ice nearly one thousand feet higher and over two miles long, with a turbid river, possibly half a mile wide, boiling up from beneath it. Could we have been here many centuries ago, we should have seen, much farther down the valley, a palisade of ice two or three thousand feet high. Many of these Alaskan glaciers are rapidly melting and are now but the fragments of their former selves. From observations made here twenty years ago by John Muir, it is known that the position of the front of the Muir Glacier at that time was about two miles below its present position, which would indicate a rate of recession of about one mile in ten years.

What we saw on that June afternoon was a broken and crumbling wall of ice two hundred and fifty feet high in our front, stretching across the inlet and running down to a low, dirty, crumbling line where it ended on the shore on our left, and where it disappeared behind high gray gravelly banks on our right. The inlet near the glacier was choked with icebergs.

What is that roar or explosion that salutes our ears before our anchor has found bottom? It is the downpour of an enormous mass of ice from the glacier's front, making it for the moment as active as Niagara. Other and still other downpours follow at intervals of a few minutes, with deep explosive sounds and the rising up of great clouds of spray, and we quickly realize that here is indeed a new kind of Niagara, a cataract the like of which we have not before seen, a mighty congealed river that discharges into the bay intermittently in ice avalanches that shoot down its own precipitous front. The mass of ice below the water line is vastly greater than that above, and when the upper portions fall away, enormous bergs are liberated and rise up from the bottom. They rise slowly and majestically, like huge monsters of the deep, lifting themselves up to a height of fifty or a hundred feet, the water pouring off them in white sheets. Then they subside again and float away with a huge wave in front. Nothing we had read or heard had prepared us for the color of the ice, especially of the newly exposed parts and of the bergs that rose from beneath the water—its deep, almost indigo blue. Huge bergs were floating about that suggested masses of blue vitriol.

As soon as practicable, many of us went ashore in the naphtha launches, and were soon hurrying over the great plateau of sand, gravel, and boulders which the retreating glacier had left, and which forms its vast terminal moraine.

Many of the rocks and stones on the surface were sharp and angular, others were smooth and rounded. These latter had evidently passed as it were through the gizzard of the huge monster, while the others had been carried on its back. A walk of a mile or more brought us much nearer the glacier's front, and standing high on the bank of the moraine we could observe it at our leisure. The roar that followed the discharge of ice from its front constantly suggested the blasting in mines or in railroad cuts. The spray often rose nearly to the top of the glacier. Night and day, summer and winter, this intermittent and explosive discharge of the ice into the inlet goes on and has gone on for centuries. When we awoke in the night we heard its muffled thunder, sometimes so loud as to jar the windows in our staterooms, while the swells caused by the falling and rising masses rocked the ship. Probably few more strange and impressive spectacles than this glacier affords can be found on the continent. It has a curious fascination. Impending cataclysms are in its look. In a moment or two one knows some part of it will topple or slide into the sea. One afternoon during our stay about half a mile of the front fell at once. The swell which it caused brought grief to our photographers who had ventured too near it. Their boat was filled and their plates were destroyed. The downfall from the front is usually a torrent of shattered ice which pours down, simulating water, but at longer intervals enormous solid masses like rocks, topple and plunge. It is then that the great blue bergs rise up from below—born of the depths. The enormous pressure to which their particles have been subjected for many centuries seems to have intensified their color. They have a pristine, elemental look. Their crystals have not seen the light since they fell in snowflakes back amid the mountains generations ago. All this time imprisoned, traveling in darkness, carving the valleys, polishing the rocks, under a weight as of mountains, till at last their deliverance comes with crash and roar, and they are once more free to career in the air and light as dew or rain or cloud, and then again to be drawn into that cycle of transformation and caught and bound once more in glacier chains for another century.

We lingered by the Muir and in adjacent waters five or six days, sending out botanical, zoological, and glacial expeditions in various directions; yes and one hunting party to stir up the bears in Howling Valley. Howling Valley, so named by Muir, is a sort of coat-tail pocket of the great glacier. It lies twenty or more miles from the front, behind the mountains. The hunters started off eagerly on the first afternoon of our arrival, with packers and glistening Winchesters and boxes of ammunition, and we had little doubt that the *genius loci* of Howling Valley would soon change its tune.

While some of us the next afternoon were exploring the eastern half of the glacier, which is a vast prairie-like plain of ice, we saw far off across the dim surface to the north two black specks, then two other black specks, and in due time still other black specks, and the conjecture passed that the hunters were returning, and that the heart of the mystery of Howling Valley had not been plucked out. Our reluctant conjectures proved too true. Just at nightfall the hunters came straggling in, footsore and weary and innocent of blood—soberer if not sadder, hardier if not wiser men. The undertaking involved more than they had bargained for. Their outward course that afternoon lay for a dozen miles or more across the glacier. They had traveled till near midnight and then rested a few hours in their sleeping-bags upon the ice. One may sleep upon the snow in a sleeping-bag, but ice soon makes itself felt in more ways than one. When the cold began to strike up through, the party resumed its march. Very soon they got into snow, which became deeper and deeper as they proceeded. Hidden crevasses made it necessary to rope themselves together, the new hunting-shoes pinched and rubbed, the packs grew heavy, the snow grew deeper, the miles grew longer, and there might not be any bears in Howling Valley after all,—Muir's imagination may have done all the howling,—so, after due deliberation by all hands, it was voted to turn back.

It is much easier in Alaska to bag a glacier than a bear; hence our glacial party, made up of John Muir, Gilbert, and Palache, who set out to explore the head of Glacier Bay, was more successful than the hunters. They found more glaciers than they were looking for. One large glacier of twenty years ago had now become two, not by increasing but by diminishing; the main trunk had disappeared, leaving the two branches in separate valleys. All the glaciers of this bay, four or five in number, were found to have retreated many hundred feet since Muir's first visit, two decades earlier. The explorers were absent from the ship three days on a cruise attended with no little peril.

During the same time an ornithological and botanical party of six or eight men was in camp on Gustavus Peninsula, a long, low, wooded stretch of land twenty miles below Muir Glacier. Here over forty species of birds, including sea birds, were observed and collected. The varied thrush or Oregon robin was common, and its peculiar song or plaint, a long, tapering whistle with a sort of burr in it, led Ridgway a long chase through the woods before he could identify the singer. Other song-birds found were the western robin, the two kinglets, a song sparrow, the Alaska hermit and russet-backed thrushes, the lutescent warbler, the redstart, the Oregon junco, and a western form of the savanna sparrow.

Gustavus Peninsula seems to be a recent deposit of the glaciers, and our experts thought it not much over a century old. The botanists here found a good illustration of the successive steps Nature takes in forest-ing or reforesting the land,—how she creeps before she walks. The first shrub is a small creeping willow that looks like a kind of "pus-ley." Then comes a larger willow, less creeping; then two or more other species that become quite large upright bushes; then follow the alders, and with them various herbaceous plants and grasses, till finally the spruce comes in and takes possession of the land. Our collectors found the first generation of trees, none of them over forty years old. Far up the mountain-side, at a height of about two thousand feet, they came to the limit of the younger growth, and found a well-defined line of much older trees, showing that within probably a hundred years an ice sheet two thousand or more feet thick, an older and larger Muir, had swept down the valley and destroyed the forests.

In the meantime the rest of us spent the days on the glacier and in the vicinity, walking, sketching, painting, photographing, dredging, mountain climbing, as our several tastes prompted.

We were in the midst of strange scenes, hard to render in words: the miles upon miles of moraines upon either hand, gray, loosely piled, scooped, plowed, channeled, sifted, from fifty to two hundred feet high; the sparkling sea water dotted with blue bergs and loose drift ice; the towering masses of almost naked rock, smoothed, carved, rounded, granite-ribbed, and snow-crowned, that looked down upon us from both sides of the inlet; and the cleft, toppling, staggering front of the great glacier in its terrible labor-throes stretching before us from shore to shore.

We saw the world-shaping forces at work; we scrambled over plains they had built but yesterday. We saw them transport enormous rocks and tons on tons of soil and debris from the distant mountains; we saw the remains of extensive forests they had engulfed probably within the century, and were now uncovering again; we saw their turbid rushing streams loaded with newly ground rocks and soilmaking material; we saw the beginnings of vegetation in the tracks of the retreating glacier; our dredgers brought up the first forms of sea life along the shore; we witnessed the formation of the low mounds and ridges and bowl-shaped depressions that so often diversify our landscapes, — all the while with the muffled thunder of the falling bergs in our ears.

We were really in one of the workshops and laboratories of the elder gods, but only in the glacier's front was there present evidence that they were still at work. I wanted to see them opening crevasses in the ice, dropping the soil and rocks they had transported, polishing the mountains, or blocking the streams, but I could not. They seemed to knock off work when we were watching them. One day I climbed up to the shoulder of a huge granite ridge on the west, against which the glacier pressed and over which it broke. Huge masses of ice had recently toppled over, a great fragment of rock hung on the very edge, ready to be deposited upon the ridge, windrows of soil and gravel and boulders were clinging to the margin of the ice, but while I stayed not a pebble moved, all was silence and inertia. And I could look down between the glacier and the polished mountain-side; they were not in contact; the hand of the sculptor was raised, as it were, but he did not strike while I was around. In front of me upon the glacier for many miles was a perfect wilderness of crevasses, the ice was ridged and contorted like an angry sea, but not a sound, not a movement anywhere.

Go out on the eastern rim of the glacier, where for a dozen miles or more one walks upon a nearly level plain of ice, and if one did not know to the contrary, he would be sure he saw the agency of man all about him. It is so rare to find Nature working with such measure and precision. Here, for instance, is a railroad embankment stretching off across this ice prairie, — a line of soil, gravel, and boulders, as uniform in width and thickness as if every inch of it had been carefully measured, — straight, level, three feet high, and about the width of a single-track road. The eye follows it till it fades away in the distance. Parallel with it a few yards away is another line of soil and gravel more suggestive of a wagon-road, but with what marvelous evenness is the material distributed; it could not have been dumped there from carts; it must have been sifted out from some moving vehicle.

Then one comes upon a broad band of rocks and boulders, several rods in width, the margins perfectly straight and even, pointing away to the distant mountains. All these are medial moraines,—material gathered from the mountains against which the ice has ground as it slowly passed, and brought hither by its resistless onward flow. Some time it will all be dumped at the end of the glacier, adding to those vast terminal moraines which form the gravel plains that flank each side of the inlet. In looking at these plains and ridges and catching glimpses of the engulfed forests beneath them, one feels as if the mountains must all have been ground down and used up in supplying this world of material. But they have not. Peak after peak many thousand feet high still notches the sky there in the north.

The western part of the Muir Glacier is dead, that is, it is apparently motionless, and no longer discharges bergs from its end. This end, covered with soil and boulders, tapers down to the ground and is easily accessible. Only the larger, more central portion flows and drops bergs into the sea, presenting the phenomenon of a current flowing through a pond, while on each side the water is all but motionless.

Not very long ago the Muir had a large tributary on the west, but owing to its retreating front this limb appears to be cut off and separated from the main ice sheet by a boulder and gravel-strewn ice plain a mile wide. One day three of us spent several hours upon the detached portion, which is called the Morse. It is a mighty ice sheet in itself, nearly or quite a mile wide. It is dead or motionless, and is therefore free from crevasses. Its rim comes down to the gravel like a huge turtle shell, and we stepped on it without difficulty. At first it was very steep, but a few minutes' climbing brought us upon its broad, smooth, gently sloping back. The exposed ice weathers rough, and traveling over it is easy.

We found a few old crevasses, many deep depressions or valleys, and several little creeks singing along deep down between blue, vitreous walls; also wells of unknown depth and of strange and wonderful beauty. We came upon a moraine that suggested a tumble-down stone wall, quite as straight and uniform. It soon disappeared beneath the ice, showing what a depth of snow had fallen upon it since it started upon its slow journey from the distant mountains. We pushed up the gentle slope for several miles until the snow began to be over our shoes, when we turned back. I had climbed hills all my life, but never before had

I walked upon a hill of ice and stopped to drink at springs that were deep crystal goblets.

The waste of the Morse Glacier is carried off by two large, turbid streams that rush from beneath it, and on their way to the inlet uncover a portion of a buried forest. About this buried forest our doctors did not agree. The timber, mostly spruce, was yet hard and sound, a fact that might almost bring the event within the century. A sheet of gravel nearly two hundred feet thick seems to have been deposited upon it suddenly. The trees, so far as exposed, had all been broken off ten or twelve feet from the ground, by some force coming from the west. In some places the original forest floor was laid bare by the water; the black vegetable mould and decayed moss had a fresh, undisturbed look. Evidently no force had plowed or rubbed over the surface of this ground.

While at the Muir we had some cloud and fog, but no storms, and we had one ideal day. That was Sunday, the 11th of June, a day all sun and sky,—not a cloud or film to dim the vast blue vault,—and warm, even hot, on shore; a day memorable to all of us for its wonderful beauty, and especially so to two of us who spent it on the top of Mt. Wright, nearly three thousand feet above the glacier. It was indeed a day with the gods; strange gods, the gods of the foreworld, but they had great power over us. The scene we looked upon was for the most part one of desolation,—snow, ice, jagged peaks, naked granite, gray moraines,—but the bright sun and sky over all, the genial warmth and the novelty of the situation, were ample to invest it with a fascinating interest. There was fatigue in crossing the miles of moraine; there was difficulty in making our way along the sharp crests of high gravel-banks; there was peril in climbing the steep boulder-strewn side of the mountain, but there was exhilaration in every step, and there was glory and inspiration at the top. Under a summer sun, with birds singing and flowers blooming, we looked into the face of winter and set our feet upon the edge of his skirts. But the largeness of the view, the elemental ruggedness, and the solitude as of interstellar space were perhaps what took the deepest hold. It seemed as if the old glacier had been there but yesterday. Granite boulders, round and smooth like enormous eggs, sat poised on the rocks or lay scattered about. A child's hand could have started some of them thundering down the awful precipices. When the Muir Glacier rose to that height, which of course it did in no very remote past, what an engine for carving and polishing the mountains it must have been! Its moraines of that period — where are they? Probably along the Pacific coast under hundreds of fathoms of water.

Back upon the summit the snow lay deep, and swept up in a wide sheet to a sharp, inaccessible peak far beyond and above us. The sweet bird voices in this primal solitude were such a surprise and so welcome. There was the piercing plaint of the golden-crowned sparrow, the rich warble of Townsend's fox sparrow, and the sweet strain of the small hermit thrush. The rosy finch was there also, hopping upon the snow, and the pipit or titlark soared and sang in the warm, lucid air above us. This last song was not much for music, but the hovering flight of the bird above these dizzy heights drew the eye strongly. It circled about joyously, calling chip, chip, chip, chip, without change of time or tune. Below it a white ptarmigan rose up and wheeled about, uttering a curious hoarse, croaking sound, and dropped back to his mate on the rocks. In keeping with these delicate signs of bird life were the little pink flowers, a species of moss campion, blooming here and there just below the snow-line, and looking to unbotanical eyes like blossoming moss. From the height, Muir Glacier stretched away to the north and soon became a sheet of snow, which swept up to the tops of the chain of mountains that hemmed it in. The eastern half of it, with its earth tinge, looked like a prairie newly plowed and sown and rolled. The seed had been drilled in, and the regular, uniform, straight lines were distinctly visible. Along the western horizon, looking down on the Pacific, the Fairweather Range of mountains stood up clear and sharp, Fairweather itself over fifteen thousand feet high. The snow upon these mountains doubtless in places lay over one hundred feet deep.

Glaciers are formed wherever more snow falls in winter than can melt in summer, and this seems to be the case on all these Alaskan mountains on the Pacific coast. If by a change of climate more snow should fall in the Hudson River valley than could melt in summer, our landscapes would soon be invaded by glaciers from the Catskills. Farther north in Alaska, beyond the reach of the moisture-loaded Pacific air currents, the precipitation is less and there are no glaciers.

JOHN KEEBLE

John Keeble was born in Winnipeg, Canada, in 1944 and was raised in Saskatchewan and California. Educated at the University of Redlands, the University of Iowa, and Brown University, Mr. Keeble has taught at Grinnell College, the University of Alabama, and Eastern Washington University. The recipient of several awards for his work, he is the author of *Crab Canon, Mine* (with Ransom Jeffrey), *Yellowfish, Broken Ground*, and *Out of the Channel: The Exxon Valdez Oil Spill in Prince William Sound.* Works of short fiction as well as nonfiction on petroleum, ecology, community, and literature have appeared in *American Short Fiction, Story, Outside*, and the *Village Voice.*

No Road

This damn town has been smeared with money.
— A Cordova fisherman, 1989.

The town of Cordova, Alaska, has a population of 2,600, although every summer it swells to 5,000 when cannery workers and fishing permit holders return after living elsewhere during the winter. Cordova is what is known to social anthropologists as a natural resources community, and here the resource is mainly the fish—herring, and the salmon that annually run to the hatchery system in Prince William Sound. The town is isolated, and its people are quintessential Alaskans. They are attuned to the natural world. Their work is dangerous and requires intelligence and physical skill. Many among them are highly educated but have chosen to live this life. They are fiercely independent, often passionately idealistic.

There is also a community within the community. Native people, Eyaks and Aleuts, reside here. It is the Eyaks' ancestral home. Many of the Natives also fish commercially, but in recent years the Eyak Corporation, which now is composed mainly of Aleuts and which owns tracts of land near Cordova, and other Native corporations, which own large tracts of land throughout the sound, have sold the rights to another resource—timber. Logging, particularly clear-cutting and the erosion that follows it, threatens spawning streams, estuaries, and tidal flats like the rich Copper River Delta not far from Cordova. Nevertheless, before the 11-million-gallon Exxon *Valdez* oil spill of March 25, 1989, divisions in Cordova tended to take the form of close-in body punching followed by clinches, as if among family members. After the oil spill, everything changed.

The town itself was protected from the spill by its location in the extreme eastern portion of the sound and by the sound's prevailing westward currents, as well as by two land masses, Knowles Head to the northeast and Hawkins Island just across the bay from the docks.

57

The nearby fishing grounds off the Copper River Delta were also protected, but the townspeople depended on all of the sound for suste-
nance, and especially on the salmon hatcheries that had been developed
to the west. Because of weak regulation and heavy company-financed
fishing during the territorial days of the first half of the twentieth century, the salmon runs had become dangerously depleted by the fifties
and sixties. In response, a cooperative effort was mounted by the state,
the fish processors, and most notably the fishing people themselves.
It took years of planning and effort, but out of it grew a flourishing
salmon hatchery system, a marriage of science, technology, free enter-
prise, and nature placed under the common proprietorship of the state
and the fishermen. The system has so far helped to restore the salmon
runs and strengthened the economic niche for a class of entrepreneurial fishermen who are in some respects an economic throwback to the
classic Hamiltonian ideal of the independent producer.

   The 1989 oil spill—the huge slick that inundated twelve hundred
miles of beaches and by the latest count has killed 3,500 to 5,500 otters,
hundreds of other sea mammals, 260,000 to 600,000 birds, unfathomable numbers of fish and shellfish, and incalculable tons of plant and
microscopic biota—both threatened the fishermen's livelihood and de-
spoiled the place they had come to love. The first response of Cordovans was a combination of outrage and despair. Through the loss, their
feeling for the beauty of their place and for the way their lives were en-
twined with the sound would take on new force. It was not uncommon
for even the crustiest among them to say, "We should have been paying
attention," or, "The environmentalists were right." They also quickly
found their own path to action. While Exxon, government agencies,
and Alyeska (the petroleum consortium that oversees the pipeline and
the shipping terminal in Valdez, and under whose purview the early
response to oil spills falls) seemed utterly paralyzed through several
days of excellent weather as the oil spill spread from Bligh Reef to the
south and west, the Cordovans established their own lobbying and information networks, took to their boats to pull stricken animals from
the slick, picked up the oil in buckets, and set up booms to protect the
hatchery sites. They formed a solid wall of protest against bureaucratic
machinations and delaying tactics. One fisherman, George Velikanje,
told me, "This is a chance for us to force a little responsibility on the

kings of capital, the robber barons of our society. They say, Be realistic. I say, What the hell do you think is real?"

Cordova is built at the base of Mount Eyak. On the mountain's lower slopes is a residential section that the 1964 Alaskan earthquake left intact. There is a dense quiltwork of walls, of roofs set at crazy angles to each other. The houses are sometimes large and sometimes tiny, sometimes filigreed and sometimes stark-looking. Among them are vestiges of narrow boardwalks from way back in the early part of the century. In the yards and driveways lie bicycles, old cars, turned-over skiffs, and heaps of fishing net. The residential tangle expresses the history of the place, recent and old. The colors are blue, white, rust, and the deep silver of weathered clapboard made luminous by the steel-gray sky. Spruce trees fringe the upper edges of the neighborhood. Between their trunks lies the dark gray rock of the mountain.

Down toward the water is Railroad Way and a line of buildings erected after the earthquake, which had destroyed the waterfront: equipment outlets and dry docks, a new brick post office, and the city hall. First Street runs parallel to the shoreline, and strung out along it to the northwest are the canneries, the ferry terminal, and at the old New England Cannery the offices of the Chugach Native Corporation. In the opposite direction is a road that leads past Lake Eyak and the neighborhood of newer bungalows where many of the Native people live, past the airport, and northerly and inland over a series of concrete bridges that span the Copper River Delta. There the country turns harsh. The river is white with froth, and the land around it—the sandbanks and muskeg, the bush, and the gaunt, windblown trees—have a scoured look. The road is the Copper River Highway, built on an old railbed. It represented another boom. Copper, discovered in 1900, brought an influx of Guggenheim money and a railroad completed in 1911 between the Kennecott Mine and the Port of Cordova. In those days, Cordova had been what the oil-shipping town of Valdez is now, a major terminus for raw materials. The mine closed in 1938 due to the collapse of copper prices, and Cordova then began the long process of reconstituting itself as a fishing port.

Practically speaking, the highway ends sixty miles out of town at the Million Dollar Bridge, a four-span steel and concrete railroad structure completed in 1910. The earthquake had dumped the end of one of the spans into the river, but the bridge has been pieced back together, the fractures in the standing spans strapped with steel plate, the collapsed span judged to be stable enough even in its wild tilt and reconnected to the adjacent span by a big steel stairway lashed with u-bolts, turn-buckles, and inch-and-a-half cable. Over the stairway are laid two-inch planks that make a bridge upon the bridge and rather tenuously per-mit single-file vehicle traffic to the shore across the river. Beyond that point the road gradually dwindles to nothing.

The question of upgrading and extending the road to the point where it would connect with the Richardson Highway and thus to Valdez, Anchorage, and points beyond has been controversial in Cordova for years. The absence of a road makes the town an island in effect, acces-sible only by sea and air, but it also eliminates the incursion of certain classes of traffic—the casual traffic of tourists and the insistent traffic of truckers. In 1989, road advocates bemoaned the fact that Cordova could not be an oil spill cleanup staging base, which reduced the amount of Exxon money that came into town. Others were grateful that Cordova could not become another Valdez. As much as anything else, the ab-sence of the road contributes to the town's integrity. Under normal cir-cumstances its absence defines motion, reduces interruption, increases continuity, and encourages reflection. It makes relationships different here because it is never easy to go away.

Beginning a few days after the oil spill and running into the early fall of 1989, the town was filled with strangers, and not just with agency and oil-industry people. A full complement of the national and inter-national press came to Cordova, and came again and again. A Cousteau Society team, filming an oil-spill special, came several times. The heads and representatives of environmental organizations came and went. Representatives from government agencies established a semiperma-nent presence. Oil observers from foreign countries came. Coast Guard admirals came. Members of Congress came, and so did Vice-President Quayle, sealed up tight in an envelope of security. For a while, it was thought that President Bush would come, but he did not, preferring to keep the same distance as had Lawrence Rawl, the chief executive offi-cer of the Exxon Corporation. The singer John McCutcheon came. John

Denver gave a benefit concert. James Naughton, the actor, appeared with Chuck Hamel, the oil broker, and there was a buzz about a feature movie to be financed by Paul Newman. Economists came to study the new contours the economic windfalls had given to so small a community. Social scientists and anthropologists came to study the effects of disaster.

Mental health researchers came to watch the course of delayed stress syndrome, which a striking number of Cordovans would eventually suffer—the consequence of a violent alarm over the threat to the substance of their lives, the long hours spent battling that threat, which stretched into months, and then the precipitous dip in energy, the confusion over simple details of daily life, the depression. In August, John Crowley, who worked in the mental health outpatient division of the local hospital, said that the number of cases had increased fivefold, but he also said, "Each case has had a history of fragility that the spill itself, the destruction of nature, or the financial stress triggered." In the realm of the human psyche, it was very similar to what scientists referred to as the tweak to nature caused by the oil spill itself. They were provocations that carried the potential to push mental or ecological systems over the edge.

Back at the end of May, the town had rolled out the red carpet for the crew of the Russian superskimmer, the *Vaydaghubsky*. The largest oil skimmer in the world, the ship was capable of recovering 200,000 gallons of oil per hour, but it was far too large to negotiate the narrows and shallows near the shorelines. By the time it arrived at Resurrection Bay on April 19 (following another in the chain of bureaucratic snarls, this one over the question of allowing a Russian vessel to enter U.S. waters), the oil had scattered and had been driven by wind and wave action into a water and oil mixture euphemistically referred to as mousse. Attempts to modify the ship's machinery to pick up the mixture and separate the oil from the water proved unsuccessful. Very little oil was collected, and finally the ship's heralded arrival became another in the line of disappointments. But the people of Cordova, learning that the superskimmer was anchored off Knight Island and doing nothing, invited the Russians to town. The ship moved to Nelson Bay, just up the coast from Cordova, and the townspeople ferried the crew and themselves back and forth between the town and the ship, threw a five-hour party with food, music, and dancing, and so entered the world of foreign relations.

Money came into Cordova as well, buckets of it, mainly from Exxon, and secondarily through Veco, Exxon's principal cleanup subcontractor, and also through the state and federal governments. By June 1990, more than a year after the oil spill, the Exxon money that had entered through the city government in the form of grants totaled $740,000. The money had been used to alleviate the housing shortage during the previous summer (a chronic Cordova problem that had become acute) and to supply child care (everyone in town was working overtime), and it was also spent on reimbursements of various types, including the considerable expenses of the Cordova Oil Spill Disaster Relief Office (COSDRO). COSDRO had been created in the first days of the spill as a volunteer organization, and it evolved into an arm of the city government.

By June 1990 the Prince William Sound Aquaculture Corporation (PWSAC), a private nonprofit corporation that administered the hatchery system in the sound, had received a total of $8 million from Exxon. The bulk of the money was channeled through Spill-Tech, a containment and management company hired soon after the oil spill to continue protecting hatcheries. PWSAC had also instituted a permanent storage system for boom and other protective gear at the hatchery sites. This eventually became part of the new and presumably improved Oil Spill Contingency Plan adopted for the region.

Cordova District Fishermen United (CDFU), a lobbying organization, would eventually receive more than $400,000 to cover its spill-related expenses. The Cordova Science Center, a new project modeled on Woods Hole and the Moss Landing Institute in California, was established early in the summer. Under the acting directorship of John Harville, the founder of Moss Landing, the science center became the crown jewel of the city's response. It received $100,000 from the city of Cordova in the form of a loan. More money would come from Congress and through donations. According to Nancy Bird, who began as a volunteer at COSDRO and then became the coordinator of the science center, the support was made possible by the presence of Exxon funds, but the energy to implement the long-wished-for center was triggered by the alarming sense following the oil spill that the community had to do something to diversify its economic base.

During the year following the spill, sales tax revenues in Cordova jumped by 22 percent as a consequence of the large doses of capital that flowed to all the niches of daily life: the restaurants, grocery stores, the liquor store, the cabs, newspaper subscriptions, boat and supply purchases, and the extra flights to Anchorage, Seattle, Hawaii, and back and forth between Cordova and Valdez. For example, CDFU went through twenty or thirty cases of photocopy paper during the year as opposed to the usual four or five. Close on the heels of the paper came the wages for additional help and overtime to run and maintain the machines and to file the copies or to find copies in the files. Information, too, in all its forms, had undergone an abrupt surge, and the expenditures connected with it were only partly the result of work being done by the CDFU itself. Photocopying services were made available without charge to anyone in town, resident or visitor.

In mid-August 1989, I had met with Brenda Guest, the COSDRO deputy director, who had come to Cordova from Anchorage. She was amazed by the way the town had kept up its spirit in the midst of the chaos. She said anyone might walk into the office and read the COSDRO correspondence with Exxon off the computer. As arrangements were being made for the visit of the *Vaydaghubsky*, she'd gone around securing supplies for the party, and local businesses had accepted purchase orders with little idea of how or by whom they would be paid. The entire town was functioning as a committee of the whole.

I was then trying to pick my own way through the confusion. I asked Brenda what she thought the heart of Cordova was. She paused, then a light came into her eyes. We went outside, got into a pickup, and drove along the old New England Road, which passes by a house filled with Filipino cannery workers, past the canneries themselves, the Veco boat cleaning lot, the ferry terminal, and toward the old New England Cannery, since taken over by the Chugach Native Corporation.

We stopped first at what some referred to as Hippie Cove, though its proper name was Shelter Cove. It was a shallow inlet and creek drainage backed by a steep slope. We looked at a sauna that had mystic symbols on its walls and a sign that said anyone could use the sauna so long as they left it clean and stocked it with wood. Just above the sauna, almost hidden in the foliage, was a small handbuilt house, and then above it another house. Brenda said there were more houses up there. She led me a hundred yards along the edge of a pool in which a lone spawning salmon struggled to enter the creek. We climbed, winding our way through the dense woods to a string of campsites and dwellings built out of salvage from a wrecked ship down below. No one was in sight, but left in the campsites and shelters were bags and cooking gear. Higher up, Brenda said, were better-built dwellings. She said something about Gene not being here, and I wondered if it was Gene we were looking for, or if what she'd already shown me, the semipermanent and strictly temporary dwellings, made her answer to my question.

From there we drove to a set of campsites COSDRO was building to help accommodate the overflow of people in town, then on toward the Chugach Corporation. We found Gene walking along the road. He was Gene Rosellini, Brenda told me, a member of a prominent Washington State family and now the unofficial spokesman for Shelter Cove. He wore a ragged pair of black shorts and a ragged brown shirt and had a pack on his back. The pack was filled with rocks. It was his practice to carry rocks in order to keep what he referred to as his "primary means of transportation" in top condition. He had carried building materials up the slope at Shelter Cove. His brown hair was cropped short. He had a weathered face and remarkably clear eyes. Behind a strap that passed across his chest was wedged a tiny plastic prescription bottle filled with water. In accordance with his principle of no excess, it was just enough water to sustain him on his walk.

He spoke with difficulty, as if he weren't used to talking. Slowly I came to see that Brenda and he were negotiating. Brenda was making arrangements to move a trash bin and two Porta-Potties to Shelter Cove and to build a fire ring there. The reason for such "development," again, was the influx of people, many of whom were camping out because of the housing shortage. Gene approved of the Porta-Potties and the fire ring but not the trash bin. He didn't want trash removed from the sites. "Besides, there's a new theft problem," he said. He meant that on general principle he didn't want people getting the idea that things could be either taken or thrown away. "I can't leave anything valuable in my cabin anymore," he said. "I have to carry my money with me."

Later, as we drove back to town, Brenda told me she was surprised that he had money. She said that some time before, when the oil spill outrage had the town in its grips, Gene had gone to the police chief, a man revered in Cordova, to inform him that he would be appearing in town a little more regularly, that he wanted to prepare the police for that. "The children love him," Brenda said. Now I understood her answer to my question: it was the campsites—spartan, exquisite, and built with Exxon money as it was routed through the city government; it was Shelter Cove, for years a refuge for those in transition who had come here seeking their future, hippies once, perhaps, but serious ones who had dropped out in the lower forty-eight in the late sixties and seventies and who now were independent fishing people, business people, and members of the city government; and it was Gene Rosellini himself, the offspring of wealth and influence in Washington come here to drop out completely, way down to the bottom, but who by the trust the town placed in him, by the duration of his presence in Shelter Cove, and by his labor had become the spokesman who negotiated the most extreme tailings of Exxon largess. Porta-Potties and fire ring, yes. Trash bin, no. It was a good answer.

A year and a half later Gene would be found dead of a knife wound in Shelter Cove. The town was shocked. It was thought for a time that he'd been murdered, but then it was determined that he had taken his own life in the Japanese fashion. His was, no doubt, a troubled psyche. A grim afterthought to his loss was that possibly the turmoil in the place he loved had carried him beyond the limits of his forbearance. Now, under the auspices of a new police chief, there is a program to "clean up" Shelter Cove.

Clearly, one of the most unsettling aspects of the spill was the uses to which Exxon money was put. In Cordova, as elsewhere, there were instances of graft, nepotism, and profit-taking as Exxon spent money hand over fist. Rifts developed over the assignment of boats by CDFU or PWSAC to the cleanup or to the defense of the hatcheries. Prices in some public establishments had been jacked up. There were tales of a Veco supervisor who skipped town with funds. Some residents billeted out their homes at exorbitant rates. There came to be what were called "spillionaires," who had survived the summer's fishery closures by making hundreds of thousands of dollars through leasing boats and equipment to Exxon and Veco. Often enough, they lived in the same neighborhoods or even next door to those who were sinking into debt. Later, some who had made fortunes would pull up stakes and leave, taking their money with them, thus further disturbing the town's delicate infrastructure.

Although instances of graft and greed were far from representative of the town's fundamental response, the money was incendiary. By the end of 1989 and on into early 1990, it was threatening to tear the town apart. Many community groups and institutions that had received funding would find themselves way out on the ends of limbs. Some, such as the Cordova Science Center and COSDRO, which had sponsored the *Vaydaghubsky* party and had paid for it with Exxon money, were created after the spill. Others, such as CDFU and PWSAC, had been in existence long before the spill. To those citizens who preferred to follow what they might call the moral high road, the use of Exxon money for any purpose not connected strictly with the cleanup and reparations was wrong. Such people came from both ends of the spectrum: those who hated Exxon and wished to have nothing to do with its money, and those who applauded Exxon's cleanup efforts and wished to prevail no further upon the company's indulgence. Among the remainder, particularly those adept at managing money, there were some for whom the presence of Exxon capital in large quantities created an opportunity to extend the meaning of reparation. The Cordova city government came to lean in that direction, and COSDRO was its arm.

In the beginning, the oil spill had startled many Cordovans into thinking that economic diversification was necessary as a defense against the unknown effects of the spill and of future spills. COSDRO hired a professional business consultant, Mead Treadwell, to head its operations. Treadwell is a resolute young man, a member of an old Alaskan entrepreneurial family, a graduate of Yale and Harvard Business School. He had previously been associated with Walter Hickel's venture company, Yukon Pacific Corporation, and would later leave Cordova to serve in Hickel's administration following Hickel's election as governor in 1990.

As the summer of 1989 wore on into August and then into September, it had gradually become manifest that Exxon would indeed live up to its promise to extract its cleanup forces from Prince William Sound by mid-September—the 11,000 workers, 14,000 vessels, 80 aircraft, and most of the offices, bureaucrats, and public relations specialists, as well as its vaults, which by then had poured forth close to a billion dollars. The Cordova claims offices were slated to be closed. The presence of state and federal agencies would be reduced. The population of observers and hangers-on would melt away, and Cordova's brief, high-velocity stint as a weird, disaster-fed company town would soon be over.

The town found itself hanging between returning to something like what it had been before the spill (a complete return was patently impossible) and putting the best face on the changes that had come to it. "Exxon," Mead Treadwell told me then, "keeps saying that they don't want to pick up garbage that's not theirs." From Exxon's perspective, garbage consisted of a range of things that ran from trash left by others on the beaches to mental stress and economic dislocation stemming from causes not clearly related to the oil spill. "But my attitude," Treadwell said, "is, Go jump in the lake, guys. You certainly won't be able to pick up all your own garbage. This city is trying to recover from an economic disaster, and I don't see anything wrong with trying to mount a deeper keel to stabilize the city."

The "deeper keel" included community development projects. One of these was the science center. Another under consideration was a deepwater port, which was tied to the interests of the Eyak Corporation, centered in Cordova, and thus to logging. Yet another was the road to Valdez and Anchorage. All three projects had been longstanding concerns in the community. But again, those who took the moral high ground said that any such project had nothing whatsoever to do with the oil spill and that even to study them with Exxon money was a form of gouging and thus of capitulation to villainy. Others said that the oil spill, the possibility of another one in the future, and the likelihood that Alyeska would again be unable to deal with it necessitated such considerations. With the help of Treadwell, among others, the city prepared economic projections. According to Treadwell, the city government remained worried about the potential long-term effects that the spill would have on fish processing in Cordova and on the number of boats for which Cordova was the home port. Both the boats in the harbor and the canneries (through a raw fish tax that brought about a million dollars annually into the city coffers) had a direct effect on the economic and social fabric of the town. "Twenty-nine families have left town because they made so much money on the cleanup that they had no reason to stay," Treadwell said. "It's what's called a pattern dislocation in our economy, and Cordova will be feeling it for years."

Some would argue that the Cordova airport—the best in the sound—was a good reason for Exxon and Alyeska to use Cordova as a staging ground for any future oil response and that they should be courted toward this end. One of these was Connie Taylor, a member of the Oil Response Committee and president of the Cordova Chamber of Commerce. Earlier, the Cordova business community had split between the old-line Chamber of Commerce people, led by Connie Taylor, and a newer, more aggressive group, Main Street Business, led by Bob Van Brocklin. A bitter rift developed between the two groups stemming from the question of who should represent Cordova businesses to Exxon and the state government. In the October municipal elections, Taylor was elected to the city council and Van Brocklin was elected mayor. The rift deepened through the following year, culminating in Taylor bringing suit against Van Brocklin and council members R. J. Kopchak and Jeff Hawley for allegedly holding secret meetings in her absence in violation of the Alaska Open Meetings Act. In turn, Taylor was accused of channeling information from council executive sessions to Exxon, including information connected to possible future suits for reparations from Exxon. The city council soon appropriated $75,000 to defend Van Brocklin, Kopchak, and Hawley against Taylor's suit. The consequence, which is still in the process of unfolding, has been that Taylor has won a portion of her original suit, the city expended about a million dollars it didn't have, Taylor was recalled from the city council, Kopchak and Hawley resigned, and Van Brocklin declined to run for office again. For a year the paralysis that had struck Exxon and the state and federal governments was echoed in the chambers of Cordova's city government. Just as the oil slick had slipped into the most unexpected places, wreaking havoc, so too did the money. Later, in 1992, a despondent Van Brocklin would also commit suicide.

A rift had developed on the CDFU board, too, over the questions of legislative lobbying, Alyeska's new Oil Spill Contingency Plan, and the appropriate level of cooperation between CDFU and the new Alyeska head, James Hermiller. The road debate percolated through it all. Connie

Taylor had been pro-road. Van Brocklin had been anti-road, or so it seemed. The lack of a road, some argued, was part of the reason the town had been passed over as a winter staging ground and that therefore less money had come into town. Proponents wanted the road built for the sake of future development. To some, the prospect of completing the road seemed the answer to all problems: expand endlessly outward.

At the same time, Walter Hickel, who had been the governor of Alaska and then the secretary of the interior in the Nixon administration during the opening of the North Slope to oil production, had become governor again, following his eleventh-hour entry into the 1990 race. He had financed his pro-development political campaign with his personal fortune and had won by carrying the principal Alaskan cities, Anchorage and Fairbanks, and the Prince William Sound region, but he lost everywhere else. The two cities are tied to development. Prince William Sound apparently supported him because of his promises to negotiate a strong oil spill settlement between Exxon and the federal and state governments and to insist that settlement moneys be devoted to restoring and enhancing damaged habitats.

As it turned out, Hickel supported a settlement early in 1991 that is favorable to Exxon. Exxon is to pay a total of $1.125 billion, most of it over a period of ten years. This is set against scientists' estimates of $10 to 15 billion worth of damage to shoreline and near-shore habitats. Later in 1991, Hickel vetoed a bill from the Alaska legislature that would have dedicated a portion of settlement moneys to the purchase and set-aside of timber rights in the sound. This idea reasons that the sound is now best left to heal itself, that logging would actually constitute another "hit" to marine habitats, which are interlocked with adjacent woodlands. Further, because of the high cost of shipping and the relatively low value of the trees, logging has so far operated at a loss in Prince William Sound. The proposal to repurchase timber rights is supported by most fishing people and many Native people as well, who do not necessarily agree with the courses taken by the corporations in which they hold shares. Hickel reneged on his promises to Cordova and quickly became a strong pro-road advocate. He takes the view, common enough in Alaska, that the state is best treated as a resource colony, and he appears much less interested in restoring the sound or in nurturing the balance of communities such as Cordova than he is in furthering his own view of "enhancement," which to him means cracking open remote regions to tourism, logging, and mining.

Most typical of the feelings of Cordovans toward the road question were those of the fishing families who were stunned at first by the destruction of Prince William Sound and who then grew increasingly outraged at the ever-deepening bureaucratic imbroglios attached to righting the wrong in which they, in order to survive, were forced to participate. First they had to get somebody to do something about the oil, then they had to do something about it themselves on Exxon's payroll. They had to try to collect their claims against Exxon for losses suffered during the 1989 fishing closures and watchdog Alyeska's new contingency plan and settlement, and in the meantime to adapt to a profoundly altered financial reality. Finally, a lot of them simply wanted to see Exxon and any other corporate interloper shut up and get out. Community polls and the election as mayor of Kelly Weaverling—an oil-spill activist and by his own description the highest elected member of the Green Party in the country—suggest that the majority of the Cordovans remain opposed to the road. Mead Treadwell, when he was still the COSDRO director, had told me that he "wouldn't touch the road question with a ten-foot pole."

The disaster that struck Cordova and the other towns of the sound is markedly different from most natural disasters in three important ways. First, rather than one catastrophic event, it was a persistent sequence of events that will remain disruptive for years because of lingering questions about the long-term effects of the oil spill and the cleanup, which, it is now generally agreed, was at least as damaging to marine and shoreline habitats as the oil spill itself. Second, many of the claims filed by fishermen against Exxon will remain unresolved for years, and they carry with them personal expense and heartache. Finally, and most important, because the spill was a technological disaster caused and compounded by a sequence of human errors and because many Cordovans participated in the cleanup sham, a haunting sense of guilt throws even the victims into the same realm of culpability as the perpetrators. The God in this, whose judgment might be accepted, is difficult to locate.

The town's roadlessness and the PWSAC-administered hatchery system speak to the deep contradiction Cordovans have been forced to confront. The lack of the connection by road to the outside world creates a dissonance in the town itself and in the imaginations of individuals. One part of the imagination wishes to keep things just as they are. It seeks continuity. Another part wishes to move outward, even to the unknown. The middle ground might be to protect, probe, and nurture what lies at hand but also to insist on seeing the inescapable chaos that always lurks at the edges. Such a middle ground is hard to locate, and once found it turns out to be a narrow path with precarious footing along a precipice that overlooks the certain ruin of water and rock. To hold one's position there requires attention and lightness of foot, and patience, and the cunning to know when to move back and when forward.

In the salmon hatchery system, the gene pools must not be allowed to weaken, so PWSAC has a program for renewing wild runs and replenishing the genetic diversity of its own stock with wild-run eggs. In particular, the fry and eggs must not be subjected to pollution, as both the fry released in 1989 and the spawning run of 1989 certainly were, although as it happened the 1988 pink salmon brood, released as fry in 1989 following the spill, produced the largest return on record (an estimated 43 million pinks). This resulted in a barrage of Exxon press releases and advertisements claiming that the oil spill had hardly damaged the ecosystem. What the 1990 pink salmon return validated, however, was what had been observed in the weeks following the spill—that the all-out effort of fishermen to protect that year's hatchery stock from instant death had been successful. It said nothing of the multitude of factors that might—for better or worse—affect a run at sea, of the effects of oil pollution on the spawning run of 1989, of the sublethal effects of the oil, of the effects of the chemicals, such as Inipol, used in experimental research during the cleanup effort, of the extensive damage done to wild spawning streams by both the spill and the cleanup, or of the fact that 1990 was not the year the biologists expected to see the greatest effects of the spill.

In 1991 the salmon returns in Prince William Sound also set records, but only for numbers of salmon. The fish were small and were three weeks late and were therefore too advanced in their spawning cycle to be of value. The bottom fell out of the market and millions of fish were dumped. The 1992 returns were extremely low—about a third of what had been anticipated. PWSAC took a loss of over three million dollars, and fishermen hauled in catches worth an average of about $20,000 — far below their needs. In 1993 the hatchery pink salmon fishery failed completely, and both PWSAC and many fishing families are threatened with bankruptcy. Explanations for the poor returns include the recurrence of a twenty-year cycle in which water temperatures in the Gulf of Alaska are colder than normal. This condition puts both the fingerling salmon released from the hatcheries and the returning mature fish in jeopardy. Salmon adapt less easily in colder water, and food systems are also stressed by the cold. An increasingly compelling case can be made, however, that the sublethal effects of oil and Inipol on the fish are finally becoming evident. The 1993 pink salmon run was about one-fifth of the anticipated harvest. These salmon, which show evidence of genetic damage, are the offspring of the fish that behaved erratically in 1991, and the second-generation offspring of adults that returned to spawn in 1989 during the oil spill. As if this weren't enough, the 1993 herring fishery was canceled. Herring that had been juvenile fish in 1989 were almost completely absent from the 1993 run, and more than a third of the returning fish were infected with bleeding lesions that may have stemmed from the same cause as the abnormalities in the salmon runs — at the least the sublethal effects of pollution in combination with harsh conditions.

Granted, the hatchery system has its own hazards: die-outs at sea, disease, high-seas drift-netting, the lurching of the marketplace. Some of these are the typical dangers of monoculture, of converting salmon into something a little like hybrid corn. The sameness of the stock accentuates its vulnerabilities. The fish arrive more-or-less at once, huge runs of them coming in like Godzilla and stressing the very habitat they depend on. Unlike oil drilling, however, and mining and timber harvesting, the hatchery system, with luck and wise management, could prove to be an indefinitely renewable resource and could sustain the lives of a remarkable group of people. The oil spill reminded them of an ever-present technological menace and of big money's sleight-of-hand, but the hatchery system has become indispensable. It cannot be given up, and it is so vulnerable that in August 1993, following the failed purse-seine pink salmon fishery, the fishermen blockaded the tanker channel with their boats. For a period of several hours, there were no tankers in

Prince William Sound for the first time since 1977 when the oil began flowing through the pipeline. What the fishermen wanted was speedy dedication of Exxon *Valdez* settlement moneys toward research, restoration, and true enhancement, speedy resolution of the outstanding suits, and attention to the financial troubles of their community. What they certainly got was their first moment of unanimity since the oil spill.

It's as if they all found themselves up there together on the narrow, slippery precipice, holding among them a big basket of eggs. The basket must be held firmly, delicately, and by the many at once. It has its own chaos, its own way of hatching trouble and of shifting its weight. It must be allowed to do that. The people must also look out for all the other Godzillas coming at them. They have to readjust their footing constantly, moving here or there as circumstances require, and yet they must never abandon their position, never let loose of their load, and most of all, never cease to be friends with themselves.

PETER KALIFORNSKY

One of the last speakers of the Kenai dialect of the Dena'ina Athapaskan language of Lower Cook Inlet, Peter Kalifornsky was born in
1911 in Unhghenesditnu, or Kalifornsky village, a village founded by his
great-great grandfather on the Kenai Peninsula. A self-taught writer
and scholar, Kalifornsky wrote *Kahtnuht'ana Qenaga: The Kenai People's
Language, K'tl'egh'i Sukdu: A Dena'ina Legacy*, and *Five Legends of the
Dena'ina People*. His numerous honors and awards include the 1987
Distinguished Humanist Award from the Alaska Humanities Forum,
the 1990 Citizen of the Year Award from the Alaska Federation of
Natives, the 1991 Meritorious Service Award from the University of
Alaska Anchorage and Kenai Peninsula College and the 1992 Ameri-
can Book Award from the Before Columbus Foundation. In 1987 the
Alaska state legislature passed a special resolution in honor of Kaliforn-
sky and his work. He died in 1993. His text was edited by James Kari
and Alan Boraas.

FROM *K'tl'egh'i Sukdu: A Dena'ina Legacy*

Unhshcheyakda Sukt'A

Unhshcheyakda be'izhi hdghelach' Qadanalchen. Gin unhshcheyakda sukt'a, ch'u ch'aduch' hghuda ki k'usht'a qetitl' qilal.

Yus qayeh q'anqeydul'uk ghu, taqiynin'un ch'u Naq'eltanich' talghel ch'u duhdeldih bek'eshchegiq'. Naqan'ijut qyaqeydin'uni be'izhi Kalifornsky.

Ch'u gu naqan'ijut ghu Fort Ross, California qech', betukda ghun duyeq ghela ch'u bequsil. "Yin tl'egh duyeq enlan," qyełni.

Hq'u "Qil," ni.

"K'usht'a duyeq eztghelal da, nach'anildush," qyełni. Ch'u beł ch'indaqna ighedneq ch'u Unhghenesditnu niqayehqit'un. Be'izhiq' qak'hdin'un Kalifornsky Qayeh.

Yet hch'a'iyusht quht'ana hdgheni: "Bech' ch'elyuyi bełenh tgheh'uh, hq'u Naq'eltani qilan bech' tulyułi, yi unhtsah ełnen quq'łuq'u," hdgheni łu.

Ch'u Yaghanenq' gu ki duyeq qighestle, ch'u ki qetitl' qusil. Ch'u Unhghenesditnu sergu nihqini'un ch'u Qezdaghnen k'u sergu nihqini'un.

Yet łu dghuni qghelah łu, ch'u shcheyadka gun k'ghudgheni łu: "Hugh ch'qeshdnik' da q'udi shqtustle. Shnula dghełkegh da, q'udi shqtustle. Shchutl'a dghełkegh da, q'udi shqtustle." Dach' qya nuqulnish en'ushna.

Shcheyakda yin k'u Nikanalguk be'ulten niłtl'eghq'u qbequsil 1926. Yethtl'egh Unhghenesditnu dnaqusil. Qech'il'eq'na Kahtnuh hdaqilchet.

Q'udi k'uych'en'i tsiq'a yeh qełu. Hq'ech' qenink'danshel.

77

Kahtnu Dena'ina Egh, Part 1

Q'udi shghuk'dunich' k'usht'a qit'aynesil, guna sez'a'ina, ch'u
Chickalusions, ch'u en'ushna, shtukda. "Gin dach' t'enlah, yi t'enlah,"
k'usht'a shhdinil. Qghednu dghu, "Gin dnil'an," qyan shhdghenih.

Q'uch'a yadi ninya qyeghusłtish dghu qyeł dnish tutnitutq'ashi k'u.
K'deyes ch'aduch' hnunes bech'ak'ghetucheł. Ch'u ch'aduch' dihu
qyede'ish ch'u qyedeseh.

Ch'u guna tuq'ina niłch'indaqna Chickalusions elgheji qbegh
qghela. Sustenh ben teh qyeghudghełt'a. Ch'u tuq'ih biqidin baydalgi
Tika'ahtnu qyeghudhgełt'a. Guna undat k'eyes badi ghudghełt'ana ey
guduh.

1933 elgheji zełchin. Niłq'atighetunt k'etnu bahkaghdeshnik
tułchuda uhu ch'el'ani ghe. Kahtnu batunghanshnik ch'u tubugh
ninełggat ch'u shtunighel.

Tik'teh k'uhughel'ih. Qadi łuq'u ghenelggeni, onions, vegetable
cheese, milk, fish, fruits.

Guna undat Dena'ina, k'eyes ch'u ush egh ghudnuhna qbe'uqa k'u.
Alex Sunrise, Knik Pete, Feodore Sasha, Max Maxim, Nick Murphy
(Quten), Simeon Sacaloff, Nick Kalifornsky. Ch'u gun qichi Tanya undat k'eyes dghesah, ch'u dukłi chik'ish ch'u hegh nasdedzi ts'ah egh
ghudnuh 1950. Yin tl'egh k'eyes ch'u q'unch'k'dałqushi q'ahdulnen.

Guduh Kahtnu gu tinitun qizlan ch'u cars qizlan. Ch'u łik'aha
nuhutelch'ix. Q'udi ggul niłtu qyiten. Ch'u ki ch'aduch'
beghuhdułt'al?

Kahtnu Dena'ina Egh, Part 2

K'usht'a qbeł ch'duqidniłt'agh k'uhu ch'el'ani. Qayeh qit'ahqidigheni.
T'qughełjaqch' q'anqudil. Qebech'eda łtaqul'i ey hluzhuna nutiha
k't'u ch'da k'u qbet'uh el ch'u k'chan. Qadi luq'u niłeh qanilyuh.
K'qulgheł łuq'u ghanalggeni k'tsen, baba, q'in, qutsagheł'i tlegha,
tleh ił nazt'ayi.

Titenh denłtsek'i ninya qghela. Yadi qanchi, k'nuy'a, qeba, elyin.
Shiłteh k'usht'a q'anqidil. Sustenh, benteh elgheji dghełjaggi sustenh
q'anqutish, bech'ehdi. Be'izin'a, k'izhak'i duguli. Be'u ghun k'u
yeqech'. Yin k'u dequldin. Ch'u eshdech' yeł ghednuyi tl'inqin
gadil'ih. Ch'anik'na titenh hquldih. Łuq'u diq'ushi qitih k'ench'ik'a
k'yes yiq'. K'usht'a nudiłtlegh.

Tika'ah tuq'ih biqidin bayadalgi n'at q'anqghunish ch'u qadi ch'aduch' titenh qadi k'qel'ih yeqech' q'u qbech'naqa qbe'iltench' qyan ch'u yeqech' q'u hqeldih.

Shchiyakda Alex zah qyeł k'uhul'ani łik'aha qusil. Quht'ana qayeh niłteh nughedełna ch'u qetitl' q'ahdulnen. Hq'u baydalgi jidqwa beghuhdełt'a. Shtukda nutih łu tika'ah q'anqyedul'uk tuq'es uhu ch'el'anich'. Ch'u tuq'es uhu ch'el'anich' q'ahdulnen. Ch'u baydalgi ki jidqwa beghuhdghełt'a Tika'ahdnuh qyuhu ghel'ihi qutsaghel'i, qunshi, ggaggashla, qiz'in.

Ch'u Dusdu Benah, Sqilan Benah yadi nuji, elt'eshi, qunsha, uhu qul'ih. Ch'u baydalgi q'ahdulnen. Dach' t'qijuq ch'u guduh ki k'usht'a k'un ilal.

Alex Wilson undat qutsaghel'i chiłyuq, Tsadni'unt. Ch'u Mrs. Austin undat Kahdnu Betnu qunshi chiłyuq, 1929. Dena'inaq' huch'ulyeshi q'hdulnen.

Heyteh qayeh q'anqudiłch'qadi yudeq ghu itch'q'u. Nubes hetl, yadi k'deyes k'u beghu duyeh t'ent'ah beqatl'uh denłqet. Sustenh dghili q'aghdeqh qayeh qit'ahqidigheni. Łik'a qebegh qighestle, yelqadi ghuda. Suk qyeł k'uhu ghel'ih.

Ch'u Chickaloon łu undat Dena'ina duyeq nutihna be'uqa ghela. Ch'u łik'aha k'nik'ghelu be'uqa tl'eh hetl aneshi.

Unhtsah lik'aha qyeł k'uhu ghel'ih. Ch'u izin tazdaq, ch'u łik'aha hetl anesh ht'ejuq.

Guduh K'uhu Ghel'ih

1927 Yaghetnuh k'uhu ghel'an. Shagelahtnu Ch'adinlent yet gheshdu. Yuduch' Russian Crossing q'anghelduk, yet q'u q'ench' ch'u Susten n'ech' Martin Qenq'a chu'u q'ench' Susten sht'uh. Ełduquzel Martin qyelnihen qenq'a qwa qghel'u, yeqech'q'u hqighezhih.

Ch'u guduh 1920–1925 hey shtukda k'uhu ghel'ih Niłq'atighetun Bena. 1929–1936 yeh k'uhu ghel'an. Suk gudach' nuhdulggesh qayeh qech' gu Kahtnu tighetih: Tsik'el'unt, Tuzqunt, Niłunkaq'dnu, Nilq'atighetun Bena, Benkda. Benkda, Quggesh Bena qyedghenih Dena'ina. Benkda daghełkegh ch'u qughusht'a k'usht'a ghednełtik', ch'u ezga, ch'u Benkda qyedghenih Dena'ina.

Denk'i shlik'aha qghela. Gu qech' teshish Kahtnu qech' q'ut'enteh tighetih: Kili Bena, kili qyedghenihen yet ghedu nuk'k'nejeht qyesh tudałtunt. Ch'u yetq'u ken ts'itnun ch'u ch'bala teh, ch'u yetq'u kiq'u kenq'; yetq'u Tuq' Bena, ch'u kiq'u kenq'; ch'u yetq'u Yaghetnu, Tahdna Nundulggesht, ch'u yun'eh bednuh; yetq'u Sustenh, Susten Bena, ch'u kiq'u Yaghetnuh; ch'u yun'eh. Ch'u gu Grishga qenq'a qwa, John Otterstrom k'u yin q'u qenq'a qwa qheł'u; ch'u yetq'u Shagela Bena; ch'u ki ken ch'u k'etnuh; yetq'u Nubendaltunt, tułchuda qayeh; yetq'u Martin t'uh, ełduqults'eł Martin qyedghenihen qenq'a qwa yet qgheł'u. Yetq'u Ggabila Bena skihnulchint qgheł'u. Yetq'u Sus Kenghełk'et ch'u Ht'uch' Dałtuni, ch'u K'ggałggats'aq' Dalchini, ch'u K'jech'aq' Dalchini, ch'u Susten, Niłq'atighetun Bena, gu sht'uh.

Yetq'u susten Unhtsadi; yetq'u Uch'eh Dałtuni; yetq'u Qeyach'en Dałtuni; yetq'u Benkda Ch'en Dałtuni; yetq'u Benkda; yetq'u Benkda Q'estsiq'. Ben yunch'dich'en ses susten Q'esdilen Bena. Benkda Ch'en Dałtuni gin k'etnu qwa ses q'aghdeq ch'u ken ch'u ben qwa teh dinłen. Yetq'u Gidaraq' Dalchini, yetq'u sht'uh.

Guduh quht'ana k'uhu qul'ih.[1] From Goose Lake to the east entrance of the Swanson Canoe Route area, Charlie Marsh, George Pederson, Henry Nelson; from the west entrance of the lake canoe route to around the Rock Lake area: Alfred and Mike Danieloff, Victor Antone, John Monfor; from Beaver Lake to around the Finger Lake area, Nick Mishekoff, the Johansens, John Alex; from Ciska Lake to the Seven area, the Wilsons; from Moose River to the West Fork area, George Miller; in the Moose River—Moosehorn area, Johnny Wik and the boys; at Torpedo Lake, Otto Schreider; across the river by Torpedo, Stepanka; in the Killey and Frisbee Lake area, the Backoffs and the Ivanoffs; in the upper Killey River and King County— Cottonwood area, Louie Nissen, Frank Standifer, Pete Knik, Alex Sunrise, Mike and Andrew Dolchok and the boys; on the upper Kenai River to Cooper Landing, the Demidoffs and Dariens; Trail Lake into Bear Creek, Moose Creek, and the Indian Creek area [on Tustumena Lake], Alex Kalifornsky, Nick Nicanorka, Semion Yunesha, Pete Carling, Andrew Berg, John Berg, Windy Wagner. Ninilchik people trapped around Nikolai Creek [on Tustumena Lake], up in that area.

---

1. The following paragraph was written in English by Peter Kalifornsky.

Niłdnayi k'uhu qul'ih yethdi htl'egh nutiha dghunigh yethdi ninya q'ahnitu.

Ginihdi Shi Sukt'a

Nudgheltant Kalifornsky Qayeh October 12, 1911. Shunkda bequsil janq'u ch'anik'en elanh. K'usht'a esh'il. Shbach'a'ina q'u shqigheten. Ts'ełt'an shitih ch'u ki ghel'en.

Yethdi sez'a Theodore Chickalusion hni'iju ch'u shighetneq. Yadi hey k'usht'a qzelnik', 1915 k'ushu. Jitq'u h'elnesh tsents'didatl' shlupch' yunch'eh ch'tunani Tikahtnu. Ts'il k'gheł'an yi Alaska packers sbayles ts'etsałi heyiq'.

Ch'u shihdi q'u quht'ana usdeth, shi qyan. T'qinalt'ah tik'u'eldush ch'u eshchih ch'u nteldeh, hneltish shtukda shuda ch'u scheyakda. Sez'a k'usht'a yuh idul. Tik'teh k'uhul'ih k'usht'a ghesdne da, hq'u shegh nink'delyish ch'at' tghesht'ił, gghelldihni ts'its'atnaq'. "Hunlk'et' ch'u ghednu, ch'u q'ench' nugh qetnashigu. Nqel'uda yetq'u tghelgheł, hna ghen dults'el ch'q'u."

Ts'iłq'u q'ut'en qanilchit shełni, hq'u k'usht'a qa'elcheł. Ezhiyi miłni stsindnulqet'. Ughasht'a qanelnik.

Ch'u Naqazhegi Cannery qiz'in dighelak. Heyi shu 1919 yethdi quht'ana ghesh'ih. Ch'u yet nuhtetnish ch'u shiqyan nindelnish heyi daghesediq', hq'u nagh qghedełi shi hnayeh k'u heyiq' daghesediq', hbesukt'a ch'u hbek'elik'a ch'u chiqul'iłch'.

Ch'u shtukda hni'iju Fedosia bunkda 1921. Yethdi sez'a nushtal'u shtukdach' duhdgheldihni. Scheyakda ił gheshduh shanteh ch'u heyteh nagheyik.

Łik'teh'i ghela tik'teh dilaq'adghelnen ch'u shi qyan, ch'u yet guduh nindanlnent hk'uch' shel ninen'i'u. Dena'inaq' ch'elqadi beqel'ani.

Ch'u henugh tanshu ghu Libby diqelasht ch'qiluq' ts'ił jan gidaytsi bu.

Ch'u shtukda be'u qusil 1925 ch'u shcheyakda ch'u Nik'analguk. Yit htl'eghhdi yina qebequsil, ch'u Unhghenesditnu dnaqusil. Ch'u shtukda tininu ch'u łuq'u qil'eh hdaqilchet. Peter Constantine yunich'enh hda'ilchet Tubughnenh. Yin ey shkela.

Ch'u shihdi tik'teh hdanelchet. Shtukda k'uhu ghel'ih gheshdnuh k'uhu el'ih yadi henu ghetghesuł. Ki heyda niłtu chik'a estsizł ch'u garbasnik yih diqelasht. Nutiha dingi qygheqit, yethdi ch'qiluq' nidal'eq'.

Łitl'enteh Kahtnu ht'ana Libby dik'elash qghutnuh. Ch'u łuq'aka'a uhu qul'ih yet May 25 to June 25. Yet tahbił ghelayi chik'a k'ents'esa ts'ah tahbił.

Yet hey thirties Alex Wilson il tahbil ch'ghel'an nutiha dingi łuq'aka'a. Ch'u Granquist niłtu tanalt'eq'i q'aghdeq łuq'u tahbił t'ghel'an. Denłts'ek'i tanalt'eq'i itena nungheshtih. Ch'u dik'elyashh hnugh nuteshjish, niłk'uch' henu ghen k'u nuk'detseden nungheshtih.

1941 hnineshju Agrafena Sacaloff ił hq'u k'usht'a yuh eshdul. 1941 henugh tanshu ghu Portage ch'u Whittier Qeghtinitunt qałnigi ch'qeldedzi. Yet htl'egh hdi Tsani'un yeh Amchitka. Yet htl'egh hdi q'ench' Whittier qeghtinitunt unch' hdanłmen. Yet htl'egh hdi qeliq' 1945 Naknek dik'elash tanshnu yi PAF. Yet htl'egh hdi naqeli tunghanshdnik Kahtnu. Ch'u q'iłdu q'u gheshdu.

Ch'u ch'bala ggats'a ch'aghełak dora ghech niłtu, ch'u dora gheshghun tahbił t'el'ana niłtu, ch'u burhut ank'dghełak ch'u qenq'ah, yadi henu shlaq'a tul'eh. Yethdi tinitun hnugh Kahtnuh heck' tinitun hqeshqa.

1956–57 hkut' qel'anh nidanlnen tuberculosis ghu Seattle Laurel Beach Sanitarium k'uych'eni beq'di hqugh. Ch'u tunghanshdnik idiłdi shqenq'a ghu k'qul: yuleq qul, hdukaq'di qul, belda qyan ez'un. Shlaq'a ghel'eq'i $30.00 ni'iq' yi beł ch'dalnigi.

Q'uch'a shnunastunen Dan France duhhdeldih q'ank'ułqes. Dnigi k'qatl'na shlaq'a ghełggat, ch'eda bach'k'elqedi gudlik ch'u qadi shlaq'a ghełdatl'. Ch'u dora buzełchin. Qughesht'a qyushiluq.

1960 tahbił ch'el'ani q'aghanshdnu sheghes egeduyi hnes t'eshjuq, hq'u yeqech' q'u ghegheshdnu ndahduh henu shlaq'al'eh. 1965 Jack Farnsworth bu henugh tanshu yi nutuyu'ułi shgaba bik'eghneltishi łuq'u beqeghyeh hqugh bik'eyeshi yeq'ahdetałtlet. Deghełkegh hqugh 20' × 60' yi bu dnuyełuq, nutiha shani begh k'egh gheshdnu.

Yethtl'egh hdi kiq'u burhut t'nuch el'ani ch'u ki dora ch'eghuni. Ch'u yet qizlan ch'u ki gheshdnuni qil sheghes egeduyi. Ch'u qadi dink'a shlaq'a ghel'eq ch'u yethdi qyeł k'nunetuhi.

Ch'u yethtl'egh hdi 1972 idashla Jim Kari be'u ił shegh niyu. "Dena'ina hnaga gheniynik'eset," shełni.

"Ch'du'inaghełt'ey shi'i," bedeshni, hq'u bech' henugh ch'tazdatl'.
Ch'u nutastnu ch'u 1973 tunghastnik idiłdi Dena'ina hnaga
ch'k'tuchek shełni. Ch'u yek'echek ch'u "Nen k'u k'ichek," shełni.
Benanltun hq'u qil egduyi shgguna shq'eya. Ch'u "Ch'hdechedigu,"
shełni.

Ch'u yethdi *Kahtnuht'ana Qenaga* niłtut'elyuyi k'yeshchex. Ch'u gin
niłtu t'elyuyi yus qayeh California łuhshiniłtan, qayeh ndahdu
unhshcheyakda yeghenik'ghadnuy be'izhi: Kalifornsky unhtsah
Tahtna ił q'anghudnesh yeh Fort Ross.

My Great-Great Grandfather's Story

My great-great grandfather's name was Qadanalchen, [Acts Quickly; literally, bounces up and out]. This is my great-great grandfather's story,
and the reason why there came to be no more potlatches.

When they took him Outside [to Fort Ross in California, a Russian
colonial post], they baptized him, and he began to believe in God and
to learn to write. When he returned they gave him the name Kalifornsky.

And when he returned here from Fort Ross, California, his father,
who had been chief, had just died. "You next, be chief in his place,"
they said to him.

But he said, "No."

"If you won't be chief, leave the tribe," they told him. So he took his
relatives and founded a village at Unhghenesditnu [Last Creek Down],
which they called Kalifornsky village from his name.

When he was leaving he told the people, "Keep on respecting the old
beliefs, but there is God to be believed in; that is first of all things on
earth," he told them.

And here on the Kenai Peninsula there was no longer a chief, and
there were no more potlatches. And at Kalifornsky village they built a
church, and also at Kustatan they built a church.

At that time there were disputes over territory, and they say that that
great-great grandfather of mine gave the people some advice: "If I were
careless, I wouldn't be here now. If I were one to worry so I couldn't
sleep, I wouldn't be here now. If my stomach were big [i.e., greedy], I
wouldn't be here now." That is what the old people told about him.

My grandfather, Alex Kalifornsky, and his partner, Nickanorga, too, died, one after the other, in 1926. After that there was no one at Kalifornsky village. The survivors moved to Kenai.

Recently, I found the graves there at Kalifornsky village. I set crosses over them.[2]

About the Kenai Dena'ina, Part 1

Here I did not know I was getting trained all the time by my uncles, the Chickalusions, the old people, and my dad. They did not tell me, "Do this" or "Do that." They would just tell me, "Watch this" when they worked.

They knew how to skin an animal so as not to damage the skin. They knew how to get more use out of the skin. And they knew how to remove the hair and tan the hides.

The three Chickalusion brothers had a canoe. They used it overland, going from lake to lake. And they used a three-hole bidarka on Cook Inlet. They were the last ones to use skin boats around here.

In 1933 I made a skin boat. Up at Where Trails Intersect [Gene Lake] I came down the creeks, hunting for muskrats. I came back to Kenai in it and left it on the beach. I don't know what happened to it.

I would go hunting out in the woods, eating dry foods, onions, vegetables, cheese, milk, fish, and fruit.

The last Dena'ina to work with their wives on skins and to use snowshoes were Alex Sunrise, Knik Pete, Feodore Sasha, Max Maxim, Nick Murphy (Qutsen), Simeon Sacaloff, and Nick Kalifornsky. One old lady, Tanya, was the last person to make slippers and fur hats and sinew thread up until 1950. After her there was no more skin and needle work.

Here in Kenai the roads came, and cars. The dogs got to take time off. Now they have dogs for racing. What else can dogs be used for?

About the Kenai Dena'ina, Part 2

Hunting was no problem for them. They knew the country. They traveled light. Bedding for eight or ten people might be two down blankets

2. In 1916 the U.S. Coast and Geodetic Survey established the map name of Kalifornsky as "Kalifonsky." For years, members of the Kalifornsky family had the pronunciation and the spelling of their surname altered to conform with this map name. In 1981, the Alaska State Board of Geographic Names changed the spelling of "Kalifonsky" to "Kalifornsky." A year or so later the road signs on Kalifornsky Beach Road were also changed.

with spruce boughs and grass beneath. Everyone carried his own food supply: dried meat, dried fish, roe, seal oil, biscuits baked with oil.

On the trail there were the small game animals: porcupine, beaver, rabbit, spruce hen. They did not travel in a hurry. They brought a light canoe to travel overland from lake to lake, one built out of willow. For tools, a man would have a rifle, a knife, and an axe. His wife would have the same tools. She, too, was a skilled hunter, and she had her own separate tools and needles. The children learned on the trail. They all had matches inside gut bags. They didn't get them wet.

Out in the inlet a three-man kayak was used, and they carried the same food supply as on the trail. The children were always with them; that is how they learned life.

Hunting dogs were given up long before my last grandfather, Alex Kalifornsky. Visiting other villages and potlatching was gone. But the three-man boat was still used some until my dad was young. He was taken out to sea for sea otter two times, he claimed. Then sea otter hunting ended, and the skin kayak was used on the Inlet for a while for seal, beluga, and ducks, and for sheep and black bear and ground squirrel. And then the skin boats ended, and it happened that they did not need this amount of game for food.

Alex Wilson was the last one to kill a seal, at Rocky Point. And Mrs. Austin was the last one to kill a beluga in the Kenai River, in 1929. The old Dena'ina lifestyle is gone.

In winter they would travel the country the same as mentioned above. They had frame toboggans with skins attached to the bottom, hair side down. They slide well. They traveled through the mountain passes and overland. They knew the country, and they used no dogs because it took too much to feed them. But long ago they used dogs for hunting.

Chief Chickaloon was the last Dena'ina with two wives. He had the dogs pull the sleds in place of his wives pulling the sleds.

At first, dogs were used for hunting, then they got guns, and dogs got to pull sleds.

Where I Trapped

In 1927 I trapped on Swanson River. I stayed at Shagelahtnu [Where Trout Creek Flows Out; Grushka Lake Creek]. I would go down to Russian Crossing, then back, and to Susten [Portage Trail; portage by Hungry Lake], up to Martin's Cabin, and back to Susten to my camp. Long ago a man named Martin had a cabin there, so they call the place that.

And up there in the years 1920 to 1925 my father trapped at Nilq'a-tighetun Bena [Trails Intersect Lake; Gene Lake]. From 1929 to 1936 I trapped there. Long ago they traveled through there to the village here at Kanai or to the trails: Tsik' el' unt [Head in Position; American Pass, near the head of the Chickaloon River]; Tuzqunt [Still Water; Point Possession]; Nilunkaq'dnu [Islands Mouth River; Moose River]; Nilq'atighetun Bena [Trails Intersect Lake; Gene Lake]; and Benkda [No-Good Lake; King Lake]. Benkda was also called Quggesh Bena [Swan Lake] in Dena'ina. Benkda is big and doesn't freeze up well, so it's dangerous, so they call it Bad or Dangerous Lake in Dena'ina.

I had four dogs, and I would go from here at Kenai in the mornings, where the trail was to Kili Bena [a pond at the head of Ryan's Creek] — a man named Kili stayed there, at the pond alongside the airport — and then straight across the flat, through the timber, and then again on the flats, and then to Tuq' Bena [Mudflats Lake; Akula Lake]; and again on the flat; and then to Yaghetnu [Good River; Swanson River], Tahdna Nundulggesht [Where the River Crossed; Russian Crossing], and up the river; then Susten Bena [Portage Trail; Hungry Lake], and again on the Yaghetnu and on up. And here was Grishga's [George Oskolkoff's] little cabin, and John Otterstrom had a cabin there too. And then on to Shagela Bena [Trout Lake; Trout Lake or Grishga's Lake], and more flats and creeks, and then Ni Bena [Island Lake; Quill Lake] and down to the river at Nubendaltun [Lake Extends Across], which is muskrat country, and then to Martin's cabin. Then to Ggabila Bena [Clamshell Lake; Embryo Lake], where I had a brush camp. Then to Sus Kenghelk'et' [Pass Extends Through the Flat]; and Hi'uch' Daltuni [That Which Lies Hidden; Owl Lake], and K'ggalggats'a Q'dalchini [The One Made Like a Fish Heart; Camper's Lake], and K'jech'a Daltuni [The One Made Like a Kidney; Swanson Lake], and Susten and Nilq'atighetun Bena. Here was my camp.

Then there was a portage to Unhtsahdi [The First One; Eider Lake], then Uch'eh Daltuni [One That Lies Obstructing It; Olsjold Lake], then Qeyach'en Daltuni [One That Lies on the Other Side; Wonder Lake], then Benkda Ch'en Daltuni [One That Lies on the Side of Benkda; Wilderness Lake], then Benkda. Then Benkda Q'estsiq' [No-

Good Creek; King Lake outlet] begins. Across the lake over a portage across the ridge is Q'es Dileni [Flows Into Outlet Lake; Wren Lake]. Benkda Ch'en Dałtuni [One That Lies on the Side of Benkda; Wilderness Lake] little creek runs between the ridge and the flat, and among little lakes. Then there is Gidara Q'dalchini [One Made Like a Guitar; Pepper Lake], and then my camp.

Here is where other people used to hunt and trap [from 1927 to 1940]. From Goose Lake to the east entrance of the Swanson Canoe Route area, Charlie Marsh, George Pederson, and Henry Nelson; from the west entrance of the Swan Lake Canoe Route to around the Rock Lake area: Alfred and Mike Danieloff, Victor Antone, and John Monfor; from Beaver Lake to around the Finger Lake area, Nick Mishakoff, the Johansens, and John Alex; from Ciska Lake to the Sevena area, the Wilsons; from Moose River to the West Fork area, George Miller; in the Moose River —Moosehorn area, Johnny Wik and the boys; at Torpedo Lake, Otto Schreider; across the river by Torpedo, Stepanka; in the Killey and Frisbee Lake area, the Backoffs and the Ivanoffs; in the upper Killey River and King County—Cottonwood area, Louie Nissen, Frank Standifer, Pete Knik, Alex Sunrise, Mike and Andrew Dolchok and the boys; on the upper Kenai River to Cooper Landing, the Demidoffs and Dariens; Trail Lake into Bear Creek, Moose Creek, and the Indian Creek area [on Tustumena Lake], Alex Kalifornsky, Nick Nickanorka, Semion Yunesha, Pete Carling, Andrew Berg, John Berg, and Windy Wagner. Ninilchik people trapped around Nikolai Creek [on Tustumena Lake], up in that area.

Our people trapped in these areas until after World War II, when the animals began to disappear.

This Is My Life Story

I was born at Kalifornsky village on October 12, 1911. My mother died when I was a baby. I never saw her. My aunts took care of me. One would keep me, and then another.

Then my maternal uncle, Theodore Chickalusion, got married and took me. I don't remember what year it was, maybe 1915. I barely remember going down to the boat to go across the Inlet [to Polly Creek]. He had a contract with Alaska Packers to cut pilings year-round.

And here I was, away from people, by myself. Many times I would go out in the woods and cry and go to sleep, lonesome for Dad and

Sister and Grandpa. My uncle never stayed home. He was in the woods hunting when he was not working, but he would instruct me in what to do every day, training me in the real old-time way. "You exercise and work, and don't answer back. If you're sent to do something, move right at the very word."

One morning he told me to get up, but I didn't get up. I got cold water over me. I was up fast!

And Snug Harbor Cannery was canning clams around the year 1919. Then I saw some people. Then, when they left, I was left alone again for all the long winter, but their visit to us was my company for all winter, their stories and their songs, and the games they played.

Then my father married Fedosia Sacaloff's mother in 1921. Then my uncle sent me back to my father to go to school. I stayed with my grandpa in the summer, and in winter he visited us.

I was wild because I had been raised in the woods by myself, and when I got back on this side [of Cook Inlet], I had to live a different life. I was used to Native food.

Then I went to work for the Libby Cannery for a dollar a day, for the Chinese crew.

Then my father's wife died in 1925, and also my grandfather and Nickanorga. After they died, Kalifornsky village died out too. And my father left the house, and everyone took off for elsewhere. Peter Constantine went across the inlet to Tyonek. He was a younger brother to me.

But as for me, I went to the woods. I hunted and trapped on my father's trapline and took whatever work I could find. I cut wood for next winter and trap poles for the cannery. They paid forty cents a pole, and later it went up to one dollar.

In springtime the Kenai people worked for the Libby Cannery. The king salmon fishing was from May 25 to June 25. In those days the nets they used had wooden floats and linen web.

One year in the thirties Alex Wilson and I net-fished for king salmon for forty cents a fish. And everybody netted for Granquist [the cannery superintendent] between the traps. I helped the owners of small hand traps. And I would go back to work in the cannery and do other kinds of work, like being a blacksmith's helper.

In 1941 I married Agrafena Sacaloff, but I never stayed at home. In

1941 I went to work on the Portage and Whittier tunnel as a rock driller. After that I went to the Aleutians, to Amchitka, and after that back to Whittier to work on widening the tunnel. After that, in the spring of 1945, I went to the Naknek Cannery for PAF. After that, in the fall, I came home to Kenai. And I stayed home then.

And I dug out spruce roots (natural knees) for ribs for dories, and I built some dories for fishermen, and I repaired boats and houses— whatever work I could get. Then I worked on the highway out from Kenai for the Alaska Road Commission.

In 1956–57 I landed in the hospital with tuberculosis, in the Laurel Beach Sanitarium in Seattle, for sixteen months. When I came home, my house was empty—no windows, no door, only a stove there. What I got was $30 a month from Social Security.

The only person who helped me was Dan France, who was driving the school bus. He gave me the hindquarter of a moose, and he gave me some blankets, dishes, and pots, and some groceries. Then I built him a dory, and he paid me well.

In 1960 I had to give up fishing because my arthritis got bad, but I kept on working wherever I could find work. In 1965 I went to work for Jack Farnsworth on a floating barge on which the freezer's chemicals had rotted everything below the decking. It was twenty by sixty feet, what I repaired for him, and I worked on it for him for two summers.

After that I repaired more boats and built more dories. Then the time came when I couldn't work anymore because of arthritis. So I went on food stamps, and later on welfare.

Then after that, in 1972, my friend Jim Kari and his wife came to visit me. "I am interested in learning the Dena'ina language," he told me.

"It is a hard language," I told him, but we got going on it. Then he came back in 1973 and at that time told me the Dena'ina language could be written. Then he started writing it and told me, "You write something too." I tried, but the pain was bad in my arm and hip. And he told me, "Don't give up on it."

And finally I wrote the book *Kahtnuht'ana Qenaga*. And [in 1979] this book took me out to the state of California, the state where my great-great grandfather earned his name: Kalifornsky, who went with the first Russians to Fort Ross.

IVAN VENIAMINOV

Ivan Veniaminov was born in 1797 in Aginskoe, Siberia. In 1823 he ventured to Unalashka, where for ten years he worked as a missionary, church administrator, and scholar, compiling the first detailed studies of the Aleut language and customs. He died in 1879 and is buried near Moscow. Veniaminov was canonized as St. Innokentii, Evangelizer of the Aleuts and Apostle to America, by the Holy Synod of the Church of Russia on October 6, 1977. His work was translated by Lydia T. Black and R. H. Geoghegan.

FROM *Notes on the Islands of the Unalashka District*

Clothing

The principal and most necessary garment of the Aleuts is the *parka*—a kind of long shirt falling below the knee, is now made of bird skins, primarily of tufted and crested puffins (sea parrots), but sometimes of murre, but, if these should be lacking, of [hair] seal straps, as Mr. Sarychev saw.

The parka for Aleuts in the local climate is an indispensable article. On the road it constitutes their bed and blanket and, one might say, home. With it they are not afraid either of wind or cold. This I can attest from my personal experience. Until I began to use a parka on my travels, I suffered very much from the cold and the winds, while using all means to keep warm which frieze cloth [*frizy*], even furs, and so forth, furnish. [Their inadequacy] is the reason why, although one can see many Aleuts in frieze cloth or cloth [*sukno*] jackets and even frock coats [*siurtuki*] (as for the last, only *toions* and notables have them), all of them when traveling carry with them, without fail, a parka, and those who are more well to do even two, one new and one old.

Another and just as necessary Aleut garment is the *kamleika*, also a kind of long shirt, the difference being only that in place of a collar there is joined to it a separate hood or sack, which, in case of necessity, in the rain for instance, is put over the head and drawn tight with a cord around the face. Cords are also attached to the sleeve ends to draw tight the sleeves. Kamleikas are made generally of gut membranes, primarily of sea lions (of the largest [bulls]—*sekachi*), and also of bear, walrus and whale [intestines]. Kamleikas are used only for baidarka travel and occasionally on [overland] passages during rain. The most durable kamleikas are the sea lion [gut] ones and the most elegant are of bear. The

Company makes kamleikas of sea lion throats [esophagi], but these are used by very few [people] because they are much too expensive.

Nothing can replace kamleikas either in terms of comfort or [serving] the purpose for which they were invented. This too, I tested by experience on several occasions. In the worst possible weather, a kamleika is light, warm and comfortable, and nothing could be better.

A kamleika, even the very best one, cannot serve as long as a parka. An active man needs two and even three kamleikas a year. (For durability the kamleika is frequently oiled but never with fish fat.) A well-worked parka, of tufted-puffin skins, can serve for an entire year, as the saying goes, without taking it off one's shoulders [in constant wear], provided one takes care to protect it [the parka] from the rain. With care it can serve even two years, because it is not worn out so much as it breaks up from washing. Urine is used for washing parkas and preparing skins, which then are usually rinsed in fresh water. Usually, for a parka, 40 tufted-puffin skins and 60 horned-puffin skins are needed. Marine animal sinew is generally used to sew parkas and kamleikas. Bird hunting will be described below.

Footwear in general use at present are the torbasa, a kind of brodni [fording boots, waders]. The leg part [golenishche] is made either of sea-lion throats or sea-lion laftaki. To these are attached the fore pieces [uppers] of yufta leather, while the soles are made either of Russian leathers or whale or sea-lion flippers. The last mentioned, being wrinkled, are most suitable for walking over pebbles [stones, rocks] and slippery places. Formerly torbasy were made without the forepart [uppers, but a vamp]—like a bag. Nowadays many of the men wear [high] boots [sapogi], while the women wear shoes [bashmaki].

Formerly, Aleuts knew no hats or caps at all, and, in general, both sexes did not cover their heads or tie them up. Consequently when the Aleuts saw the first Russians, who covered their heads, they called them, before [knowing] any other name, saligungin, that is, the ones having caps or hats [shaposhnye or shliapniki].

Now, however, all men commonly wear visored caps [furazhki] made of cloth or [hair] seal skin, the visors sometimes fashioned of baleen and quite skillfully. Married women, widows and old women bind their heads with kerchiefs, and only young, unmarried girls go about with uncovered heads.

The clothing of the old-time Aleuts consisted formerly also of bird skin parkas, but then these were also often made from the skins of fur seals and sea otters, variously ornamented. The cut and so forth of these hardly differed in any way from the men's parkas. Now they have no sea otter and fur seal pelts and therefore women's parkas are nowadays made of the self-same bird skins or of some cloth material such as ticking [tik], etc., but preferably of dark-colored nankeen [kitaika]. This kind of garment, [also] called a kamleika, replaces the former [ceremonial] festive parkas. In cut, they differ very little from parkas, except that in front a small slit, similar to a shirt opening, is made from the collar down. Elegant kamleikas [of this kind] are ornamented with narrow bands of red, sky blue or green cloth, which are sewn around the hem at the cuffs and below the collar.

Shirts were wholly unknown to the Aleuts in former times, but now they have come into common use. However, not everybody has the means to own them. Prosperous Aleuts even wear waistcoats, trousers (of which previously they had no conception), and neckties. Wives and daughters of such men, on holidays, wear fashionable Russian dresses and shawls (which, because of their clumsy gait and stooped posture, sometimes appear rather comical).

The Aleuts use no belts except when it is necessary, in a parka or kamleika, to go on foot.

The parkas of small children almost always are made of eagle skins with [just] the down on them. For adolescents ordinary parkas and occasionally even frock coats [siurtuki] and dresses are made.

Aleut bedding consists of several tserely, or grass mats, one better than another; on top of these there are [hair] seal skins. In former times, in place of [hair] seal skins, sea-otter and fur-seal skins were used. Now many Aleuts have woolen blankets and down pillows, even featherbeds.

In general, Aleut men and women do not know [how] to take care of their clothes and to wear them with discrimination (sometimes this is, however, because they have not many changes of clothing). Very often one may see an Aleut man, having put on a jacket or an Aleut woman her kamleika, wear them until they fall apart. Not too long ago, many even wore clothes without mending them so that sometimes one would see a person wearing a good jacket or a fine kamleika, but torn and ripped at the seams.

Lately they have begun to become more discriminating and careful about this because it is not always possible nowadays to acquire a dress or a new outfit, and if so, then only with great difficulties. This is so especially recently when clothing cannot be obtained except in hard cash.

The Aleuts almost never wear gloves, except for old men, who wear leather [skin; *kozhannyia*] mitts on baidarka trips in cold weather. Instead of lining, soft grass is stuffed inside them.

To male attire belong the wooden hats or caps used only on baidarka travel. These hats are used specifically to protect the eyes from the seawater spray. They are of two types, one with a closed, the other with an open crown.

The first are made from roots of tree stumps cast up by the sea and are bent into the form of an irregular (elliptical) funnel. Then they are painted with different colors [in] longitudinal stripes and adorned with sea-lion whiskers, *korol'ki* [trade beads] and various carved bone figurines. Such hats in olden times, that is, when they did not have the present tools, were a great rarity. Only the toions and the notables could have them, as the best hat cost one to three slaves.

The other hats with open crowns are nothing other than large, long visors, like a crownless cap with a large visor, worn over the kamleika hood. Some of them are also adorned with sea-lion whiskers, trade beads and bone [ivory ornaments]. The first [sea-lion whiskers] are usually attached on the left side only [in order] not to interfere with spear throwing, but those who are left-handed attach the whiskers on the right side. Such hats of large or small size are owned by every seagoing Aleut.

In a strong wind, large hats can cause the death [*gibel'*] of an inexperienced person, since a wind can very easily get in under the cap and by its force overturn his baidarka. Consequently, as a precaution at such a time, many take them [the hats] off.

In former times there was also in use a small round cap made of [hair] seal skin, embroidered with caribou hair, with a long braid of thongs in back and with an embroidered *tongue* in front. These hats were used only in the dances and now no one has them.

Baidarkas

As island dwellers, the Aleuts must have some kind of boats or skiffs [lodki ili boty] for moving from one island to another and so forth. Nature, however, has denied them the requisite material for boat building, that is wood, but on the other hand, as if in recompense, has given them the intelligence to perfect a flotilla of a very special—and new—[invention], the baidarkas. Who first invented it, the Aleuts or their neighbors, that is, the people of Kad'iak or other North Americans, is not known. However, it is known that the first Aleut baidarkas were so imperfect that they were able to cross from one island to another only with difficulty and then only in calm weather. These [baidarkas] were wide and short and, therefore, very heavy afloat. It is beyond dispute, however, that it was the Aleuts who perfected the baidarka. One has only to look at the baidarkas of the Kad'iak people, the Aglegmiuts and other northern inhabitants, and even at [the baidarkas] of their compatriots [Aleuts] living on the islands nearest to Kamchatka, and at first glance, the advantages of the local baidarka over them all are apparent. It is necessary to state, however, that the baidarka of the present-day Aleuts is not as perfect as the baidarka of the former Aleut [sea] riders [naezdnik]. In those times, excellent riders had baidarkas so light that they were not outdistanced by birds. The baidarkas were narrow and sharp-keeled in an upright position. They were so light that a seven-year-old child could easily carry them. By my time, I was not able to see such baidarkas built for speed [skorokhodki].

In the best one-hatched baidarka, in order to make it speedy, up to 60 small bones [shims] were set into all its joints to serve as nuts [vtulochki], pivots [vertliugi], mortise-locks [zamochki], and plates [plastinki], etc. In a baidarka so constructed, when underway, almost every member was in movement. Nowadays no one has such bone parts [kostochki] and, with the exception of some old men, knows how to make them or how to use them properly. I had a three-hatched baidarka made with bones, but it was in no way better than an ordinary one. As proof of the lightness of an old-time baidarka, I shall quote a well-known example.

During the sojourn here of Captains Krenitsyn and Levashev, one of the best Aleut sea riders was sent from Kapitanskaia Gavan' to Issanakhskoi Strait with a most important message. He made it in 25 or 30 hours, traveling a distance of about 200 versts, but after arrival he soon died from a chest hemorrhage. It also frequently occurred that the distance between Ugamak and Sannakh was traversed in 12 to 18 hours.

The best present-day baidarka can go against the fastest current in the straits, as for example, in Unalginskoi Strait, where off the capes the current runs up to 6½ knots.

It seems to me that the Aleut baidarka is so perfect of its kind that even a mathematician could add very little if anything to improve its seaworthy qualities.

Presently the baidarkas are of three kinds: that is, with one hatch [iqax], with two and with three hatches [ulyuxtax]. All said above about the baidarka is to be understood as pertaining to the one-hatched ones because the three-hatched baidarkas began to be made only after the Russians' arrival and are their adaptation. While the Aleuts always had two-hatched ones, these were only for transporting light cargo or for an old man to go to sea with a minor. But there was no precedent even up until this time for two young and healthy oarsmen of their own volition going hunting sea otter in a double-hatched baidarka. This is considered a disgrace.

The principal part of any baidarka, in general, is not the keel, as Mr. Sarychev says, but the rods [shesty] or upper frame [gunwales], together with several transverse stretchers [rasporki] or thwarts [beams; bimsy] [spaced] from 2½ to 4½ chetverts wide in the middle but brought together at the ends. The greatest width of a good baidarka is not in the middle but nearer the bow. The keel [keelson] is fastened to the lower side of the frame. The baidarka in motion should have flexibility or, as they say, be able to bend over the wave. Then, above the keel [between the keelson and the frame], ribs [rebra] or luchki are inserted into the rods [shesty] [of the upper frame] at a distance of from 3 to 7 inches from one another, and over and on top of them several very thin rods are placed lengthwise of the baidarka and fastened with filaments of baleen.

When all this is done, the reshetka [grating], as the baidarka without its sheathing is called, is ready. The sheathing, or [outside] covering, of the baidarka is made of sea-lion or [hair] seal skin [laftaki]. It is cut to fit, and on the baidarka itself [all seams are sewed] except only the [long] upper seam from the hatch to the stern, and in two- and three-hatch baidarkas [it is left open] from the forward hatch to the stern. This last seam is sewn [when the covering has been stretched] over the baidarka itself. It is self-evident that every item, and even the sheathing, of a baidarka requires an experienced master. Not every Aleut can be a master. Therefore, not every Aleut baidarka has all the good qualities. No [additional] sheathings are made on the inside. But, when traveling, inside over the grating an old skin [*laftak*] is spread, topped by various pads [*podstilki*] and then cargo.

To ensure the durability of the baidarka cover, it is, on clear days, oiled. However, no matter how carefully one preserves it, a single baidarka cover is not enough for one year. The grating, however, can serve for several years, naturally with repairs.

The dimensions of the baidarkas are as follows:

	Length in *arshins*	Width in *chetverts*	Height in *chetverts*
Three-hatched	8½ to 9	4 to 5	2½ to 3
Two-hatched	8 to 8½	3½ to 4½	2¼ to 3
One-hatched	6 to 7	2½ to 3	2 to 2¼

Indispensable for a baidarka are the close-fitted coverings [*obtiazhki*], or drip-skirts [*tsuki*], without which it is not possible to travel, not only on a distant voyage but with wind even a close a distance. These drip-skirts are always made of sea lion intestines or occasionally throats [gullets]. These are from ½ to ¾ arshins in height or [rather] width. One edge is placed over the hatch and fastened to the baidarka with baleen. The other edge the rider, in case of need, draws tight under his breast with a sinew drawstring, which is then passed across the left shoulder.

The oar [paddle] for the baidarka is always made two-bladed, from 2½ to 3 arshins long, depending upon the stature of the paddler and, whenever possible, always of California *chaga* [cedar] as the lightest wood. However, some old men, with two-hatched baidarkas, use one-bladed paddles as among the Kad'iak people.

The kamleika and the wooden hat are also indispensable appurtenances belonging to the baidarka, but they were discussed above.

Also, it is considered absolutely necessary to carry in a baidarka a pump or a sea sponge to bail out the water. The pump is made of wood. It is nothing other than a cylindrical tube about a half arshin long, a little thicker in the middle than an arm but tapering gradually toward the ends so that the end itself can be taken into the mouth. In a single-hatch baidarka, the second oarsman [paddler] does the bailing. He is always more experienced and stronger than the forward oarsman [paddler] because it is his business [duty] to steer the course.

In the single-hatch baidarka, if they are without a load, many carry a stone or two as ballast.

Among the articles indispensable for a baidarka, there formerly belonged the bladder [puzyr'], that is, the cleaned [hair] seal or sea lion stomach, which was necessary if the baidarka [was] overturned. When this happens, it is not too difficult to climb out of the baidarka and [right it] put it again on keel without swamping it. But it is absolutely impossible to climb into a righted baidarka without an outside point of support [fulcrum]. An inflated bladder in this case is very useful. With its help the paddler could support himself on the [surface] and climb into the baidarka. It has happened that, when occasionally the baidarka sheathing split somehow, the paddler, with the help of the bladder, climbed out of the baidarka, turned it over, repaired the tear, and then climbed in—provided the weather was calm. With a fresh wind, however, under unfavorable conditions, the bladder was put inside the baidarka and inflated as much as possible. It [the inflated bladder] supported the baidarka on the surface even when it was full of water [swamped]. Nowadays, I observed such bladders in possession of very few, because now a baidarka almost never goes out by itself, but always two or three [set out] together: in case of danger, one is able to render help to another.

Formerly, sails were never used on baidarkas, and even now only some of the toions have a small sail on their three-hatch baidarkas. The undertakings by some Russians to equip the baidarka with several sails are absolutely useless.

Mr. Sarychev says that when an Aleut casts a spear, then with the other hand he supports the baidarka with the paddle, preserving its equilibrium. This is an error, because no one ever does this. All Aleuts are able to keep their balance under any circumstance, and some are so skillful that they can stand up[right] on their feet in a baidarka if only they have a paddle in their hands. Such a feat as, for example, to cast a spear while setting out from shore, or [and] in a small surf with one foot in the baidarka to shake-off [otriakhivat']; the other [overboard], and so forth, is an ordinary occurrence.

All travelers are unanimous in stating that the Aleut in full attire and in his baidarka has a handsome and indeed a majestic appearance. Then he is in his proper element. If the Californians are the best horsemen among Americans, then the Fox Island Aleuts are the best baidarka riders. No force of wind nor rough seas, and not in fact any impact by an outside force, if only the Aleut anticipates it, is able to capsize him, provided he has his paddle in his hands. The only thing which the Aleut fears — and which he is not able to fight — is a strong suloi [whirlpools and tidal rip] in the straits and also heavy surf at the landings. But in the latter case, too, an experienced and dexterous paddler can very often land or cast off and save himself as well as others. But in the first event, if he does not know how to avoid the suloi and passes between them, his doom is inescapable.

The Aleuts of old also had baidarkas for transporting large cargoes, but their construction was completely different from that of the present-day colonial baidarkas. They had a uniformly steep and low stern and bow and a very narrow bottom, while the ribs were sometimes bent in the same manner as in the baidarkas. In such a case, there were no special thwarts [rasporki — crossbeams] on the keel. There were no shelters [besedka] or benches in them, and the oarsmen sat on the sides [po bortam]. They had short, single-bladed and small oars. [Their] baidarkas, it is said, were very unsteady or easily upset but far lighter in movement than the present-day ones. I had no opportunity to see their former baidarkas.

Food

Nature's bounty here is extremely meager and scant in terms of land products. The local climate hardly will allow introduction of any cereal plants. Consequently, the products of the animal kingdom alone constitute the food of the inhabitants here, predominantly the sea animals, specifically whales of all kinds (except the sperm whale), sea lions, fur seals, [hair] seals, sea otters, and to some extent walrus[es], and fish: cod, kalaga, red sculpin, halibut, Atka mackerel, sea perch, nalim, salmon trout, King salmon, humpbacked salmon, dog salmon and silver salmon; mollusks: sea urchins, clams, black mussels, etc., and two kinds of crabs; birds: ptarmigan, geese and ducks of various kinds, murres, tufted puffins, fulmars, horned puffins, sea gulls, red-legged kittiwakes, and others.

In order to have a full list, let us include caribou, bears, porcupines (one Aliaksa and Unga), and domestic animals, that is, swine and chickens. Of the vegetable kingdom they use for food: berries — crowberries [shiksha], raspberries [malina], and, to some extent, other berries; roots: sarana, makarsha, chagitka, the sweet root, and sea cabbage [kelp] of two kinds.

At first glance, such an enormous inventory of the various products may create the impression that the inhabitants here have plentiful means for their subsistence, approaching even luxury. In reality, their food supply is very limited and even scant, because, in general, it depends upon circumstances and chances incomparably more unpredictable than for inhabitants of terra firma. And there is nothing which could always be, so to speak, fundamental and unfailing food — with the exception of the water and air. It is even impossible to define exactly what is the Aleuts' staple food [what they eat most]. In the best of summers, no more than 500 of the seasonal fish are stored for each family, and although ocean fish in many localities are abundant, means and circumstances do not permit the Aleuts to store much because the only possible method of fish preservation is by [air] drying, to which the weather, however, very often is an impediment. In winter the fish go into the deep waters, [and] strong and almost incessant winds do not permit going out after them.

Very few sea lions are taken, and then in few localities. [Hair] seals, although they are found everywhere, are but few in number. Fur seals are only on the Pribylov Islands, while the sea otters are here only in the summer and besides are consumed by the hunters themselves.

The whales in summer sometimes are in great numbers, but only at Unalashka and to some extent at Akun. There, although they hunt or wound from 30 to 60 every year, no more than 33 and sometimes no more than 10 come to hand. Certainly, to the eye, 10 or 20 whales comprise a huge quantity, but generally the whales here are only of the small kind so that it is easily possible to load a whole whale into one baidarka. Besides, even with the greatest abundance of whales, only inhabitants of the immediate vicinity obtain stores of whale meat and blubber, and then such stores are not rich. Their reserve never lasts a whole year, because some are careless and waste it to no purpose, others live too open-handedly beginning with the autumn, but more so because there are no containers in which the blubber could be preserved. The containers in general use for fat [blubber] are sea-lion or [hair] seal bladders [puzyri]. Since these animals are few, so are the vessels. Moreover, to [our] misfortune, since 1828 there have been rats here, which sometimes in one night strip the householder of his whole year's reserve.

Wooden vessels are very few because, although many of the Aleuts could make them for themselves, there are no necessary materials available (specifically hoops).

The main food of the Aleuts is fat [zhir—oil, blubber] of any [sea] animal except the sperm whale.

However many fish an Aleut puts up, if, at the same time he has no fat, one can say with certainty that he is going to suffer either from actual hunger or illness, because with long usage yukola, or dried fish, without fat is not too nourishing. On the other hand, even if an Aleut does not have a single dried fish, if fat is sufficient, he will not experience hunger. Because with fat, he can use everything—roots, sea cabbage [kelp] (which is, without fat, very harmful, especially the latter) and mollusks [rakushki], and the driest yukola and straps, in brief, everything which the stomach can possibly digest. Those who believe that the plentiful and abundant Aleut food consists predominantly of fish are in error. True, they eat more fish than meat, but this is due, however, only to the scarcity of marine animals. Besides, whenever possible they always eat fish only with fat.

The best Aleut dishes are crowberries with fat, beaten until white; the heads of seasonal fish fermented to some degree and fish roe prepared in the same way as the heads; the heads and fatty parts of the halibut; nura (a small seaweed), cooked with fat; and good-quality yukola with whale blubber [zhirovaia kitovina]. The second mentioned dish especially is considered excellent eating which even one accustomed to Russian cooking will not refuse.

The Aleuts eat almost everything raw except codfish, which, raw— and particularly not completely cooked—is very harmful. The meat of sea mammals, though cooked, or rather stone boiled, may be said only to be warmed up.

They use absolutely no salt on food. Only nowadays, those who are workers in the main village have begun to use salted fish, but this is only from necessity. But no one refuses bread, tea and sugar.

Although the Aleuts eat almost everything and are not too fastidious about cleanliness, still, for all that, it is not possible to call them omnivorous — as they say about the Kamchadals — because there are things produced by their land which they absolutely do not eat, for example, mushrooms of any kind in any form. Also, at first when they saw that for several vegetables the Russians manured the land with ordinary dung, they did not want to eat vegetables which were produced in such soil. Even nowadays, when they have become accustomed to seeing this, they themselves will not do it even if there is a need.

To lay in fish for yukola is always woman's work. For this purpose they settle with their children in good time along certain rivers in which fish are especially plentiful. Each party is accompanied by one or two of the elderly or ailing men, not so much to help with the fishing itself as with the transportation of the indispensable things and to guard them from the vagabonds [beglye].

Laying up food for the Aleuts, it can be said, does not constitute the sole object or the exclusive aim of their existence, as it is possible to say about very many Russians of the common people if one looks upon both from such a point of view. Every Aleut lays up food for himself, but he stocks it up as if he worked for hire and not for himself, and as was said earlier, having put by a supply for two or three months, he meets the winter without a care. Notwithstanding the fact that each spring teaches him in the most intelligible manner to be more active and careful about storing food, he does not learn from such lessons. This lack of concern springs from the fact that living by the sea, this inexhaustible and rich storehouse for all around it, available always, they expect at every season to obtain something from it if only the circumstances and the available means would permit. Consequently, such unconcern of the Aleuts about storing food for themselves is, on the one hand, laudable, because, more or less, it is a sign of trust in All-Sustaining God. On the other hand, however, this attitude is by no means superior to that type of care which has as its sole concern only the stomach: it can serve as an excuse for idleness, and idleness is always worse than any bustling about and carefulness.

With the exception of supper, the Aleuts have almost no regular times for eating. They never eat in the morning, especially before a long voyage, in order, they say, to drink less, as otherwise they will suffer a serious shortness of breath.

During a voyage they eat very rarely and very little and just, so to say, snack on this or that. At the camp, however, they set free their appetite, but it is not true, as some say, that they eat all night without interruption and that one eats as much as ten. True, one ordinary portion must take into account their uninterrupted labor and fasting, which lasts sometimes up to 18 consecutive hours. At ordinary times, in general, Aleuts eat very moderately, even less, it appears, than [they] ought.

All the mollusks, and especially sea urchins, which are used for food in great quantity, cause excessive drowsiness.

The only drink of the Aleuts is water. Until the Russians came, they knew nothing intoxicating, but since then they have come to know vodka and tobacco, which, in some way, replaces intoxicants [khmel'noe].

Vodka and all spirit beverages the Aleuts call *tangam daqulga*, that is, fool's for stupefying water. Now the use of tea, even daily, is spreading. They get it from the Russians in exchange for work or fish and so forth. The habit of drinking tea is growing so strong among Aleuts that many are ready to exchange a shot of vodka for a cup of tea.

Tobacco is in general use nowadays and for the most part as *lemeshina* [chewing tobacco], that is, it is put behind the lip. A few take snuff, but no one smokes.

LIBBY BEAMAN

The daughter of a prominent Washington, D.C., family, Libby Beaman at the age of thirty-five became the first non-Native American woman to travel to the Pribilof Islands. In 1879 and 1880 she wrote and sketched detailed studies of the seal life and the lives of the Aleuts while her husband, John, helped supervise the fur seal industry for the national government. She died in 1932 at the age of eighty-eight.

FROM *Libby: The Alaskan Diaries of Libby Beaman, 1879–1880*

June 30th

The Aleuts believe that they are descended from the seals! Never having seen a monkey in their lives, this belief is much more logical for them and is a part of their legend and folklore—that is, what little they have retained of a folklore from the time before the Russians. Dr. Kelly says it is a logical belief and in many ways more valid than ours, because the seal has a far larger brain box in proportion to the body than has a monkey. The seal's eyes express human emotion where a monkey's do not, and since the Aleuts always have worn seal fur, eaten seal meat, and used the skin for boats and the blubber for fuel, they are entirely identified with the seals. If they have any theology left from the old time, their god or gods were no doubt giant seals, and they themselves have been seals in other incarnations.

While they do not have too many legends for their race, they do have a few strange customs that are not Russian. The men wander about at night in a sort of a trance, not kvas-induced. Of course the nights are light, so one can see them. They are not frightening, just eerie, moving about unseeing. No one has been able to account for this, and as they never do any harm, no one has ever tried to stop the habit. It is a bit disconcerting to run into one and have him look right through you without acknowledging a greeting. The womenfolk never wander like this and don't seem to mind when the men do. Usually the next day, the man will recount ghostly encounters he has had or visions of almost mythological beasts. I've heard them pad past our windows on occasion and wondered what they could be up to. Sometimes they are actually clairvoyant when they are traipsing about in a dense fog and suddenly scream out, "Ship's light! Ship's light!" which they cannot possibly see with their physical eyes. And always, sure enough, when the fog lifts, a ship is lying offshore!

One screamed "Ship's light!" about two this morning, sending chills up and down our spines. There's a dense, dense fog, but we think the St. Paul may be in. She's due within a few days.

July 2nd

The St. Paul was riding at anchor when the mists finally dissipated. What a welcome sight! What a truly beautiful sight! A first link with home! Letters and messages and gifts and the purchases Captain Erskine made for me. All our dear ones seem so close in the letters they have written and by the little luxuries they have sent. They hadn't received our letters that went back from Onalaska on the St. Paul. But they thoughtfully had written anyway, so letters could be brought up on this trip. I won't ever mind that startling cry in the night, "Ship's light!" again. This is a beautiful day.

Another great surprise the St. Paul has brought is in the person of Henry Wood Elliott himself. He was the first Treasury Department agent sent here. During his two years here, he mapped every inch of the two islands. But because he took his drawings directly to the Government Printing Office, I did not get to see them first. Mr. Elliott found the fur seal herds so completely decimated by the Russians that, when he returned to Washington, he pushed for legislation to prohibit any killing of seals until the herds could be reestablished. Congress passed such a bill before the writing of a treaty with Japan and Russia forbidding any sealing on land or in the waters around the islands. Mr. Elliott's greatest claim to fame, in my estimation, is the fact that he married a native Pribilof Island Aleut and took her back to live in Lakewood, Ohio, his home. She has come back to stay with her family while he goes to St. Matthew Island. He will spend several days with us at Government House. Fortunately, the sa's [senior agent's] room has two beds. Then he will go over to St. George to await the Reliance, which is to take him up to St. Matthew Island some five hundred miles north of here. He is still gathering material for the book he plans to write about the fur seals, and he wishes to make sure that the Pribilofs are their only breeding ground.

Mr. Elliott is also on official government business and business for the Smithsonian, so the *Reliance* has been put at his disposal. He says that he would like to visit the Commander Islands, seven hundred miles southwest of us, but he is afraid he'll never get there—the *Reliance* is not permitted in Siberian waters. The vast amount of sailing he has done in these waters is a courageous act, heretofore unheard of in the interests of accurate, scientific knowledge about our possession and the wildlife of this area. He is also a very fine artist. His watercolor sketches and pen and ink drawings easily could be compared to the Old Masters'.

I shall be spending a great deal of time with Mr. Elliott while he is here. He is quite interested in the seal book I have begun and has asked me to make specific observations for his book at times when he cannot be here. I am flattered.

I had not realized that the excellently drawn map of St. Paul on the office wall is his work; there is also a map of St. George on that island. I've insisted that he sign them. This one is truly a work of art, with its profile of the approach to the island as he first saw it. He has promised to sign his name if I will do a proper job of lettering. "Yours is far more accurate than mine . . . and finer," he said. I will letter the maps for him, as well as the copies he will take back with him for his book. My lettering is finer, smaller. He shades his letters so that they do not print out as precise. Thus he has set me tasks that will keep me busy all winter.

July 12th

The men have begun the final week of killing. The St. Paul has departed to deliver Mr. Elliott to St. George and to load the skins taken there. The work is at its heaviest in order to get it all done soon, for the pelts get too gamey if not taken early in the season. Even this is a bit late, except that the weather has remained cool enough to prolong the work. Though I am spared the actual sight of the slaughter, the noise is so terrible that I am constantly aware of what is going on. It is an awful time to live through. The whole idea upsets me, and I am in a state of nerves that has me worried. After all, I must have visualized some sort of slaughter to get the pelts, but I never dreamed that it all would take place so close at hand. I probably thought, if I thought about it at all, that there was some remote spot for, and dainty way of, expediting the poor seals— far from any personal experience or involvement for either of us—and that John would have to stand at some warehouse door, after it was all over, counting the skins that came in and billing the company for the number of pelts in the name of the U.S. Treasury. How sadly different!

John is sick at heart over the real job and physically sick, too, for he hardly eats, just picks at the food on his plate. He does not join in the conversation around the table, which is a little louder and more boisterous than before. He is so silent, stooped, and white that I worry about him.

"It's a messy business, Libby, ugly and contrary to anything you or I have ever been taught. It's just no place for us. Yet what can we do now? I feel as trapped as one of those animals—more so I guess—because I know what's happening. Fortunately they don't." This John said a few days ago. He hasn't said much since.

While I watch him grow more morose and disgusted with his job, I have sensed a rising tension among the men of the company and among the natives, too. Perhaps the men have become so restive because of the very bestiality of the job they have to do—selecting the animals, directing the drives to the killing grounds, directing the flensing operations, making sure the skin is taken the moment the animal is killed, being right on the field in the thick of the blood and offal, coming in spattered with blood and dung, and reeking of decaying carcasses with almost nothing but the putrefaction of death in their eyes and minds and nostrils.

Each night, by the time we arrive for dinner at the Lodge, they are gruff, less careful of their language, and less carefully attired. Though I have seen none of them take a drink, I have smelled alcohol on some breaths, and I have noted many blood-shot eyes. The natives, always so docile and well behaved in front of me, also are more keyed up. Neither the SA nor John can find any kvas, but they know that the Aleuts have been drinking more heavily. Their tyones (they also call a native foreman tyone) have been warned to keep them in order or they will lose their jobs. But each day grows more difficult to get through, and I wish the whole business was over with.

Naturally I could not write all this to my family, who would be shocked and worried as I am shocked and worried.

July 13th

I am afraid to write, yet I must write, what happened today. I write with the hope that perhaps the whole episode will become clear. I try to understand why it happened, why I let it happen. But some things are beyond human calculation, beyond human control. I know these are difficult days. The killing season should be ended, but because we have had extremely bad weather at times, it has been prolonged. Fortunately it has been cool enough to keep the pelts from rotting, which they usually begin to do about now. The men are tired and excitable, and so are the animals, especially the bulls at the height of their mating season. They fight constantly and viciously over the matkas, and one of the favorite pastimes of the natives is to stand at the edge of the harems and bet on the fights just as men at home might bet on a cockfight or a wrestling match. Aleuts will bet on anything that presents a challenge. So they pick their favorite bulls and spur them on from the sidelines.

I've stayed away from the rookeries because I do not like the noise and heat of battle. Yet now that the baby seals are being born, I've wanted to watch them closely so I can write fully about them, which means, of course, that I have to spend some time close enough for careful observation.

Walking is not easy on this island. There are no well-worn paths anywhere except to the spring, where we get our drinking water, about a mile and a half away from here. I am tired of always walking in that direction, which is inland, because no seals are to be seen along the way. The longer walks I had once anticipated taking so far have proved to be short excursions only. Some obstacle—such as slippery rocks, deep ravines, sudden fissures, or bogs—always stand in the way of going on to the farther rookeries.

Today started out to be such a beautiful day, the clearest we've had so far. Since I couldn't stand the din from the killing grounds and knew that the men had just finished driving the seals in from Polavina across from the island, I decided I would take advantage of the path the animals wore down. Mr. Elliott told me that Polavina is the most beautiful sight on the island and an interesting rookery. I wanted to see it before the rains washed away the seals' path and while the weather still permitted sketching.

John did not, as was his custom, ask what I would be doing all day. If he had, and if I had told him, he would have forbidden me to go. Instead, and with a certain amount of resentment in his voice, he announced that he had been ordered — "Ordered, Libby," — to supervise the killings at Novastoshnah.

"You knew you would be sent. The log records that the assistant agent always supervises the operation at Novastoshnah."

"But it means that I must leave you alone here, alone and unprotected."

"I can manage. Do not worry." I had assumed he'd be gone for just the day so I made my plans accordingly.

Past Kamminista's volcanic peak I climbed, seeing dead and dying seals along my path, rejected seals that had been left to find their way back to the sea or perish in this high, unfamiliar region so unlike their natural habitat. Flesh flies swarmed thick upon them, and white foxes lurked among the rocks, shy of me, but waiting to scavenge as soon as I had passed. I have no fear of the white foxes. They will not harm a living, moving creature. They are the island's sanitation corps.

I've had no real fear of meeting any Aleut. I know them all by name. They've all been friendly to me even when they've had kvas. We mumble a greeting — possibly *spasibo* for an answer — and go our separate ways. I've come upon children hunting birds' eggs. They are less silent, less secretive. I hear their laughter before I come upon them. Their elders sometimes give me quite a start. But I've known no real fear of anything so far up here on the islands. That is why I could not understand why John was so fearful for me.

But later, when I began to reconstruct the horrible day, I could understand. Three times I thought I saw a slight motion out of the corner of my eye. Something, or someone, kept disappearing behind a rock like a wraith. None of the natives would act that way. Then I suddenly remembered that Mr. Morgan had brought up a few stranger Aleuts from Attu whom the natives did not like. I dismissed the thought of them because they were all employed. I'm not sure whether I'd really have been frightened if I had met a strange Aleut face to face in that high rugged place. I breathed more freely when I came onto the open dunes. No further thought of danger crossed my mind.

How still the air was on the high dunes, away from the din and stench of the killing grounds. Then as I approached, I could hear the noise of the bachelor parade ground below me, and even that seemed wholesome. The wheeling, screaming birds had a hypnotic effect. They calmed me. I followed the recent driving trail over the last tumbled rocks, down to a broad plateau above a seacoast shelf. This plateau extends about a half mile inland from the edge of a sheer cliff, which drops directly down several hundred feet into the sea. This bachelor parade ground teemed with hundreds and hundreds of holluschickie that had escaped the killings for another year. The herd seemed scarcely decimated, and the bachelors appeared particularly happy on their pink sand and highly polished basalt playing field.

I passed between Polavina Sopka, a high conical peak, and a lovely little lake with a margin of jagged rocks on one side and great grass-covered dunes on the other. Vivid flowers dotted the grass like confetti — giant nasturtiums and great patches of deep blue gentians, early brilliant phlox such as I've never seen before, pulse with its delicate odor (when the wind was not from the rookery), and other flowers I must learn.

I sat on a ledge at the very edge of the cliff, at this point a highly polished red rock that goes straight down to steely blue-black ledges far below, where bull seals exercise full rein over their harems. Below them the surf boomed tremendously against the rock, polishing it to even greater smoothness. At first I could not figure out how the seals could get back and forth to the ledges, or how the holluschickie could get way up on the high parade grounds. Every other rookery I had seen had a slow and gradual rise for approach; this one had a forbidding perpendicular wall.

Then I saw them coming up the face of the wall using little ledge-like outjuttings for stairs. These small steps seemed to present no problem to the seals in spite of their clumsy gait, which is an inching movement. They seemed to have established some order of precedence for those going up or down. Here and there, where a few had forgotten the rules, they just climbed over each other or turned and went in the same direction. I saw not one tumble off those narrow ledges.

The cliff gentles off far to the south and as soon as I had made a rough sketch, I clambered in that direction to get nearer to the baby seals, which I wanted to sketch accurately and from close up. I came to a place where many newborn pups nursed contentedly. I decided that they are about the most adorable baby animals anyone could wish to watch.

I sat on a rock close to and slightly above a small harem, a good vantage point for working. Fortunately the wind came from behind me and blew the stench out to sea. I sat for a long time just watching, fascinated by the ways of the pups with their soulful human eyes and their bleatings like little sheep when their mothers pulled away from nursing them and left them. After a while I began to sketch.

Naturally all around me, I could hear the barking and hissing, the spitting and coughing of the bulls, some challenging others for invading the boundaries of their harems or fighting over their wayward wives. But the problems of the adult seals were remote from the objects of my concern — the little pups. I could not help noticing how beautiful the young matkas looked, sleek and docile except for a slight whimper now and then when one gave birth to a kotickie or was bumped into by a clumsy bull ten times her size. The screaming birds and the *baroom* [the sound of the surf] of the sea added to the din. But in spite of the commotion, I managed a few fair sketches of several pups.

"Seal mating is no sight a lady should have to witness," is what one of the men at mess probably wanted to say to me the night before. Instead he had again warned me, "Don't go near the rookeries during the mating season, Mrs. Beaman. The bulls are somethin' fierce then and mought do ye some harm. They have no use for anyone who interferes. They'll charge ye and tear yer ta bits."

"Aye," said another. But I caught the glance between them and knew they were trying to spare me the sight of actual mating.

Well, this day so much of it had been going on around me that I had little curiosity about it. I wanted to do my sketches of the little kotickie. But suddenly the bull right below me challenged the bull of the next harem over a sleek little matka that was escaping his domain for the other's. I had to stop and watch; the drama was such a human one and so close that I felt personally involved and ready to root for the bull of the little cow's choice. The hissing and spitting and swaying of the two battling monsters became so vicious that I stepped to higher ground. I should have continued sketching the babies, but the fight was too fascinating not to watch to the bitter end. Those two bulls were out to kill each other, and they set about using their powerful shoulders and teeth in such a way that neither could come out of it whole, no matter who won.

But in the middle of the row, my attention was diverted to a third bull who had taken advantage of the fight to carry off the little seal the other two were fighting over. I hadn't realized that I was sitting on the edge of this new seacatch's harem until he brought the trim little matka to my feet and plopped her down on the very ledge I had so hastily vacated. There he gave her a most ungentle trouncing, thumping and scolding her, while I retreated to still higher ground, now more curious than ever about what the other two would do when they discovered their prize gone. But the scene so close to my feet was even more intriguing.

The matka's new lord and master, after several more thudding blows that sent her yelping against the rocks, began to caress her by rubbing his long neck along her sleek body. Immediately she wriggled and snuggled up to him, as if to acknowledge his overlordship. They nosed each other all over, especially about the face, and she did not struggle to get away or to go back to the two suitors still warring over her. Instead she slithered up and down beside him. They fondled each other more and more excitedly. The expressions in their eyes were all too human expressions of passion and desire. I could not help myself. I had to watch, with not even a scientist's impersonal interest or an artist's justification, but with frank curiosity and a sense of personal involvement.

Suddenly the little matka flattened out on the pinkish sand and let the great bull cover her. Their mating lasted a long time, with frequent convulsive movements that set their whole bodies to quivering. I grew limp with my own intense absorption in the scene, my sketchbook and crayon forgotten in my hands. Slowly I began to realize the enormity of what I had stopped to watch and was ashamed of myself for succumbing to such an unladylike experience, so contrary to my careful upbringing and even my own convictions. I wanted to run from my shame. I stood up, bent on going back to the dunes and away from this mass of mating, fighting seals.

I turned to face the Senior Agent standing silent, just behind me!

"Interesting, isn't it, Elizabeth?" he asked with a thin smile on his lips and mockery in his eyes. I wanted to faint into nothingness, to disappear beneath the sand and the tufa, to be anywhere but there on that spot. A blush of embarrassment and confusion spread from the roots of my hair down to my toes. I tossed my head and ran past him up the rise toward the parade ground and the little lake. But the earth was so uneven and my eyes so blinded by tears of anger and shame that I stumbled often and could not run from him with the dignity I wished to show. I lost my sketch pad and crayons clambering over a particularly difficult rock in my path. He, following more easily, picked them up and handed them to me.

"Thank you," I said coldly and turned away from him toward home, wondering if he would follow me all the five miles back just to mock me. But a sudden storm, such as come quickly and go quickly, struck violently, making of the seals' driving trail a river of mud through which I floundered. Lightning on these islands is always terrifying. The Pribilofs are noted for the most harrowing electrical storms in the world, and this morning's was the worst since I've been up here, more so because I was out in it and unprepared for it. The sheet lightning spread steely blue over us with a hiss that ended in deep thunderous rolls out over the Bering. The direct lightning hit in great, vivid darts against rocks and crevices as though intent on blasting the island into bits. Thunder cracked instantaneously with the darts. It has deafened many natives and company men in the past, and I was afraid for my own hearing with each deafening crack.

There was nowhere to take shelter on the dunes of the open plateau, nowhere until I reached Boga Slov, "Word of God," with its great boulders and ledges. But Boga Slov got its name because it attracted the lightning more than any other spot in the Arctic, and this morning was no exception. Lightning illuminated the peak, which looked like a finger of God pointing a warning to all those who would break the rules.

I kept straight on toward home, floundering in the awful mud, stumbling over the jagged basalt, drenched to the skin without my oilskin, and, most of all, angry with myself for now being vulnerable to the Senior Agent's scorn.

As I came past the mountain and onto the road that forks to the spring, I think I would have fallen but for the firm grasp he took on my arm to help me over the little flash flood between us and the final stretch of the road. He had been following me all the way! And in silence he now followed me the rest of the way. How can I ever hold up my head again or look the man in the eye?

But—he called me Elizabeth, my first name!

CAROLYN KREMERS

Carolyn Kremers writes creative nonfiction and poetry and teaches at the University of Alaska Fairbanks. Her writing has earned her a fellowship from the Alaska State Council on the Arts and a special citation from the PEN/Jerard Fund Award for emerging women writers of nonfiction. The essay that follows is included in her book manuscript *Place of the Pretend People*. Much of the book was inspired by her experiences living in the Yup'ik Eskimo village of Tununak on the coast of the Bering Sea.

We Are All Paddling a Kayak Through Open Tundra, Not a River

"Reindeer hairs," Linda had said when she came to my house to visit a few weeks before Christmas. It was my first year on Nelson Island. Linda had brought her daughters, Charlene and Nora, with her on the snowmachine. The three of them sat on the sofa in fur-lined parkas like a row of fluffed-up birds on a wire in winter, their faces flushed red with cold and heat.

Linda slipped a plastic bag from the front pocket of her bright green parka. Without saying anything, she handed it to me. I knew it must contain the dance fans she had been making. Gently, I drew them out.

"Reindeer hairs. Those are the ones we use," Linda said, laughing as I stroked the fans. "You know, the white hairs under the neck. Those are special hairs. From the reindeer's throat. They are not always easy to get."

I turned over one of the fans, looking at how it was made. Coarse white hairs, eight inches long and gray at the roots, sprouted from a thin strip of hide no wider than my little finger. The hide was stitched neatly to a circular mat the size of my palm, creating a halo of long white hairs that flared around the fan like a flat beard. The mat was tightly woven in a spiral pattern with quarter-inch coils of tundra grasses, some a shiny, natural straw color, others dyed dark red, green, or brown. Two coils at the top of the mat departed from the spiral in a graceful triangular arch, creating a hole for slipping the fan between the fingers or for hanging it.

Charlene and Nora, third- and fifth-graders, watched closely as I admired their mother's work. I had never seen them so quiet, at my house or in music class. I knew they were waiting for me to say they could sit in the mustard-colored chair and spin around in it, then choose an herbal tea from the colored boxes on the shelf in the kitchen. I smiled.

"These fans are beautiful, Linda," I said, standing up to get my check-book. "I like them very much. How much shall I pay you?"

"Oh, I don't know," she said, laughing again. "You should pay what-ever you think you should pay."

I always noticed when people in Tununak talked this way about money. Money was a relatively recent addition to their culture. Yup'ik Eski-mos had lived on or near the site of Tununak for two thousand years, but cash had not come to the village until 1930, when the Northern Commercial Company established Tununak's first store. Even then most people bartered, trading furs, carvings, and grass baskets for cloth, chocolate, and iron pots. I knew Linda did not want to obligate me by asking a particular price for the fans. For her, buying and selling were forms of sharing.

Linda reflected the values of many Yup'iks, before white missionar-ies, teachers, government officials, and twentieth-century technology came into their world. I had seen how people in Tununak cherished things like family, laughter, contentment, a close connection with the land and sea, the present and the past. At the same time, like people any-where, Tununak people valued cash. Cash could be turned into gasoline, pop, heating oil, Pampers, Bingo pull tabs, Rit dye, dental floss, mari-juana, videotapes, fishing nets, snuff. It could be turned into whatever the people wanted or needed, or didn't need, and sometimes cash was a good thing, and sometimes it wasn't.

For the first time in my life, I felt I had cash to share. I was no longer a struggling flutist but an English and music teacher earning thirty-two thousand dollars a year. Now, however, I was living among people who had always shared, even in times when they had nothing. What they had acquired freely, from the land and sea and from each other, they gave freely, in order to ensure its return.

"It is believed that the things we give will come back to us," I had heard an elder say, "in bigger amounts."

I thought of the needlefish story. A needlefish has sharp teeth and is about the size of an index finger. One of my high school students, John, had tape-recorded the words of an elder, Martha Flynn, as she told him stories in Yup'ik. John had chosen a few of the stories to translate into English for the school newspaper.

"Starving is very painful, suffering, and sad, which makes you feel real sick," Martha told the student. "That is, the stomach's shrinking is very painful. Even if a person is a great hunter, if a food is not available, the great hunter would starve. When animals and other living creatures were real hard to find, the two great hunters looked for other pieces that were left. When they found a small needlefish, they cut the needle-fish in half and shared the needlefish. That was to fill their stomach."

Among Yup'iks, sharing wasn't a function of plenty, it was a function of survival. It was essential in the Arctic, and besides, sharing made people feel good. Sharing was more visible in Tununak than any other place I had lived. People shared naturally, and they expected others to reciprocate. To save for the future, as I had been taught, was not to share.

"Share with your little sister," my mother had said many times when I was a child, so I had grown up to be someone who shared.

"You'd give someone the shirt off your back if they asked for it," she had said more recently in a long-distance phone call. "Be careful."

But I did not want to be careful, and I loved living among these people, who in good ways weren't careful. Whenever anyone brought something to my house to sell, if I wanted to buy it, in the spirit of sharing I always asked the same question next.

"How much do you usually sell these for?"

"Fifty dollars, usually," Linda said. "Here. In Anchorage I can get more. But fifty dollars here."

Ten dollars an hour was a standard rate in Tununak for janitors, teacher's aides, and other people with indoor jobs. I tried to think how long it takes to grow a reindeer herd, harvest tundra-grass, learn to weave, invent songs and dances to be handed down, generation to generation.

I had seen that Linda's fans were some of the most beautiful in the village. She had grown up in Mekoryuk on nearby Nunivak Island, where the reindeer hair came from. She had fallen in love with a man from Tununak, and when she had married and moved to Nelson Island she had brought her talent for making fans with her.

Reindeer hairs were not easy to get in Tununak. All the reindeer on Nelson Island had died off in the 1960s when severe winters weakened the herd, making them easy prey for wolves. After decimating the reindeer, all the wolves had died off, too. Now the managers of the Tununak village corporation bought frozen reindeer carcasses from their Nunivak neighbors. They cut the carcasses into twenty-pound pieces with power saws, and the meat was sold for three dollars a pound at the Tununak Native Store. Sometimes men in the reindeer corrals on Nunivak Island saved the throat skin during butchering, and sometimes they did not. It depended on how they felt that day, how bad the weather was, how much the reindeer spooked. Sometimes Tununak women could not get reindeer hair for their fans, and they used wolf or dog hair, or synthetic fur, instead.

Dance fans. The Yup'ik word is *taruyamaarun*, "like a person's face." I knew I would not always live in this rich place, that one day I might need some of its spirits on my wall. I wrote a check to Linda for fifty dollars, the price she had implied. Then Nora picked Orange Zinger tea and took turns with her sister, spinning in the chair.

I drove out Farmers Loop Road to the forest above Fairbanks and pulled into the driveway outside my landlord's garage. Breathing a murmur of thanks that my old Subaru had started and chugged safely home, I got out and plugged in the timer that would turn on the engine-block heater early the next morning. Thirty-seven degrees below zero and falling, the radio announcer had said. A round, yellow moon burned above the blanket of ice fog that had settled downtown.

I stood a few minutes, watching. Such clarity. The moon glowed like a face filled with flames. Under the lit sky, I unlocked the door to my apartment. Then the phone rang.

"You sure are hard to get ahold of," a voice said. It was my friend Troy. "It's after eleven o'clock. I called several times, but you weren't home."

I smiled. Sometimes people who live alone are hard to reach.

"Two elders are coming to my Native dance class at the university tomorrow," Troy continued. "From Tununak. Do you want to come and see them, come and dance?"

My heart quickened. I had been gone from the village almost a year and missed it more than any place I knew. Troy was a geologist, but he had decided he would rather be a high school teacher in the bush, and he was taking courses at the university to get certified. He and his wife knew how much I loved the village.

"Who's coming?" I asked him. "Do you know?"

"Yeah, I have the name here somewhere. I wrote it down for you." He sounded out a Yup'ik last name. "Does that seem right? That's all I know."

It took a few minutes, but I did not panic, and the first names came to me, suddenly, unconsciously. James and Christine, Mary's parents. It had to be them. They had raised ten children in Tununak and were known throughout the Yukon—Kuskokwim Delta for their music and dancing.

"I'll be there," I said. "And, Troy, . . . thanks."

I hung up the phone and took my dance fans off the wall. Then, as if I were no longer in Fairbanks but back in the village, Linda's laughter filled the room.

Listening, I put the graceful fans in a plastic grocery bag, the way the women in Tununak always do. I didn't want to forget them in the morning. Then, still holding the bag, I sat on the sofa and closed my eyes. Perhaps people in Tununak were dancing at that very moment. They could be, for it was February, the heart of winter, the dancing season. Perhaps they were practicing in the community hall.

I listened until I could hear James singing in his powerful nasal voice and beating the drum steadily with a stick. Between dances he drank Pepsi and spit chew into a giant Bumblebee tuna can. John-Hoover-on-his-knees, the elder who always laughed and called "Halloo!" when he saw me taking a walk, sat on his heels on a mat in front of the drummers. Crippled by polio in childhood, he led the men's dance with rhythmic movements of his broad chest and muscled arms. Christine stood with the women, swaying gently to the music, her qaspeq (an Eskimo blouse-dress) the color of robin's eggs. She smiled and teased, sometimes closing her eyes. She had been the first woman in Tununak to invite me to dance.

One January evening during my first winter in the village, John, the student who translated the needlefish story, had telephoned. It was almost eight o'clock.

"Maybe they're having Yup'ik dancing tonight," he said. "I saw the elders going over."

Since arriving in Tununak in October, I had wanted to see some dancing. This was the first I had heard of any. Excited, I bundled into warm clothes and set off down the hill for the community hall, enjoying the glitter of the Milky Way and the crunch of my boots on the snow. No wind for a change. The village generator buzzed in its trailer like a trapped fly, and lights on the two school buildings and a few lampposts revealed parts of the way. I kept a small flashlight in my parka pocket but used it less outdoors than indoors, when the generator broke down, which it often did.

In good weather, nights in Tununak vibrated, alive. Voices in the darkness said "Hi, Carolyn" as people passed, going home or out to visit, or to practice basketball at the gym, take a shower at the laundromat, wash clothes, haul water, take a steam bath, rent a video, or buy something at Charlie's Store. Children and adults had a keen ability to recognize a person in the dark by small signs: a profile, a gesture, the sound of a voice. They delighted in my inability to recognize who they were until after they had passed. I had never lived in such a small community — only 330 people — where everyone knew everyone else, sometimes from birth to death, nor had I ever needed to develop the sensory awareness that was crucial for survival in wind, cold, and unbroken space.

Children in Tununak played late into the night, chasing, hiding, sledding, building snow forts. Sometimes ice covered the hard-packed snow that people and snowmachines travelled, and under a bright moon, kids could skate all the way from the high school, down the hill, across the bend in the frozen river, up and down drifts between houses, past the post office and the church, and out to the bridge and the airstrip. Teenaged couples walked the frozen beach of the Bering Sea, holding mittened hands. Other youths walked around "downtown," listening to pop music on a boom box or Walkman, laughing and talking.

"Hi, Carolyn. Hi, Carolyn."

Just past Sally's corrugated-tin-covered house opposite the church, snatches of drums beating and men singing escaped into the night. A scattering of snowmachines waited ghostlike on the drifts, lit by the glare of a single bare bulb. I slipped through the outer door of the plywood building and into the entryway.

The community hall felt mystical to me, and I knew that it was. It is a modern version, above ground, of the traditional qasgiq, or Yup'ik men's house. In earlier times, men of the village ate and often slept in the qasgiq. They spent whole days and evenings there, making tools for hunting and fishing and weapons for war. They took sweatbaths in the qasgiq, played games, smoked pipes, told stories, and performed rites and rituals there.

Sometimes, for special ceremonies and celebrations, all the people of the village gathered in the men's house. They came to share a circle of songs, stories, dances, and masks. They danced to communicate with the spirits that inhabited their world and to relieve the dull ache of winter, ease tensions, nurture community, welcome visitors. Often, they danced for sheer joy.

The qasgiq where they gathered was built half-underground, like a sod-covered family dwelling but larger. Log walls kept back the dirt and surrounded a square floor covered with planks. Trees did not grow in Tununak, yet wood was plentiful. Logs from Alaska's interior forests drifted down the Yukon and Kuskokwim rivers, into the Bering Sea, and up onto Tununak's beach.

In the old days, the walls of the traditional qasgiq rose in a gentle dome to a single window at the top, which was covered with a piece of walrus gut that could be used as a skylight or removed to let in fresh air. Sleeping platforms and benches lined the side and back walls, and a deep fire pit gaped in the center of the plank floor.

Outside, the qasgiq was covered with a thick layer of tundra sod. In summer this spongy mound turned green with sedges and grasses. In winter the sod accumulated snow and ice, creating layers of insulation. With a fire crackling inside, the qasgiq could get so warm that men and women dancers stripped to the waist, a common practice indoors. Sometimes men dancers wore no clothes at all. Faces, bodies, and masks came alive, lit by the flickering fire and the glow of seal-oil lamps.

In Tununak, the last traditional qasgiq was abandoned in the late 1970s, when its functions were replaced by single-family government housing, a pre-fabricated "city hall," and the frame and plywood community hall. Now the community hall was used for village potlatches, Alaska Department of Fish and Game meetings, city council meetings, elders' council meetings, Calista Corporation shareholder meetings, elections, bingo, rock dancing, and Yup'ik dancing.

Sometimes, out for a walk, I would hear loud squeals escaping through the walls of the hall as the young men in one of Tununak's two rock bands turned up their synthesizer and electric guitars full blast and jammed. And sometimes, on particularly desolate winter Sundays, I would step inside the hall for a few minutes just to see the elders and parents sprawled on the broad plywood floor, every inch of it covered with bodies, fur parkas, bingo boards and cardboard pull tabs, the entire qasgiq listening closely for lucky numbers.

Now I stood by the inner door in the drafty entryway to Tununak's modern qasgiq, thinking like a classical musician. Don't enter during a performance. Wait for the applause.

When the drumming and singing stopped, though, there was no applause. Instead, I heard shouting and laughter. I opened the door anyway, and walked in. Feeling more than ever like a giant in my noisy Gore-Tex wind pants and heavy felt-lined pac boots, I slid into an empty folding chair.

The air was hot. I unzipped my parka and fleece jacket and took them off, thinking I must look suspiciously clean, like a model in an L. L. Bean catalogue. I had lived in Tununak less than four months and spent much of my time working in the school, so I was not accustomed to being the only kass'aq among twenty Yup'ik adults.

Kass'aq, the Yup'ik term for white people, comes from the Russian word Cossack, which Yup'iks often heard used by early Russian explorers and fur traders. I did not mind being called a kass'aq, for I knew it had good-natured connotations as well as negative ones. But among elders I felt especially conscious of my kass'aq-ness.

The rustle of my clothes seemed deafening as I shed layers and settled at last in the chair. I thought of a popular Yup'ik saying and its implications for other kinds of noisiness: "Don't let your rustlings be heard." Yup'ik people seemed to me fundamentally still sometimes, and I liked that. I remembered the nickname they had given Edward Nelson, the naturalist who had visited Tununak in 1878. Big Mouth.

I smiled.

Several middle-aged women around me smiled back, their shorter legs and smaller feet dwarfed and delicate next to mine.

Six suspendered men, all elders, sat in a row of folding chairs opposite us. They sipped cans of Coke and Sprite, resting, their faces weathered and wrinkled with smiles. Several wore baseball-style caps—black, green, navy—emblazoned with captions like ALASKA, ANCHORAGE, and TRC. A few of the men conversed in Yup'ik, and one spit snuff into a red coffee can by his foot. The men wore layers of shirts—flannel and wool—and heavy work pants. Their feet were bundled in plain sealskin mukluks, gum rubber boots, or felt-lined pac boots smaller than mine. Three elders hacked with deep coughs, reminding me that tuberculosis is endemic in Alaska Native villages, and that teachers are required by law to be tested every year for infection.

What grabbed my attention most, though, were the drums. They looked like giant tambourines.

Each man held a drum and a slender stick in his lap or between his knees. I knew that Yup'ik drums used to be made of stretched walrus stomach, but walrus gut was hard to maintain and had been replaced by synthetics. Each of these drums was made of a piece of dark-green ripstop nylon stretched over a wooden hoop about two feet across. I saw that the nylon was held in place by a cord wound around the outside of the hoop in a sunken groove, and I guessed that the drumhead could be tightened by pulling on the corners of the material. The nylon-covered hoop was screwed to a long wooden handle, giving the impression of a huge, dripping, Sherlock-Holmes-style magnifying glass. I had seen pictures of how the drummer held the handle in one hand and, with the other hand, tapped the drumhead or the rim with a stick.

In the anthropology book about Nelson Island that my friend Mark had loaned me, I read that frame-drums are relatively lightweight and easy to transport. In earlier times their handles were carved in animal shapes from walrus ivory or whalebone, or from caribou, moose, or reindeer antler. According to the book, the round shape of the frame-drum reflects the circularity of the sun and moon, the seasons, and life itself. Similar drums have been used by musicians and shaman healers all over the world—in Siberia, Guatemala, Northern Ireland, Mozambique. Yet, though I was a music teacher, I had never heard a frame-drum played except in films. I did not know that when all the drummers beat together, something ancient and booming would fill the room, pushing like a boulder through the walls, into the night, halfway across the village, deep into my soul.

I glanced around the rest of the community hall, listening. This modern qasgiq was a prefabricated plywood shell, but it could never be empty, even when no one was in it. Like the night, it vibrated.

Instead of a fire pit, a fat furnace hurled hot air from one corner of the rectangular room. The gray metal box connected with the outside world by a patched flue that snaked several feet to the ceiling. Nearby stood a silent yellow-and-white popcorn machine. At the room's other end, a dilapidated set of blue-sparkle drums waited, temporarily abandoned.

The bare walls of the hall had been decorated with tundra-grass mats and scenes painted on stretched sealskin. Villagers had also painted pictures directly on the blue plywood: jigging for tomcod, hunting seals · with kayaks and harpoons, dog sledding, berry picking, life in the sod-house village. The emphasis on traditional activities was not accidental. People in Tununak knew that the knowledge and customs that had sustained their culture for two thousand years were in danger of being forgotten and lost.

Yurarluni, traditional Yup'ik dancing, was an example. Moravian, Presbyterian, and other Protestant missionaries considered Yup'ik dancing a dangerous pagan practice. They said it was a way to avoid work, that it encouraged gluttony at accompanying feasts, and that shamans used it for extortion. By the early 1900s these missionaries had banned Yup'ik dancing in all the Yukon—Kuskokwim villages they served. Only villages visited by Russian Orthodox and Jesuit priests were spared.

Friends of mine who taught in villages where Yup'ik dancing was forbidden said I was lucky to have been assigned to Tununak. Now I began to realize that the traditions and power of Yup'ik music lay deep in Tununak people's souls. Though I could not see it, Yup'ik dancing glowed like a banked fire inside the children and teenagers I taught every day in school. This music was part of Tununak people's collective unconscious, I thought, the way Bach was part of mine.

Since arriving in the village, I had tried to discover more about this musical heritage unmentioned in the school district curriculum, but almost nothing was written down or available on recordings or film. Among the hundreds of unused textbooks and piles of teaching materials stacked in school closets and storage rooms, the only Yup'ik songs I was able to find were traditional children's tunes like "Hickory-Dickory

Dock" or "Mary Had a Little Lamb" set to Yup'ik words in the 1970s by school district people in Bethel.

One day, while looking at textbooks in another teacher's room, I came across a dusty book of Yup'ik story and game songs. These had been collected on Nelson Island in 1972 and compiled by an ethnomusicologist at the university in Fairbanks. The songs had musical notation. I was elated. I chose two of them to teach my elementary music classes and carefully copied the Yup'ik words in big colored letters on butcher paper.

When I introduced the first song to the fourth-, fifth-, and sixth-graders, though, only a few could read Yup'ik well enough to make out the words even though most of them spoke the language fluently. None recognized the tune when I played it on the piano. How were the dance songs, which were more complicated than these game songs, being passed on? Or were they?

"People are respectful of the old songs because the songs have power," said an elder from another village in a film I would see later. "People say some songs are good because their meanings are good."

I liked this idea, that something could be good—simply, inherently good—because its meaning was good.

"Many of these old-time songs has been passed on to us before we were even born," the elder continued. "And that song there, it keeps moving. Pretty soon there's songs from way back. But you would never know who made that song. The guy is way underneath the ground, he's past gone. And still his song is going."

This was like a Bach flute sonata, it seemed to me: something special and powerful that had been handed down carefully and that continued to be passed on. These Yup'ik songs and dances were not 250 years old like Bach's music, though. They were much older, some of them, and they were not written down. They were passed on orally, as if Bach had taught a flutist his A Minor partita, for instance, and then that flutist had taught another flutist, and that flutist had taught another flutist, and that flutist had taught another flutist until my teachers had taught me—all by ear and by imitation, not by written notes. No wonder my students in Tununak learned so quickly by watching and listening.

I knew from reading Mark's book that Yup'ik dances could be about anything, traditional activities or modern-day experiences. A dance might celebrate winning at bingo, escaping a ghost, catching a seal, building a kayak. It might make the audience laugh as the dancers played basketball, cleaned fish, strummed a guitar, dumped the honey bucket. Or it might make the audience sad as the dancers traveled to Bethel by plane, got drunk, felt lonely. A dance could make fun of kass'aq ways or even, in the old days, ridicule a person who had done something unacceptable, thereby nudging him or her to change.

Cauyarvik. November. Time of drumming. On Nelson Island the winter season is still referred to as *cauyaq,* "drum." I had been hired to teach music, and that was what I had been doing, but there was much I needed to learn. At last, on this winter night, a gift would come to me.

Lightly tapping a drum, one of the men began singing in a soft nasal drone, apparently signaling with this incantation the end of the rest period and the start of another song. I watched as the mothers of several of my junior high and high school students walked out on the floor and formed a line facing the drummers.

There was Sally, who had sold me my first tundra-grass mat and who would surprise me on St. Patrick's Day with a green qaspeq embroidered with shamrocks; Wendy, whose four teenaged daughters were learning to play the clarinet, piano, xylophone, and saxophone; Ruth, who ran the village clinic and who had been taught by Father Deschout to play the church's organ by ear; Naomi, who would make me a large, lidded grass basket covered with colored butterflies, and whose grown son would later freeze in a blizzard, lost on his snowmachine a few miles beyond town; Athena, the wife of Nicolas whose family I had watched after school, butchering a musk ox; and Christine.

John, the student who had telephoned me, got up from a folding chair and walked to the space between the women and the drummers. He and two other men, both elders, knelt on blue vinyl exercise mats. From the mats they picked up circular wooden fans. White ptarmigan feathers stuck out around the rims. At the end of the solo incantation, the other five drummers joined in with gentle singing and tapping, and the dancing began.

Like most dances I would see on Nelson Island that winter and the next, this one began quietly. The women kept their heads down, looking modestly at the floor by their feet. They swayed gently with the drums and song, moving up and down and side to side. Their feet stayed flat on the floor, knees bending in time with the music, while their arms and heads floated like breezes. Their bodies mirrored the motions of the men kneeling before them, but the effect of their fans was different. The women's soft tundra-grass and reindeer-hair fans brushed the air gently, while the men's stiff wood and feather fans sliced like small knives. I could feel the fans' connections with hands, faces, spirits—the women's fans reflective of female activities such as weaving and skin sewing; the men's, of male activities such as woodworking and bird hunting. Covered by fans, each person's hands were protected, perhaps, from too-close contact with the spirit world.

In Mark's book I had seen pictures of masks worn by men during Yup'ik dancing. Until the 1970s, masks were made on Nelson Island for particular performances and then thrown away after. Carved of driftwood, ivory, or bone and decorated with natural dyes, shells, fur, and feathers, some masks represented the animals or spirits seen by the village shaman during his or her spiritual hunting trips. Other masks were half animal and half man and were thought to bring good luck to the hunter, who became half animal himself when he wore one. Women sometimes wore finger masks, often carved to resemble the men's large masks. Sometimes these miniature masks contained shells, and the shells rattled like masks talking.

The Jesuits tried to understand many aspects of Yup'ik dancing, but they could not accept masks. To them, dance masks represented something pagan and evil. The people of Tununak were devout Catholics. They loved and respected the church and the priests and sisters who served it. By the 1970s, the wearing of dance masks on Nelson Island had disappeared.

I watched the women and men before me, moving with dignity to the gentle beat of the drums. Everyone shared the same dance language. They brushed and sliced the air with their fans, first on the left, then on the right, as if paddling a kayak. Right arms swung forward, then left arms, beckoning someone or something to come. Hands circled to rest on hips and all heads turned to the right, then to the left. Everyone shaded their eyes with the fans in their right hands, looking, looking.

Again on the left. Finally, all arms stretched to the center—with only drums playing, no singing—and all the fans brushed something away four times.

At the end of this sung verse and instrumental chorus, the sequence began again and the motions of paddling, beckoning, looking, and brushing away were repeated at the same slow tempo. This time James said things quietly in Yup'ik during gaps in the singing, making a few women smile.

The dancers stopped at the end of the repeated verse and chorus, glanced around, and smiled, but James did not let them rest long. After perhaps thirty seconds, he started drumming and singing, a little faster and louder this time, and the dance began again. James teased the dancers less quietly, and by the third round he was almost shouting. Other drummers joined in, and people giggled.

I looked around. Throughout the dance, people had been coming into the hall and going out. Teenagers looked in to see who was there. Children ran in to get warm, their faces red from the night. Young women in their twenties, some with babies bundled in their parka hoods, sat with relatives, and young men perched on the counter next to the furnace. One of the boys poured cooking oil into the yellow-and-white popcorn machine and kernels rattled down the chute. Soon a buttery smell drifted among the other odors of warm bodies, damp fur, wet wool, and fish.

I looked from the audience back to the performers, wondering why no other white teachers had come. I noticed Mary sitting several rows away, laughing with friends, enjoying her parents' performance. She held a pair of dance fans in one hand. Perhaps I would get to see her dance.

I had read that Yup'ik dances give everyone a chance to tease— dancers, drummers, audience. Now I saw how. By the fourth verse, the singers and the people around me were egging the dancers on, laughing and joking, even yelling.

"Amik patuu!" one of the drummers called to a bevy of small boys who had flung the door open and were piled against it, watching, while a wall of cold air rolled in. Close the door!

The door slammed and the drums beat in unison, louder and louder —thum, thum, thum. The men's nasal singing and chanting bounced like balls off the blue plywood walls and steamy windows, hurling us all into a power as ancient as the sea beyond the door. Drummers pushed dancers to move—faster, faster—paddling, beckoning, looking, brushing something away.

"Ampi!" James called. Faster!

Some of the little boys, sitting and standing among the chairs now and munching pilot crackers, shouted, "Kiiki! Kiiki!" Hurry! Hurry!

Sweat ran down the dancers' faces as they laughed and concentrated on their moves: to the right, to the left, arms up, arms back, faster, faster. Then, at the end of the fifth verse, like a foot race—suddenly, breathlessly—everything stopped.

Sinking into the chair beside me, an elder in a sky-blue qaspeq panted for air and dropped her fans into my lap. Christine.

Mary's mother. What can I say?

I knew Mary had been disappointed after Christmas, when the principal had assigned her to the junior high and me to the high school English classes. Mary was not certified to teach English, but she had been doing it for two years and was a good bilingual teacher. She had never told me she was unhappy about having to give up her high school students, but she had not been particularly friendly, either. Sometimes I felt uncomfortable around her, but I had not known what to do about it.

One day, after I had been in the village for about a month, Christine had come to the school to work with some students, and Mary had introduced us. After that I recognized Christine in the post office and the church and I smiled, but we never struck up a conversation. Now, without hesitating, Christine smiled and nodded at the fans she had just offered.

"Do you want to try?" she asked.

Naomi and Ruth grinned and nodded, encouraging me. I stammered, then grinned, too. I picked up the fans by their small, triangular handles. The white hairs brushed the air like butterflies.

"Well, . . . sure," I said. "Thank you."

I wanted to say more, have a conversation, but one of the men began singing softly and lightly tapping his drum. Several young women and a few of my high school students stood to form two lines, and I joined them in the second row. I could see Mary in front, down on one end.

None of the men drumming looked at me. Were they being polite? The dance began.

I watched the women in front, especially Mary, and tried to follow their arms and heads without thinking too hard. I knew not-thinking was a key to any kind of dancing, and anyway, I did not want to look like a clumsy kass'aq. I had chosen the back row on purpose, so I would not feel so conspicuous, but I knew people would be watching me, just as I watched them.

I was glad the dance began calmly, so I could feel for a center. Years of flute playing guided me. Soon I felt my arms floating, slowly, gently, my fingers laced inside Christine's fans, the soft reindeer hairs caressing the air. I followed Mary's arms, making waves like water, on the left, the right, the left.

I was more accustomed to even-numbered dance rhythms and repetitions than odd ones, and I faltered sometimes when motions were repeated three or five times. But there was no stopping, and always the chance to get a motion right on the next verse.

With each repetition the music got faster, and so did the dancers, and so did I. The audience and drummers teased, louder and louder, but I hardly heard them. We were swept up together, whirled out of winter and the community hall, and I was lost within the spell. Inside my throat, my heart thrilled. And like so many other times in Tununak, it seemed I had scarcely begun when the dance ended.

"You dance very good for your first time," Christine said afterward, accepting her fans and sharing a smile that I knew was sincere. " 'Specially for a person not from here. I am surprised. You should learn."

I was lucky. That winter and the next, two dance festivals were celebrated on Nelson Island. One was hosted by the people of Tununak, and one by the people of Toksook Bay. Yup'ik families came from all over the island and its neighboring villages, mostly by snowmachine, a few very old elders by small plane. Several hundred people from Toksook, Nightmute, Chefornak, Newtok, and Stebbins stayed with relatives in Tununak for a week. Children came late to school or not at all, and homework and practicing were forgotten. I was glad.

Women danced in polyester slacks or jeans half-hidden by qaspeqs

—blouse-dresses of calico in all colors: pink, lavender, orange, blue, green, tan—trimmed with rickrack, bias tape, ribbons, and beads. All kinds of mukluks brushed the floor—spotted sealskin, black wolverine, brown and white calfskin, tan wolf, white rabbit—decorated with fur tassels, braided yarn ties, beaded flowers, appliquéd designs of birds and animals, hunters and kayaks. Women wore tall beaded headdresses of tan and white wolf fur, dangling white ivory and brown mastodon earrings, and intricate beaded necklaces called "fancy beads." They waved grass dance fans dyed a hundred colors.

Elders danced as if their bodies were young and flexible again, and small children, dressed in miniature headdresses and red-topped mukluks, danced with them, intent on imitating each motion. The crowd and I pressed together on the floor, surrounded by unzipped parkas. Elders hugged grandchildren, unmarried young people craned to see who was there, parents gave children money for pop and cupcakes, teenagers drifted in and out, flirting and teasing. A few of the teachers came, and the priest. People beamed, especially at the priest, and insisted he sit in a folding chair. Jokes and laughter rang into the inky night as each village tried to out-dance the other, whirling past midnight into the hours of early morning. And all of us laughed and laughed.

"You should learn," Christine had said. I learned a little, but there were so many things I wanted to learn in Tununak. How to speak Yup'ik so that I could talk with the elders more, understand their stories and songs. I wanted to learn how to make a pair of children's mukluks, cook a ptarmigan, jig for tomcod, hunt for mouse food (the roots and seeds that Arctic voles hide away for winter). I wanted to fish for herring and halibut with Mark and his father in the new boat. I wanted to visit more, talk less, listen better, watch. Slow down, share without thinking, laugh lots. Think less about the future. Dance.

I learned some of those things. But time travels quickly without us, through thick grass.

It was a little before five o'clock when I walked into the Great Hall at the university in Fairbanks and found Troy and the Native dance class gathered in a corner. I was pleased to see several Yup'ik students I knew from classes I had taught at the university: Sara from Tununak, Anita from Toksook, Lynn from Kasigluk, Alice from Chefornak. I tossed my jacket and mittens in the pile on the floor and took Linda's dance fans out of the plastic bag.

Something was vibrating, hungry to be shared. I had never thought of the Great Hall as a qasgiq until then.

The glass doors swished open and James and Christine walked across the carpet, shrugging off their parkas: James's from a catalogue, Christine's hand-sewn, calico-covered, thick, and sprouting fur. Shyly, I walked over to shake hands, not knowing how well they would remember me but knowing that everyone in Tununak remembers everyone. Then Christine hugged me, her face splitting into that big smile, eyes closing behind the thick black-framed glasses, her thin, graying hair matted on her head where the silver- and white-furred hood had been. I heard her reminding James, in the beautiful language that I will always be able to listen to for hours, that it was me, the *elitnaurista*, the woman who used to teach with Mary. James smiled, too, and shook my hand.

Then once again Christine surprised me, making me feel as pleased as a child. "It's like home," she said in English. "I'm so glad you came. It's just like being at home."

James sat in a chair, Christine stood in front of him, and the rest of us—six kass'aqs and twenty-five Natives—formed lines behind her. James began singing and she began dancing, and soon I was lost again, floating with Linda's and my fans and the fans of all the others, following the pictures in Christine's body and the ancient beat of James's drum. Swaying in place on the red and green carpet in a corner of the spacious hall, we became kayak paddles, birds, hunters, a river—all of us gathered in the arms of a very large and very old family.

When the dance ended and the teacher translated the song, I remembered what I already knew. My heart beat fast, inside my throat, the way it had at that first dance in the community hall and so many other times on Nelson Island. The words are right, and the dance:

We are all paddling a kayak through open tundra,
not a river.
The grass is high.
And there is just enough water
to make it through.

Bibliography

I would like to acknowledge the contributions of the following resources to my understanding of Yup'ik Eskimo music and dance.

Fienup-Riordan, Ann. *The Nelson Island Eskimo: Social Structure and Ritual Distribution.* Anchorage: Alaska Pacific University Press, 1983.

Fitzhugh, William W., and Susan A. Kaplan. *Inua: Spirit World of the Bering Sea Eskimo.* Washington, D.C.: Smithsonian Institution Press, 1982.

Johnston, Thomas F. "Yup'ik Eskimo Dance in Cultural Perspective." Unpublished essay. University of Alaska Fairbanks, 1988.

————. *Yup'ik Eskimo Songs.* Anchorage: National Bilingual Materials Development Center, 1982.

Morrow, Phyllis. "Symbolic Actions, Indirect Expressions: Interpretations of Yup'ik Eskimo Society." Ms. prepared for Seventh Inuit Studies Conference, Fairbanks, Alaska, August 1990.

Nelson, Edward. *The Eskimo About Bering Strait.* 1899. Reprint. Washington, D.C.: Smithsonian Institution Press, 1983.

Ray, Dorothy Jean. *Eskimo Masks: Art and Ceremony.* Seattle: University of Washington Press, 1976.

Uksuum Cauyai: The Drums of Winter. Videocassette. Presented by the Alaska Native Heritage Film Project and the Emmonak Dancers. Written, produced, and directed by Sarah Elder and Leonard Kammerling. 1988. 90 minutes.

Wallen, Lynn Ager. "The Face of Dance: Yup'ik Masks from the Sullivan Collection." Ms. prepared for the Glenbow Museum Ethnology Department, 1990.

PAUL TIULANA

Paul Tiulana was born in 1921 on King Island and spent his early years learning to fish and hunt in the traditions of his forefathers. Completing six years of formal schooling, Mr. Tiulana was drafted into the U.S. Army in World War II and was stationed in Nome. A noted storyteller, skilled craftsman, ivory carver, and umiak builder, he is an expert on traditional Eskimo culture and presently lives in Anchorage. In 1983 he was honored as the Man of the Year by the Alaska Federation of Natives. In 1984, he received honors from the National Endowment for the Arts and was presented with the National Heritage Fellowship Award for his contributions to the preservation of our nation's cultural diversity and the promotion of artistic traditions. *A Place for Winter* was written in conjunction with Vivian Senungetuk.

FROM *A Place for Winter*

People on King Island did not know what was happening in the world. We did not have the political knowledge to try to understand other places. We had radios at King Island, and the teachers had a two-way radio. Whenever we wanted to report from King Island, we called Nome on the two-way radio; and when people in Nome had news, they called King Island. Sometimes we sent some telegrams to our relatives to ask them how they were, and they answered back. That is how we got news from outside, by two-way radio. We had a schedule for calling in the morning and in the afternoon. If the reception was bad in the morning, we called in the afternoon.

During the Second World War there were two guys on King Island who understood a little bit about English. They wrote down what the news was and gave the information to our priest, Father LaFortune. He was a white priest, French Canadian, but he spoke English, and he spoke Eskimo like us. He was with the King Island people for maybe fifteen years or more. He lived in a little house all by himself. He ate just like us. He spoke just like us. He gave half the sermon in Eskimo. He told us what was happening in the Second World War.

We did not understand what was wrong, why countries were fighting each other. What was the cause? What was the reason that they were fighting? We did not have the knowledge to try to understand these problems.

A lot of times people would say, "What the heck are they doing, fighting each other, killing people? They cannot eat human beings. They should come here to Alaska and hunt some animals for their food." That was the reaction that I used to hear from the older folks at King

Island. "How come they kill each other? They cannot eat the bodies of the human beings they kill."

I was drafted into the army during the Second World War. I spoke a little bit of English. I was Class A when I went into the Army. Same way with some others; there were quite a few men from the village that passed the medical examination. The ones that really did not understand English were not drafted, and those who were too old or had medical problems were not drafted. I was sent to Nome for basic training. Some were sent out of Alaska, over towards Japan. Other than that, most of us were stationed in Alaska. One of the King Island boys was stationed in Dutch Harbor in the Aleutian Islands when the Japanese bombed the town. He said he was really scared because he could hear the bombs whistling down.

One summer the people on King Island saw Japanese artillery in the area. There was one man walking on top of the island, and he saw the boat coming in. He went to warn the villagers. They waited and waited and waited, but nothing happened. It was a submarine that went down before getting to the village. They never saw it again.

It is very hard to land a boat at King Island. There is no sandbar to land on; there are only boulders. Even though we had been at King Island throughout our lifetimes, we had to look for the right place to land sometimes. We had to land in seconds, before the breakers came in. If we did not pull the boat out of the water right away, the waves would break the boat. Anyone who did not know how to land would lose his boat. So it was not likely that King Island could be attacked by sea.

Only one bush pilot ever landed a plane on the island. He landed on top of the island, going uphill. Taking off, he just slid down the hill. This guy was a really good pilot, I would say. He said that it was no problem landing on King Island. The only way for a plane to land most of the time was on the shore ice. Sometimes we made a temporary landing strip down on the shore ice. We moved rocks and snow to make a flat runway. There were a few bush pilots who knew how to land on the shore ice.

We were ready for any kind of action at King Island. We had our army rifles, we were trained. Everyone at King Island knew how to shoot anyway. We did not have to train, except maybe for a surprise attack. We knew the island just like the palms of our hands. If the Japanese had ever tried to get into King Island, we knew what to do, where to hide, how to sleep on the ice. We would have had no problems.

I had only been in the army, training in Nome, for one month when there was an accident that broke my leg. I was helping to unload a transport ship, moving some lumber. The sling slipped out from under some timbers, and the lumber fell on me. I was put into the hospital in Nome, but the doctors did not set the fracture properly and infection set in. That month the Japanese invasion started in the Aleutian Islands, and the doctors were trying to make room for wounded soldiers. So they transferred quite a few patients, including me, to Barnes General Hospital in Vancouver, Washington. By this time gangrene had set into my leg.

The doctors at Barnes said that if I had been sent sooner, they could have tried to save my leg, but it was too late. So they had to do three operations to amputate my leg. It was very painful.

I was sent down to Bushnell General Hospital in Brigham City, Utah, to be fitted with a wooden leg. I was there about five months. I felt that I wanted to die. All my preparation to be a good hunter was lost. I had lost everything. I could not go out hunting in the moving ice anymore. The Bering Sea ice moves all the time—north, south, east and west— and it is very dangerous. It is a very dangerous place to be even with two legs.

After I was discharged from the army and sent back home, my cousin made me crutches. I was just completely disappointed at that time, frustrated and depressed. Most of the people who had a very close relationship to me said that they had lost somebody who would have been a successful hunter. They had tried to prepare me especially to be a polar bear hunter. That is partly what all the running was for, to build my muscles to run after polar bears when they tried to get away. And I had lost that. I was twenty-one years old and I had lost everything.

I decided that I would hunt anyway. What else could I do? I made myself heavier crutches so that I could walk on the ice. Starting out, I tried to hunt mostly on the shore ice because the ice was not moving. I was able to carry my rifle and my hunting bag over my shoulders and to move through the shore ice using my crutches.

One day the weather was really nice, the current was not moving fast, and the wind was calm. When the wind is calm, the current is slow. I went out hunting and I got myself a seal. I felt pretty good about it. I had gone out into the moving ice and I had been successful in hunting. I started to drag the seal toward the shore ice. I took a line from my hunting bag, tied it around the seal and around my waist, and headed home. I did not get very far. A lead opened up in front of me, open water, and I fell in, inside the moving ice. I could not get out. Good thing there was somebody nearby. I hollered at him and he came running and pulled me out.

Another time I went out hunting on the moving ice and I lost my rifle. I was catching a seal and I had some of my equipment out near its breathing hole. My hunting bag and my rifle were some distance away. The ice cracked between my rifle and myself and I could not jump it; I could not go over to get my rifle. The lead was only about two or three feet wide. Anybody else could have jumped it, but I could not. So I made a really long walk around the lead to try to get my hunting bag at least, but the ice cracked again and the rifle sank. The hunting bag was floating in the water but I could not get it. It would have been saved if I had not been handicapped. So I said to myself finally, "If I try to go out hunting on crutches, one day I will not come back. It is too dangerous."

So I built myself a little skin boat about sixteen feet long. My nephew —my brother's son—and my brother helped me make the wooden frame, and some of the women of the village sewed the split walrus hides to cover the frame. I thought I could hunt from a skin boat more safely than by walking on crutches. Whenever the north wind blew, I hunted in the open water on the south side of the village. That way I started getting more seals. I had used a kayak to hunt seals before my accident, but I could not balance myself anymore in a kayak. I had more weight on my good leg and less weight on my wooden leg. In order to balance my kayak, I had to lean towards one side, and it was very hard on my back. So I never used the kayak anymore. I used the little skin boat.

Even though I became handicapped, people at King Island tried to be helpful to me in every way that they could. One winter my nephew, my brother and I went out hunting on the east side of the island. We went out until we could not go out any farther because the area was closed with ice and the skin boat could not go through. We pulled our little skin boat on top of the ice. I looked north and I saw some object above the pressure ridge of ice off in the distance. And above the object were two ravens flying.

Now when I was young, my mother used to tell me that whenever my father saw two ravens playing with something on the ice, that meant that an animal was present, maybe a fox or maybe a polar bear! And I saw those two ravens go down and go up and go down and go up. I just kept looking where they went down in the distance and I saw that object, and I knew right away that it was a polar bear. I told my brother and my nephew, "There is a polar bear coming toward us. Maybe we should pull our skin boat up some more so that it will not be carried away by the ice." So we pulled it up a little way from the water.

We went over behind the big pressure ridges and we hid. We saw that there were three polar bears, a mother and two cubs almost the same size as the mother. Every time we looked, they had come closer. They could not see us, only our skin boat. They may have thought the boat was a seal or a walrus. Finally, as they started to move away from us, we each took aim at one polar bear and we shot all three.

My mother was still living then, and when we came home she asked me, "Did you kill that polar bear, son?"

I said, "Yes," and she began crying for joy. She thought I was not able to kill a polar bear because I was handicapped, but I managed to get one. We used the meat for food and we sold the furs.

We had a polar bear dance about one week later. We gave away food, rawhide and furs from the animals. I was store manager at the village then, and I had ordered an ice cream maker for that year, to make ice cream the white man's way. That is the first time we served ice cream at a polar bear dance. And the next day one of my really close relatives said, "Paul, you should get another polar bear so that we can have some more ice cream."

I think I killed every type of animal at King Island—seal, walrus, polar bear, birds. I did what I had prepared for before I became handicapped. My preparation to be a good hunter was not wasted at all. When I started to hunt from my little skin boat, I could compare with the other hunters. I never tried to be a great hunter but only to compete with the others. But I proved myself to be a hunter—not a handicapped person but a hunter.

JOHN MUIR

Naturalist and explorer John Muir was born in Scotland in 1838 and was educated at the University of Wisconsin in Madison. The author of *A Thousand Mile Walk to the Gulf*, *The Story of My Boyhood and Youth*, *The Mountains of California*, *Our National Parks*, *Stickeen*, *My First Summer in the Sierra*, *The Yosemite*, *Travels in Alaska*, and *Steep Trails*, Mr. Muir was a leader in the forest conservation movement and was president of the Sierra Club from 1902, the year of its formation, until his death in 1914.

Villages of the Dead

St. Lawrence Island, the largest in Bering Sea, is situated at a distance of about one hundred and twenty miles off the mouths of the Yukon, and forty-five miles from the nearest point on the coast of Siberia. It is about a hundred miles in length from east to west and fifteen miles in average width; a dreary, cheerless-looking mass of black lava, dotted with volcanoes, covered with snow, without a single tree, and rigidly bound in ocean ice for more than half the year.

Inasmuch as it lies broadwise to the way pursued by the great ice-sheet that once filled Bering Sea, it is traversed by numerous valleys and ridges and low gaps, some of which have been worn down nearly to the sea-level. Had the glaciation to which it has been subjected been carried on much longer, then, instead of this one large island, we should have had several smaller ones. Nearly all of the volcanic cones with which the central portion of the island is in great part covered, are post-glacial in age and present well-formed craters but little weathered as yet.

All the surface of the low grounds, in the glacial gaps, as well as the flat table-lands, is covered with wet, spongy tundra of mosses and lichens, with patches of blooming heathworts and dwarf willows, and grasses and sedges, diversified here and there by direr spots, planted with larkspurs, saxifrage, daisies, primulas, anemones, ferns, etc. These form gardens with a luxuriance and brightness of color little to be hoped for in so cold and dreary-looking a region.

Three years ago there were about fifteen hundred inhabitants on the island, chiefly Eskimos, living in ten villages located around the shores, and subsisting on the seals, walruses, whales, and water-birds that abound here. Now there are only about five hundred people, most of them in one village on the northwest end of the island, nearly two thirds of the population having died of starvation during the winter of 1878–79. In seven of the villages not a single soul was left alive. In the largest village at the northwest end of the island, which suffered least, two hundred out of six hundred died. In the one at the southwest end only fifteen out of about two hundred survived. There are a few survivors also at one of the villages on the east end of the island.

After landing our interpreter at Marcus Bay we steered for St. Michael, and in passing along the north side of this island we stopped an hour or so this morning at one of the smallest of the dead villages. Mr. Nelson went ashore and obtained a lot of skulls and specimens of one sort and another for the Smithsonian Institution. Twenty-five skeletons were seen.

A few miles farther on we anchored before a larger village, situated about halfway between the east and west ends of the island, which I visited in company with Mr. Nelson, the Captain, and the Surgeon. We found twelve desolate huts close to the beach with about two hundred skeletons in them or strewn about on the rocks and rubbish heaps within a few yards of the doors. The scene was indescribably ghastly and desolate, though laid in a country purified by frost as by fire. Gulls, plovers, and ducks were swimming and flying about in happy life, the pure salt sea was dashing white against the shore, the blooming tundra swept back to the snow-clad volcanoes, and the wide azure sky bent kindly over all—nature intensely fresh and sweet, the village lying in the foulest and most glaring death. The shrunken bodies, with rotting furs on them, or white, bleaching skeletons, picked bare by the crows, were lying mixed with kitchen-midden rubbish where they had been cast out by surviving relatives while they yet had strength to carry them.

In the huts those who had been the last to perish were found in bed, lying evenly side by side, beneath their rotting deerskins. A grinning skull might be seen looking out here and there, and a pile of skeletons in a corner, laid there no doubt when no one was left strong enough to carry them through the narrow underground passage to the door. Thirty were found in one house, about half of them piled like firewood in a corner, the other half in bed, seeming as if they had met their fate with tranquil apathy. Evidently these people did not suffer from cold, however rigorous the winter may have been, as some of the huts had in them piles of deerskins that had not been in use. Nor, although their survivors and neighbors all say that hunger was the sole cause of their death, could they have battled with famine to the bitter end, because a considerable amount of walrus rawhide and skins of other animals was found in the huts. These would have sustained life at least a week or two longer.

The facts all tend to show that the winter of 1878–79 was, from whatever cause, one of great scarcity, and as these people never lay up any considerable supply of food from one season to another, they began to perish. The first to succumb were carried out of the huts to the ordinary ground for the dead, about half a mile from the village. Then, as the survivors became weaker, they carried the dead a shorter distance, and made no effort to mark their positions or to lay their effects beside them, as they customarily do. At length the bodies were only dragged to the doors of the huts, or laid in a corner, and the last survivors lay down in despair without making any struggle to prolong their wretched lives by eating the last scraps of skin.

Mr. Nelson went into this Golgotha with hearty enthusiasm, gathering the fine white harvest of skulls spread before him, and throwing them in heaps like a boy gathering pumpkins. He brought nearly a hundred on board, which will be shipped with specimens of bone armor, weapons, utensils, etc., on the Alaska Commercial Company's steamer St. Paul.

We also landed at the village on the southwest corner of the island and interviewed the fifteen survivors. When we inquired where the other people of the village were, one of the group, who speaks a few words of English, answered with a happy, heedless smile, "All mucky." "All gone!" "Dead?" "Yes, dead, all dead!" Then he led us a few yards back of his hut and pointed to twelve or fourteen skeletons lying on the brown grass, repeating in almost a merry tone of voice, "Dead, yes, all dead, all mucky, all gone!"

About two hundred perished here, and unless some aid be extended by our government which claims these people, in a few years at most every soul of them will have vanished from the face of the earth; for, even where alcohol is left out of the count, the few articles of food, clothing, guns, etc., furnished by the traders, exert a degrading influence, making them less self-reliant, and less skillful as hunters. They seem easily susceptible of civilization, and well deserve the attention of our government.

SALLY CARRIGHAR

Born in Cleveland, Ohio, in 1905, Sally Carrighar attended Wellesley College and wrote radio dramas and feature articles before dedicating her life to biological research and nature writing. She lived and worked in a wide variety of villages in Alaska including Barrow, Kotzebue, Wales, Shishmaref, Unalakleet, and Nome. Her many books include *One Day on Beetle Rock, One Day at Teton Marsh, Icebound Summer, Moonlight at Midday, The Twilight Season, Wild Heritage, Wild Voice of the North*, and *Home to the Wilderness*. Ms. Carrighar died in 1986.

Outwitting the Arctic

It's not fair to describe the satisfactions of Northern living without telling what some of the problems are. For there are, of course, problems. Three stand out: housing, securing supplies, and the making and stretching of money. Houses do very peculiar and unpredictable things at fifty degrees below zero. One must study them, learn their tactics, and outwit them if that is possible. And supplies, many of which come direct from the States — doesn't one simply order them and then wait? No, the process is not that logical. Nor is it true, as so widely thought, that Alaska wages and prices can be depended upon to balance. In finding the answers to these elementary questions, people who choose the arctic lead strenuous lives. But was any frontier, anywhere else, ever different?

Even after a year at Unalakleet I did not have all the information about arctic animals that was needed to finish a book about them. I had not seen the big humpback whales, walrus, or lemmings, three of the key species. I was telling the facts in fiction form, but I wanted the picture of Northern wildlife to be accurate, as it only could be if the author had seen the main characters at first hand. Therefore I went down to San Francisco, closed my apartment, and came back to Nome, supposedly in the interest of science, but I already thought that probably I would stay in the North permanently.

The final transition from naturalist into "pioneer" came when I bought a house. One week all the questions of food, heat, electricity, water, and plumbing were taken care of by paying a hotel bill; the next week I was making a list of staple groceries for a year, to be radioed to Seattle so they could come on the last summer boat; and frayed wiring, smoking stoves, cracks under doors, and the faucet through which water would cease to flow with the freeze-up — these had become pressing problems, with an arctic winter approaching fast. The time was late August.

I rented the house at first, but after three months of preliminary expense and labor, on a very cold night, as a bush pilot broke a bottle of champagne over the front door, I became its owner. About that time the late Senator Howard Lyng, meeting me on the street, said, "I hear you are buying the Berger house. There isn't a house in Nome that will give you more trouble." "I am sure by now that you're right, Senator Lyng," I said, "but it makes me a little envious when I see how comfortable other Nome houses are, and I know the reason is that you've all outsmarted the North. You've worked your own ways to live like civilized people up here in the arctic, and I want the fun of doing that too." "Well, if that is the kind of fun you want, you will have it," the Senator answered, and added, "But go ahead. You won't regret it."

The house was built during the gold rush by Jacob Berger, a miner who had made three lucky strikes. He and his bride planned the house with taste, at least taste in a period that did not excel in its appreciation of simple design. I was not delighted with the exterior, but the rooms were large and light, and there were good floors, exquisite moldings, and many attractive details, like white pillars supporting a beam in the living-room.

The trouble was that the house was old, about fifty years old—adolescence as houses are judged in New England but tottering senility in the weather of northwest Alaska. Not tottering really; the house stood firm on its mammoth timbers, with 2" × 10" joists, many-layered walls to keep out the cold, and floors of solid wood four inches thick. The skeleton was sound. Fifty years of heaving and dropping permafrost had opened a thousand cracks, however, and recent owners had not taken care of the house. It needed new plumbing and wiring, a new heating system, new insulation, and decorating throughout.

I owned it for five years, till I moved to Fairbanks. By then the house was completely practical and inside rather beautiful. During the time I lived in it there were some very chaotic hours, but not one when I ever was sorry that I had bought it. I did have more than the average difficulties. In that Senator Lyng had been right: the maximum difficulties. They gave me a chance, however, to claim that I'm an authority on arctic housing.

An Alaska house is what a home is anywhere, a center that helps to cement a family together, a place where a woman expresses her talents, and a setting for friendly gatherings. In the far North it is also, in the most elementary, cave-man sense, a life-giving shelter. These walls, only wood and some tar paper, and this roof from which shingles fly off like birds in each arctic gale, these hold off a whole skyful of lethal cold. Sometimes in winter they separate temperatures that are more than 100° apart. When all our utilities function well, the electric lights on the inside of the house glow and the thermometer registers above 70°. Less than a foot away, if there is any wind, exposed human flesh freezes in less than a minute. This protective house is, then, home as it is idealized, and our interest in it is almost, if not quite, an obsession.

The utilities do break down, with results so alarming that friends greeting each other in stores or the post office are less likely to ask, "How are you?" than, "How is your house holding up these days?" In this climate a house can become uninhabitable in a dozen ways, but the emergencies we dread most are those that deprive us of heat. Within a few hours the temperature in the house will be well below 33° and the plumbing will freeze, including the pressure pump and the water tanks; also the canned goods and crates of potatoes and fruit. The food will be lost, perhaps several hundred dollars' worth if it is near the beginning of winter. A pair of newcomers had been so well warned of the dangers that when a Nome hostess asked them to dinner, they said: "Oh, we wouldn't dare leave the food that long!"

Our troubles arise because we, the white settlers, want mechanized homes in a climate for which they were not designed. Few of the Eskimos have tanks and pumps and oil lines to freeze. We fight the country; Eskimos go along with it. On trips to the States I have been asked if I live in an ice igloo. I always think then of a white man in Kotzebue who, remembering old geography lessons, showed his young daughter how a snow house was built. Eskimos stood around photographing the curious project. But, though they don't live in houses of snow or ice, some of those they do have can be built in a day.

We who grew up with mechanical comforts, however, still want them, and so, in Nome, there is a lively competitive effort to see how close we can come to the life in Stateside communities. Ever since the first miners arrived with the gold rush, the techniques have been worked on, and some have not been improved in the last fifty years. Others are still evolving; and every house has its adaptations.

A home-owner's principal problems are cold and the permafrost. Of the two, permafrost may not be the greater, but coping with it requires the more ingenuity. In some places permafrost is true soil, frozen as much as a thousand feet down, even into the bedrock; rocks will freeze, one learns in the Arctic. Or the permafrost may be clear blue ice; or often the upper layer is frozen plant fibers, dead but not much decayed, for bacteria have as hard a time to survive in the North as most other organisms. Whenever I open a package of quick-frozen spinach, I think of the way the permafrost looks where it is composed of plants. The plants would be different from spinach, however.

In summer the surface crust of the permafrost thaws down a bit. Then the top is about as limp and spongy as spinach when it is cooking. Or if it's composed of silt, the permafrost acts like quicksand. One sinks into it almost as fast to the welcome spot where one's foot finds the ice. The lower layers remain frozen solidly, at near zero Fahrenheit, although that temperature fluctuates, even as far as fifty feet down, with the season. At all times the permafrost heaves and subsides, never predictably and sometimes quite fast. The house resting upon it tilts, first one way, then another way, to such an extent that, for example, the feedlines that carry the oil to the stoves sometimes loosen or break. Or during the night a stovepipe will disconnect at a joint. One may wake in the morning to find a layer of oil all over the carpet, or oily soot deposited upon everything in the room, including upholstered furniture.

Floors always are tipped, but we get used to that. One man says that his kitchen floor banks just enough to make it easy for him to hurry through on his way to another room.

About doors, on the other hand, frequently we become desperate. Doors have to fit snugly to keep out the cold. But as a house shifts, doors get so far out of plumb that wide cracks open under them or at the top or side; or they jam shut perhaps during a single night. When the doors then have been adjusted, the house may shift back again in the same length of time. We have long narrow wedges which can be put on or taken off the tops and bottoms of doors, and also another solution such as I had on my own front door. The ends of the door were sawed off so they didn't meet either the sill or the top of the casing. The spaces were closed up with two stainless steel plates screwed onto the ends of the door, outside. The screws went through slots in the plates, so that the plates could be loosened and pushed up or down, at an angle perhaps, to make the door tight.

In a house constantly on the move, walls can't be plastered or papered. In the old days the walls often were covered with tongue-and-groove paneling, which would give. Now we use one of the wallboards or plywood. The panels will shift as units, but the seams where they join, of course, open and close. All the seams in the house, in fact, spread. Wind gets into the walls then and, unless we keep the cracks well filled up, into the rooms.

One time, in a program to eliminate wind in my house, I found breezes that almost would wave a flag pouring out of the unused sockets in baseboard electric plugs. Wind blew in through the cracks at the top and bottom of baseboards, at the edges of door and window casings where they line up against walls, and through cracks under sills. Finally, for the temporary present, all the cracks and seams were closed up with moldings and with expansible fillers like caulking cotton, plastic putty, and a clay that comes in long rolls the width of an earthworm. When the work was completed, the temperature in the house went up fifteen degrees.

Besides rolling a house about, the permafrost creates other difficulties. Thawing because of the weight and warmth, the permafrost under the house will cave down. Anything placed on the frozen ground, in fact, from a tin can to a building or road, tends to sink. The natives at Barrow put much of their trash into empty oil drums left out on the tundra, and in a surprisingly short time the drums disappear. Houses subside in the same way, fairly fast since the heat from the stoves within hastens the thawing.

This, then, one tries to do: make a house firm and stationary on ground that moves and in summer is spongy. One way is with piling. At considerable expense piles can be driven into the frozen ground. They have to go very deep and, even so, will not remain where they are indefinitely. For a while they will hold a structure in place. Nome's Federal Building, a block square and three stories high, was set on piling as recently as 1937 and by now has shifted so much that it has been declared unsafe and is being replaced. At still greater cost the permafrost can be thawed artificially and a basement constructed. But the basement will crack, and so will the building on top of it.

These problems do not apply to the beach, where the sand does not deeply freeze. Nome of the gold-rush days was several miles long but only as wide as the beach, since the miners had no solution to putting up homes in the summer swamps. It was the mining itself that made such homes possible for the later settlers. Nome is ringed with gold-dredges, all digging the permafrost up with bucket lines, crushing the rock in the process, and spewing it out after the gold is extracted. The tailing piles formed in this way soon were the size of natural hills, of crushed rock in effect all made ready to firm up the tundra. Uncounted thousands of truckloads have been brought to town through the years, so that Nome stands on tailings now. All of the houses do.

The tailings sink into the permafrost also. They sink faster if warmth from the houses thaws the permafrost. Therefore, to keep a cold space beneath the floor, most houses rest on huge timers or skids. Nevertheless, within a few years the crushed rock under a house will have disappeared; then the structure is raised and tipped and a crew of workmen sling many cubic yards of new tailings into the basin of muck beneath. My own house stood upon fourteen inches of frozen soil. Under the soil was clear glacial ice, I was told, and along through the ice, through its layers, a flowing stream ran. Other such strata of moving water occur in the permafrost. They are due, one suspects, to springs that don't reach the surface. If the heat from the stove in a house should thaw down the permafrost far enough so that one of the streams could seep up to the top, the stream never could be contained again. There have been cases where water released in this way has come into a house and, freezing as it was rising, became an ice skeleton around which the walls were shells. Those houses were not in Nome, but we knew of them and were cautious.

Some of the streams and springs do reach the surface. On the outskirts of Nome are several—water heavily laden with minerals but delicious and fresh to taste. They are warm springs that happily do not freeze in winter, and they are the city's water supply.

Neither water nor sewage pipes can be laid in the permafrost, where they would freeze, but there is a system of mains, running along on the surface, which transport the spring water to homes in the summer.

Every street has a main on one side, in the gutter, and householders, doing their own plumbing, connect pipes and for about two months have an almost conventional water supply. The mains are owned by the U.S. Smelting, Refining and Mining Company, the organization that operates the big dredges. They sell water at one standard rate, $4.50 a month—$7.50 for a household that has a bathtub. By September 15 all these pipes are frozen. Then our water is brought to us, also from springs at the edge of town, in the tank trucks owned by two "water men," Pete Reader and Lester Bronson.

For storage a simple household gets by with a barrel. The water man fills it by carrying bucketfuls into the house at 2½ cents a gallon. Other houses have storage tanks holding up to 500 gallons, with intake and overflow pipes to the tanks through the outside walls. The procedure is this: First, the water man comes with a snowplow and dozes the driveway. Then he brings his truck, fastens his hose to the intake pipe, and connects a cord from the pump on his truck to an electric plug we provide on the outside wall of the house. The water starts pouring in— when delivered that way, at 1½ cents a gallon.

In the beginning, however, the water man blows into both the pipes. If he finds either blocked with ice, he goes away and we start to wrestle with one of the more desperate problems. My own storage tank was up on the second floor, and in the original plumbing arrangement the intake and overflow pipes looped around the eaves with several elbows before they came down to the water man's level. At the point where they broke through the roof, cores of frost, which became ice, would build up. A blow torch would loosen the cores from the pipes, but the cores would not pass the elbows. Whenever the pipes were blocked, as they always were at temperatures lower than −30°, they all had to be taken down. I revised the system, with two new, plastic pipes which were contained for most of their length in the heated house.

We have one dread that rises at times nearly into hysteria: that the intake pipe will be clear but the overflow pipe will be clogged. Then the tank will run over and, if it is on the second floor, ruin the walls. Most houses in Nome have had one or more holes drilled in the first-story floor, as an easier way than sweeping to drain off an interior lake.

After the water gets into the tank it flows to the faucets by means of gravity or a pressure pump. En route it passes through coils in a stove and perhaps then through coils with a fan behind them, to heat a room. The whole arrangement is so connected with summer lines out in the street that a valve can be turned one way to have water flow from the tank; turned the other way, the supply comes from the mains. Since I was having *all* the housekeeping problems, they included one that bothers some residents but not everyone: electricity from the ground wire of a telephone pole got into my outdoor lines and through them into the interior plumbing system. I didn't know what caused the trouble, only that every time I touched the water coming out of a faucet it all but threw me across the room. An electrician found that there was enough current in the water to light a 15-watt bulb. It was eliminated by simply disconnecting the outside pipes. Ordinarily the electricity would disperse itself in the soil, but solidly frozen ground does not conduct well, and the electricity gets diverted into some surface pipes.

Most of the plumbing in Nome is planned and installed by the owners. It is one of our favorite topics of conversation. When new acquaintances call, there is soon, inevitably, a leading question like, "Where do you have your water tank?" With it goes an expectant look, and it is only courteous then to ask, "Would you perhaps like to see the plumbing?" The callers are up on their feet in an instant.

After a house has had several owners, the plumbing is apt to be rather marvelous—more elaborate than necessary, no doubt, but they've all had the satisfaction of adding pipe. I had little to do with mine except to complain and then listen to other people's experience. But it seemed an amazing, ingenious system that various functioning non-plumbers had suggested: hot water that rose and cold water that sank where it should; wonderful tangles of pipes that began at the driveway and ended in conventional faucets. The entire tangle was visible, for water pipes never are hidden inside the walls. If they were, they would probably freeze. Mine, like everyone else's, were silvered.

It is not as hard to get waste water out of a house in Nome as to get fresh water in. An official brought a young bride to town. On her second morning she happened to look out the window as she was emptying water into the sink. She cried out to her husband: "The plumbing's been disconnected! The drain is just pouring the water out into the yard!" The young husband explained, tactfully, that the drain was not broken. Bathwater and dishwater simply are cast outside onto the tailings.

Formerly most of the lots were bordered with wooden sluice boxes. Drainage went into them and was carried to larger ditches beneath the boardwalks. Now the boxes have fallen into disuse. The water just disappears in the crushed rock, where it evaporates rather fast, since the air in the North is dry.

The equipment is elementary—only pipes through the wall from a shower or bathtub, lavatory, and sink. The problem is to prevent ice from clogging these pipes. We say in this climate that it is not a cold day unless boiling water poured out the window has frozen before it can reach the ground. I never have seen that experiment tried, but in some of the temperatures only a full, fast flow will get through the pipes. In all but the summer months a drip or a trickle will quickly stop them up. It is customary to pour salt into the drains at the end of day, but mine often froze until, as a friend advised, I had new ones constructed of six-inch galvanized stovepipe. So much wind entered the house through the drains that when they weren't stoppered my kitchen drain always hummed, in the key of D.

Other waste is disposed of through what is called the facility, or the honey bucket. This is a chemical toilet, a pail of heavy-gauge steel enclosed in a large metal box. The box extends through the wall in such a way that the bucket can be removed from the outside by the "sanitary man," who empties and steam cleans it. For this purpose there is a small door of familiar design. A subsidiary problem is the fact that the little door can be opened, the bucket lifted out, and a child, or a man with some effort, can enter the house through the interior metal box. When Nome people leave town, most of them block any chance of intruders by standing a pole tightly braced between the top of the toilet seat and the bathroom ceiling. The total arrangement fills many newcomers with dismay. To some of them I have quoted what was told to me when I arrived: "As time passes, this will recede in importance."

With these various improvisations, from the adjustable plates on the entrance door to the bathwater draining out of a stovepipe, it is possible to outwit the permafrost. In combating the cold, Northerners are a longer way from success. In some states the thermometers drop as low as ours, but they do not stay down as long; the sea off Nome has been frozen as late as the first of July. And when, week after week, the temperature never rises as high as 30°, as happens occasionally, the very materials of which a house is made become frozen. Before I came North I did not know that an ancient, dried-out piece of wood could freeze, but it will. One evidence is that when struck, it will chime. The board-walks of Nome clang under one's footsteps, and when the wind hurls a piece of ice onto the wall of a house, the whole house seems to ring.

My neighbors across the street woke one morning to find that their blankets had frozen to an adjacent wall. Inside walls do not always freeze, but they become so cold that one's body loses its heat to them by radiation. The discomfort is lessened by using electric fans. A fan mounted close to the ceiling blows down the warm air that rises, and a fan set high in a wall sends excessive heat from a room like the kitchen into another room that is cool. Fans blow across hot-water pipes to dis-tribute their warmth; other fans are incorporated in heaters installed on the smokestacks. Too much of the heat from a stove is lost up the stack. To capture it, one section of stovepipe is replaced by a piece of equip-ment that separates the ascending smoke into metal chambers. They be-come very hot, and a fan behind them will drive a blast of warm air out into the room. The effect is the same whether real or illusion: a lively circulation of heated air seems a barrier between us and the chilly walls.

Most houses in Nome have some insulation. In the newer ones some of the modern products were used. Houses that date from the gold rush have walls made of several layers of wood, with tar paper between, or walls filled with sand, sawdust, or ashes. Sand and sawdust were not effective; ashes were better except for one disadvantage. Last year a man in Nome bought and tore down an early-day structure in order to salvage the timbers. It had been insulated with ashes, and too late he learned that the lye in the ashes had eaten away most of the struc-tural wood.

Is it a kind of fear, a mental block, that leads me to speak last of the stoves? A woman I know never mentions the subject because, she confided, if she discusses stoves she becomes hysterical. Another wife always goes to a hotel when her husband leaves town because, she says, "I wouldn't stay alone in the house with the stoves." During the winter I spent at Unalakleet the stove in my room exploded one evening. By morning the indoor temperature was 10° below zero, and everything in the room had frozen, including the ink and the hand lotion. Only one such experience is needed to give any woman, and some men, an irrational tension regarding the stoves.

A few houses in Nome have oil furnaces, but not many. The furnaces can't be installed easily in houses that were not planned for them, and since Nome is not growing at present, few new houses are built. Two kinds of stoves are used: the range, which not only must cook the food but heat the kitchen; and space-heaters in other areas of the house. Both kinds, if modern, are too well insulated for Northerners. The enameled sides of the cookstoves are cool to the touch, so that it's necessary to leave the oven door hanging open. Much of the time the cook's shins are bruised, and in winter some women do not bake potatoes or pies—the kitchen would get too cold. The old cast-iron ranges were better, those covered with bulges and curlicues, every one of which radiated welcome and lovely warmth. The space-heaters now being made are enclosed in trim metal boxes, boxes pierced, it is true, with slots and louvers, but more warmth got out through the old-fashioned screens made of sturdy wire mesh.

Eskimos as a rule do not have much money and therefore burn driftwood. There is no local supply of timber in Nome, no road to the groves where the last small spruces grow. Natural gas has been found in Alaska but so far is not available in the Northern cities, and coal is being mined but there is no coastal steamship line that will bring it out to the Bering Sea. The fuel used by white families is oil. Fuel bills average from $45 a month to $145 or higher—at Barrow four times as much.

The oil tanks are outside because of the dread of fire; a fire is a frightful experience up in these Arctic temperatures. Since the tanks cannot be underground in the permafrost, they are placed up on racks and feed to the stoves by gravity. They are exposed to the ice and snow, of course, and these frequently block up the air vents. If one forgets to uncover the vents, as the oil level drops the vacuum inside sometimes causes the tanks to collapse. There is another threat: in the spring and fall, temperature changes are rather extreme, and moisture condenses inside the tank and collects in the bottom as water. Every tank has a trap with a petcock for draining the water off, but it does often get in the feedlines and freezes, and then stops the flow of oil.

With an outside tank it is not easy to keep other people from pilfering. I still have as souvenirs the equipment one neighbor used to siphon oil out of my air vent. He had left the gear hanging above my tank for his convenience.

The oil feedline runs under the house, where it branches to each of the stoves. The stoves burn well if all the conditions are quite ideal. But we live with the fearful knowledge that if anything stops the draft, if soot in the stove does or soot or snow in the stack, then the stove will explode. Stoves with electric blowers, the forced-draft type, soot up within minutes when power lines blow down. Stoves may also explode if they are lighted when they are warm.

The problems of Northern housekeeping are, therefore, numerous, but the truth is that maintaining a house is easier almost anywhere else in the North than at Nome. In the larger cities one can summon an expert mechanic. Nome has a few, only three or four, and at times they all vanish. Bad weather, the cause of most kinds of breakdowns, affects everyone. The mechanics are swamped with calls, until suddenly they may disappear, reportedly to some inaccessible room equipped with a deck of cards and a case of everybody-knows-what. In the larger towns there are more mechanics and pleas for help do not fall so heavily upon any one.

Although Fairbanks is colder than Nome in winter, through some ingenious engineering it does furnish modern utilities, and those greatly ease the problems. The Fairbanks municipal water circulates in a loop system, with pumps that prevent its freezing by keeping the water running at least three feet per second. Connections to customers are through double lines, one in and one out, and the water continually flows in these also. Each service line is insulated and, further, an electrical connection is provided to charge the line and thus thaw it if necessary.

The Fairbanks sewers are made of wood-stave pipe (concrete breaks in the permafrost), and they sometimes freeze up. Then the city sends out steam boilers on trucks, which will open the flow. Fairbanks generates its electricity by steam, and the steam is saved and piped through the downtown area to heat apartment and business buildings and a few homes. Everybody in Fairbanks wishes that he could live "on the steam line."

In the villages smaller than Nome few people try to have the more civilized comforts, except in the housing the missions and government furnish. But the white population of Nome aspire to have push-button households, and to a surprising extent they do create them. Perhaps they have the most satisfaction of any settlers, since they achieve comfort and strictly by their own efforts—gaining that feeling of competence which is one of the chief rewards of being a pioneer.

Sharing my house was Bobo, a blue-eyed Siberian husky. He was one of the compensations, part of what made the house seem such a warm and protective shelter. But any house in the North has the special meaning of holding away the cold. When Bobo and I would take our late-evening walk, each of the lighted homes we passed meant more to the owners, I thought, than homes do in most places. Beginning at about fifteen degrees below zero, the hot air from the stovepipes vaporizes and for some reason is luminous. In the usual winter wind from the north, the white plumes level down: "The smoke is lying on the roofs," people say of those nights. And the little houses of Nome are close and neighborly under this cover of driven and shining mist, which flows away into the night, over the icy width of the Bering Sea.

RICHARD NELSON

Richard Nelson is a cultural anthropologist who spent twenty-five years studying cultural relationships to the natural world among Eskimo and Athapaskan Indian peoples in Alaska. His books about Alaskan Native lifeways include *Hunters of the Northern Ice*, *Hunters of the Northern Forest*, *Shadow of the Hunter*, and *Make Prayers to the Raven*. He also wrote *The Island Within*, which received the 1991 John Burroughs Award for nature writing.

The Embrace of Names

I was born in Madison, Wisconsin—a place named for a politician who had never been there. The city is nested among four lakes—Wingra, Waubesa, Mendota, and Monona—names whispering the language of ghosts. Who among the living hears them?

When I was twenty-two years old these whispers finally came alive for me in the voices of hunters speaking names that rooted them deeply in the land. An aspiring cultural anthropologist, I had come to Wainwright, a village on the arctic coast of Alaska to live with Iñupiaq Eskimos. On a midsummer day, six of us were hunting walrus in a traditional sealskin-covered boat. We had traveled so far offshore that the flat expanse of land first became a thin stain along the eastern horizon and then sank completely out of sight.

Sitting beside me was a man named Kuvlu, who had designated himself my benefactor and teacher (partly, I suppose, to keep me from dying on the tundra or sea ice and partly to savor the endless entertainment of my blunders). Kuvlu gestured toward the hard seam where water met sky. "Before the White Man came, Eskimos knew the world was round," he said. "The elders warned that if you went too far offshore, it was hard coming home, because you'd have to paddle uphill." Later on, after we shot and butchered two walrus, a solid wall of fog swept in around us. For hours we groped blindly through congested ice floes, relying on one man's genius for dead reckoning to keep us headed toward land.

Then, suddenly, a clay bluff loomed ahead, like the prow of an oncoming ship. Kuvlu inspected the land for a moment, turned to the others and challenged: "Who knows what place this is?" To me it looked like everywhere else along this coast—the same high bank, the same gray beach, the same capping fringe of tundra grass, and a narrow ravine that seemed indistinguishable from a hundred others I'd seen on earlier hunting trips. To my amazement, Kuvlu's older brother had it immediately: "Aqlagvik," he said with assurance, Place to Hunt Grizzly Bears. I was incredulous. How could anyone know the country so well? But Kuvlu only smiled and nodded as we turned to follow the shoreline home.

Over the next hour, Kuvlu recited the names of camps and abandoned settlements along the coast: Nullagvik, Pauktugvik, Milliktagvik, Avgumman, Aqisaq, Imnaurat. For a few he offered translations— Qilamittagvik: Place to Hunt Ducks with Ivory Bolas; Mitqutailat: Arctic Terns; Nannugvik: Place to Hunt Polar Bears; and Iñuktuyuk: Man-Eater, a spring hunting camp used by those willing to overlook its ominous name. The fog cleared as we traveled north, and finally we saw the village—a scatter of weathered houses in a place called Ulġuniq, Where A Standing Thing Fell and Left Its Traces.

Reflecting on those times twenty-five years later, my mind whirls with Iñupiaq names and the memories they bring: how each place looks, events that happened there, and stories I heard about it—Qayaiqsigvik: Place Where a Kayak Was Accidentally Lost; Piŋusugruk: Big Pingok (a hill thrust up by heaving permafrost); Kaŋiich: Where Tributaries Join at the River's Headwaters; Aluaqpak: Big Coal Outcrop; Anaqtuuq: Many Droppings; Qiqiqtasugruk: Big Island; and Umiŋmak: Musk Ox. Some names I remember without knowing what they mean: Siŋauraq, Miñŋuqturuq, Aquliaqattat, Aqiaġuġnat, Kaulaaq, Ivisauraq, Amaktikrak, and dozens more. Each one evokes for me a place set apart from all others and braided into the events that have made my life.

On my first caribou hunting trip, a man named Annaqaq gestured away from the frozen river where we stood. "Take your dog team to the top of that hill," he said. "We call it Nasiqrugvik, High Place Where You Look Out at the Land."

I was confused by the name and by his instructions. Unaccustomed to the subtleties of a nearly flat tundra plain, the hill was completely invisible to me. What would it mean, I wondered, if the people who carried its name disappeared like the ghosts of my Wisconsin birthplace? In a deep and vital way, Nasiqrugvik would vanish into a monotonous, undifferentiated terrain. And the earth would be diminished as a consequence.

During the years I spent with Iñupiaq people, I was interested in place-names because I loved the language and because they were vital as a map when I traveled alone by dog team or kayak. I didn't consider writing down the names, making them part of my work as an ethnographer—not until years later, when I began recording them as a way of establishing people's tenure on their traditional homelands. I did this first with the Iñupiaq and then with the Koyukon Indians, who live in Alaska's forested interior just below the Arctic Circle. Koyukon place-names chart the landscape and color it with beauty and meaning, much in the way of Iñupiaq names. I spent long evenings with Koyukon people in their village cabins, maps scattered across the floor, penciling in names, listening to stories that gave each place history and significance.

I also traveled widely in Koyukon country—hunting moose from camps along the rivers, searching for bear dens in the fall, following traplines through forested wildlands, fishing in lakes and sloughs. In a small way I experienced how their lives were connected with places we discussed in our map sessions, and I was left with an array of names that are still lodged in my mind—not empty words but *names*, filled with memories, filled with the land's beauty, filled with stories from ancient times. What little I know of these things is at least a shadow of how the Koyukon people and their natural world are conjoined through names.

In the Koyukon tradition, many names tell something about the places to which they belong—how the terrain looks, what animals or plants are found there, what has happened there in the recent or distant past. These are names born from the land itself, as much a part of it as the spruce forests, the bedrock outcrops, and the twisting rivers. They are also rich in sound and sometimes aglow with spiritual power that renders the landscape sacred.

Let them speak for themselves: Sis Dlila': Black Bear Mountain; Bidziyh Kohunaatłtaanh Dinh: Where a Caribou is Lying on Its Belly; K'itsaan' Yee Hukuh: Big Grass Lake; Ts'eydla: Black Spruce Hill; Tin Loołeetna: Hanging Ice Place, a creek so named because dwindling streamflow in early winter leaves a hollow space under the ice, so an unsuspecting traveler could easily plunge through; Dolbaatno': River of Young Geese, where people hunt fledglings in midsummer, when the birds are big and fat but cannot fly; Diniyh T'oh: Bearberry Place; Oonyeeh Tilaah Dinh: Where the Blackfish Run in Season; Gguh Tłitł't'o Tiya: Hill Named After the Nape of a Snowshoe Hare's Neck; Łookk'a Ts'ilyaan Dinh: Lake of the Fat Whitefish; Dilbaagga Ts'oolneek Hu: Where Somebody Grabbed a Ptarmigan; Toneets Ts'ibaa La'onh Dinh: Spruce-Covered Island in the Middle of the Lake; Ts'atiyh Dinaa Dakk'onh Din: Where a Forest Fire Burned the Hill to the River; Dotson' Kkokk'a Gheeyo Din: Where the Great Raven Traversed the Length of a Lake.

Each of these places is aswarm with stories, and the landscape is infused with invisible meanings known only through the minds and memories of Koyukon people. At a place called Tsotłyeet there is a one-room cabin, half-hidden among birches and aspens, a cabin that would vanish entirely if left unused for a few decades. But Tsotłyeet is the place where one of my Koyukon teachers grew up, where he spent all the years of his childhood and early adult life. The surrounding woods and thickets, muskegs and lakes, creeks and rivers were the neighborhood for young William and for his mother and father, his sisters and brothers. This is where he acquired his intimate knowledge of moose, bear, grouse, whitefish, wolverine, caribou, and the rest of the living community to which his family belonged. It is where William perfected his skills as a hunter and trapper. In later adulthood he often stayed there with his wife, and in the forty-odd years since they settled in a nearby village, Tsotłyeet has remained the family hunting and trapping headquarters. This place is the nexus of William's life. It would be impossible to understand one apart from the other.

Yet sometime, perhaps not long from now, Tsotłyeet could cease to be a place. Without the Koyukon people and their collective memory, it would vanish from the significant world. And the same is true for literally thousands of other places named and intimately known by Koyukon villagers.

One night I was poring over maps with William and his old friend Joe. During a break from our work, Joe looked at me, his eyes filled with sadness, and he said, "I'm really glad we're putting these names on the maps, because our kids don't know a lot of them." He thought quietly for a moment. "The names might get lost. And if I died, that country would die with me."

By this time I knew the Koyukon homeland was saturated with names—the hills and mountains, the lakes and sloughs, the river bends and islands, the ridges and valleys—places where animals congregate; places where people fish or gather berries; places known for wind or calm or deep winter snow; places with trapping cabins, hunting camps, or burial sites; places of historical importance; places known from Kk'adonts'idnee, stories of the Distant Time, when animals and people shared one society and spoke a common language; places alive with sacredness, where the land listens and the earth underfoot can feel.

As Joe and William turned their attention back to the maps, my own thoughts slipped away, to imagine the entire North American continent in a time before living memory—this enormous sprawl of land, sheathed and cloaked and brilliantly arrayed with names. Names covering the terrain like an unbroken forest. Names that wove people profoundly into the landscape and that infused the landscape profoundly into those who were its inhabitants. Names that gave a special kind of life to the terrain, as Joe and William knew so much better than I.

I imagined how these names had dwindled with the deaths of elders, beginning five hundred years ago; a growing impoverishment of names as Europeans spread west, knowing too little of the land and its people to realize what was being lost. The continent was plundered of its names, left desolate, emptied of mind and memory and meaning.

But all is not lost. Many Native American names survive, others are now being recorded, and some are finding their rightful places on maps. North America is also embellished with thousands of European place-names, although many are opaque to the land itself, as if the earth were shaped into mountains and rivers as a way of commemorating the famous and the dead. There is no better example than Mt. McKinley, our continent's highest peak, named for a little-known politician who would later—coincidentally—become president. McKinley never laid eyes on the mountain, which Koyukon people know as Deenaalee, The High One. Our maps are littered with such names. One of my favorites is Goulding Harbor on the southeast Alaska coast, named by Captain Nathaniel Portlock to honor, flatter, or court favor with the publisher of his book.

I can think of few more worthy endeavors, few gestures that could better show our respect toward the environment that sustains us, than to remove this blight of numb, invading names. Where elders remain to teach us, we could resurrect original names and put them back where they belong. If all memory has vanished, we could find names through the land's own guidance and inspiration, as countless generations of inhabitants have done before us.

We could also follow the examples given by trappers, prospectors, lumberjacks, fishermen, homesteaders, and others who bequeathed to us names reflecting the land and its nexus with humanity. The wild country of Alaska is filled with wonderful examples. Some are purely descriptive: Dogtooth Bend, Flapjack Island, Splitrock Point, Skull Cliff, Naked Island, Ottertail Ridge, Coffee Can Lake, Three Tree Island, Ragged Cape, Bearnose Hill, Twoheaded Island, Bay of Pillars.

Some carry useful information: Hell Roaring Creek, Moose Pasture Lake, Dog Salmon Creek, Over-the-Hill Portage, Rotten Fish Slough, Peril Strait, Walrus Island, Logjam Creek, Whalebone Cape, Caribou Snare Creek, 197 ½ Mile Creek, Crab Trap Cove, Fishless Creek, Sealion Rocks, Plenty Bear Creek.

Some are warnings for travelers: No Thoroughfare Bay, where extreme tides create terrific currents and reversing falls; Williwaw Point, named for its sudden and violent winds; Boiling Pinnacles, where tidal currents thrash over a shallow reef.

Some commemorate personal experiences or historical events: Slaughter Island, Easy Money Creek, Cow-and-Calf Moose Lake, Strangle Woman Creek, Threetime Mountain, Lost Temper Creek, Deadman Reach, No Grub Creek, Sore Finger Cove, Tired Pup Mountain, Broken Snowshoe Creek, and Saddler's Mistake, where an erstwhile navigator guided his ship into a swale joining two mountains, thinking it was a pass between neighboring islands.

The meanings of some, of course, are anybody's guess: Big Skookum Creek, Dull Ax Lake, Seven Egg Creek, Blue Mouse Cove, Helpmejack Lake, Zipper Creek, Mooseheart Mountain, Red Devil Creek, Bear Blanket Slough. And we can speculate about the whimsies that brought forth Seduction Tongue and Doctor Beaver Creek.

Look at a map of any state and you can find dozens of names like these, expressing every possible connection between humanity and earth. They are a powerful source of hope. Given time and a return to intimacy, we newcomers to this continent may yet learn to inhabit its myriad places, may yet become worthy of the gifts it offers us, may yet find the humility and grace of those who lived here for millennia before us, may yet learn to honor the land that nourishes us, gives flight to our imaginations, and pleasures our highest senses.

The names we choose will be a fair measure of our success.

Note

I am grateful to the people of Wainwright, Huslia, and Hughes, Alaska, for sharing their lives and traditions with me over the years; and to Eliza Jones and James Nageak for help with Koyukon and Iñupiaq translations. I am solely responsible for any inaccuracies and awkwardness that may remain in the place-name translations. An anthropologist writes with the air of an expert but is seldom more than a raw apprentice, so I can only hope the elders will be patient with the inevitable errors and shortcomings in my work. Personal names used in this text are pseudonyms.

LOIS CRISLER

Lois Crisler was born in Spokane, Washington, and taught at the University of Washington in Seattle before venturing to the Brooks Range with her husband, Herb, to study and photograph arctic wildlife. Author of *Arctic Wild* and *Captive Wild*, she spent much of her active life working for the preservation of the wilderness. Mrs. Crisler died in 1971.

We shouldered our packs and climbed away from camp, setting our course for the distant headwaters of the Kugururok. As we gained the high tundra, ahead to the south rose the nameless peaks of the Range. To east and west rolled the tan land, empty, formidable, vast.

This was the tundra, the great arctic meadow that flows for thousands of miles along the top of this continent, between Arctic Ocean and arctic mountains and even far up their slopes. It is cut by streams, dotted with ponds and lakes, inhabited by the ever-moving caribou herds, the tundra grizzly, the tundra wolf, and smaller creatures that have chosen the fearsome Arctic to abide in.

The tundra is carpet and table for them all, alike for the prey and the predators. The latter do not live in some other compartment but lay their fur and step their paws on the same mattress and carpet, far-spreading under the pale-blue arctic sky. It is hard for housed humans to understand this houseless, tolerant community of danger.

The tundra is a world out of this world, a thin moss-and-lichen blanket spread over fathomless ice, beneath a sky where in summer the sun does not set and in winter does not rise, and the aurora speeds or drifts in ghostly white across the stars.

The distance walked on tundra is not commensurate with distances walked in other lands. On tundra one cannot get into a rhythm or swing, or take even two steps together without looking, on account of the tussocks. Those under our feet now were not big, but small, hard and wobbly. One's foot slipped sidewise, slipped back, slipped forward. One's legs got two miles tired for every mile traveled.

Our first arctic backpack camp seemed wild and strange to me. The strangeness began the minute I knelt on the dry sand—a patch Cris had found in boggy tundra—and started to unpack my board. I saw the shadow, heard the wings and knew a bird had alighted on my back. I glanced around and it flew. Cris stood looking at me. "Did you know a snow bunting lighted on your back?"

As soon as Cris had pitched the mountain tent—and even exuberantly lugged up a boulder as boots-off-and-on seat at its door—off he went exploring. Dutifully I cooked the rice.

I felt lonely. Once I saw him small and faraway on the end of a ridge. Like every bush on the tundra, he was gilded on one side, black on the other. The level sun came in under a fog ceiling that cut off the mountaintops, leaving their bases in light-blue shadow.

Against this vast backdrop passed twelve antlered bulls, white in sunlight. They swung by camp with hardly a glance at the tiny layout or me. Going to where? Coming from where?

After supper, instead of sacking in, we went for a walk. I felt an odd stealthiness, as well as delight, as if I were prowling in someone's house.

We came to inhabitants of the "house." A pair of long-tailed jaegers sat side by side on a high bank, black against the night sun. Incredulously, Cris walked to within ten feet of them. Their bright wild eyes looked at him with fearless indifference. We were of the house.

Everything was so interesting I hated to go to sleep that night. Cris as always fell asleep instantly. But I lay looking out. At Noluk, dark canvas had closed us in. Here the whole end of the little tent was tied wide open. Golden plovers talked. A ptarmigan grated out his bullfrog noise, as Cris called the "coffee-grinder." Even Cris's black-and-gray-lichened boulder by my head looked interesting.

In the morning we left this bivouac, Camp One, in opposite directions, I to bring up the last load from Noluk, Cris to scout ahead for our next campsite. He carried a light load to cache there.

Before setting out he had to make the decision that would hound us daily—take the camera and camera pack and leave them ahead, or leave them here? To carry them both ways was unthinkable. He left them.

I resented the weight of the camera outfit because it seemed needless in this day of light metals. There were even cute nickel trimmings, and Cris had to add to his pack a vial of black paint to keep them from flashing an alert to animals as far as two miles away. Only I can know the labor Cris has performed over the months and years and miles, carrying that camera always at the ready on the tripod over his shoulder except in settled rain or fog—through trailless wilds, along mountainsides where I used both hands but he used one and steadied the camera with the other.

When we met at Camp One that evening his first words dismayed me. "I saw something today that could make us sorry forever after." He told me this story.

"I saw a wolverine going lippety-loppety along the wet grass on the far side of a marsh I was about to cross. I watched him a few minutes, then walked forward. I supposed he would be gone when I got over there. But he stopped and worked at a certain place. I kept walking closer.

"When I was about a hundred yards away, he looked up and saw me, and stood up like a little bear to watch me. And did he run away? He started toward me! Came about twenty-five yards toward me and growled. Came closer and growled some more.

"I was a little worried. You could tell he could put up a mean fight if he wanted to. And then what did he do? He went back to his work, digging at something. I walked to within fifty feet of him and he went on digging. Paid no more attention to me. He had found a little colony of voles. I watched him catch three and eat them. Saw the vole's white belly. Saw it shake itself and wriggle, trying to get out of his mouth."

He added the crowning frustration. "And there were no heat waves."

It would have been the photographic nugget of a lifetime—it was a nugget of wilderness experience at that. So! The "busy little wolverine" was also brave. He did not fear and probably did not know humans.

This caused us a sober wonder whether the grizzlies here were equally uninformed. If so, they might be dangerously brave. There had been no grizzlies around Noluk, but they would be present up here.

The next morning Cris threw me out on the tundra to find his cache at the site of Camp Two. Casually he directed me. Proudly I refrained from asking reassuring amplification. To Cris, the situation informs you, only a fool needs more than a clue. However, he was unusually liberal with words today.

"You go through that pass on the skyline. You can go up that canyon to it—no crags or anything. On the other side of the pass, contour left and hold your elevation. After a while you'll see a ridge running right.

The cache is in the side of a peak at the far end of that ridge." He sealed these instructions with the inevitable cachet, "You can't miss it."

Proud of my responsibility but a bit anxious I set out, carrying a heavy pack—the five-gallon can of Blazo and dried foods.

As I neared the foot of the canyon a grizzly was ahead, going my way. I stood unconscious of my pack, watching until he crossed the mouth of the canyon and waddled off. I was unarmed. The far view, which gave me a chance to avoid a grizzly, was my only protection.

As the hours passed I began to wonder anxiously if I could have overlooked a ridge leading right. Then I came to it. I was tired but the ridge was such a paradise that it nullified fatigue. For one thing, it was flat and hard, paved with the shale of eons. I appreciated that footing after the rough tundra and mountainsides. But its glory was flowers. They were in flat clumps of color, blue, rose, yellow, white. The forget-me-nots were denser and tighter to the ground than any others I had ever seen. Actually I was deadly tired, but I had a kind of enchanted feeling as I picked my steps among the patches along that endless ridge.

At the far end of it I had some worried minutes. I could not find Cris's cache. I climbed up and down and at last blundered onto it. In a damp black niche, brisk and improbable, stood red and white cans of butter, powdered eggs and powdered milk.

The next day I had an odd, solitary adventure. In the morning Cris and I together carried packs to the site of Camp Two. On returning to Camp One for our final night there, we found we had packed all the food ahead, except a starvation supper and breakfast for one person. One of us ought to fall clear back to base camp. There was no question which it would be. Big bulls were passing Camp Two and Cris wanted to get back there early in the morning.

I was still soft. The day's trip had drained me to healthy exhaustion. Now I prepared to go beyond my strength. I collapsed purposefully on the sand for a few minutes—in the sun, for the wind was cold—and accepted two of the four prunes that were here. Then I shouldered my packboard and set out for Noluk, taking along all of Cris's exposed film to date to leave there. Every roll of film we could free ourselves of lightened our load for crossing the mountains. Ounces count in backpacking.

A few hours later I was nearing the lake but still hidden from it by the high ridge we called Noluk Mountain when I heard a noise that stopped my heart. A plane was behind the ridge, over base camp. Had Tommy come this soon to remove our camp? If so, I was in a predicament. The nearest sleeping bag was at Camp One and the nearest food was hours of walking beyond that, at Camp Two. Of course Tommy might be landing, not taking off. But it was useless to run to try to intercept him. I had a mile to go yet.

A Cessna flew into sight. I tore off my pack and parka and ran stumbling over the hummocks, whirling the parka above my head. The plane flew levelly away toward the south without even a wing dip of recognition. I was unseen. I stood still. A yell of frustration burst from me. The unforeseen noise brought me to self-consciousness. "Scare every caribou in half a mile," I thought sheepishly. I shouldered my packboard and trudged on. It was useless to worry about camp until I rounded the side of the ridge and saw whether it was there or not. Besides, I was preoccupied with that uninhibited yell. Ripping through layers of lifelong "niceness," it had given me a kind of organic surprise.

I contoured in shadow around the edge of the ridge. Ahead in sunlight stood a speck in vastness, our little old tent beside the frozen lake.

The next morning I awoke in white fog. In case Cris too was socked in I carried a pack of food back to Camp One. I emerged from fog as I neared it. The sand was bare in the sunshine, except for a neatly rolled pack standing ready for me to take on to Camp Two.

I would not abandon the food I had brought. I roped both packs to my board, sat down and slipped my arms into the shoulder straps, rolled over onto hands and knees and staggered to my feet. A strap broke as it took the weight. I mended it, shouldered the pack again, and, bending forward to balance the weight, made as good time as usual to Camp Two.

Or rather, to where I supposed it would be. The cache was gone. There was not a trace or sign of human passage on the mountains. Go left or right or up or down? Without setting off my pack I prowled uncertainly. Coming around the end of the ridge, I saw ahead, on a shelf among gray boulders and dryas flowers, the prettiest little camp you could imagine. Cris had the tent pitched taut and trim at the foot of a steep snowfield, overlooking a tundra valley encircled by the Range.

He met me beside the tent. An unexpected feeling took charge of me—pure peevishness. For two days I had done something not often truly accomplished—gone beyond my strength. I sat leaning against my pack without taking it off, to rest a minute before starting supper. Cris's eyes looked tired but gay—his day, too, had been hard. He slipped away and returned, holding his hands cupped.

"Make a big hand," he commanded, smiling. "Both hands!" He opened his and into mine showered iridescent and smoky and double pointed crystals. "Crown jewels!" he said, pleased. "Tomorrow I'll take you up where I got them and you can pick yourself out all you want."

Irresistibly I giggled. In spite of my best efforts, my peevishness leaked through my fingers. Rocks to backpack across the Range! That was all I needed.

After supper Cris added the following works to those of his day. First he ascended the little peak above the snowfield to scan the country for caribou. He came back for his camera and started off along the ridge; he had seen a band coming. "They're going to climb that draw at the far end of the ridge and come down over the snow cornice there."

I looked at him in wonder. How did he know which way they would come? Their easiest way would be to circle the base of the ridge, as other bands had done. I dragged after him for a mile, then lay watching. He went on and set up his camera in a dark evening shadow, the only cover there was.

Sure enough the caribou were coming as he had predicted, at first mere sunlit dots far off in the sunlit tan valley below but keeping close to the foot of the mountains. I could hardly spot them with field glasses. Cris had observed them with the naked eye. They deserted the easy way, disappeared while they climbed the draw, then came into sight on the skyline above the snow cornice. They hesitated along it, looking for a way down, then lunged over the brink and wallowed downward. Cris filmed them.

There was something big about the way Cris spent himself. Never bothering to put it in words, he understood you paid for things. What he wanted was big—"I'd like our life to be big and gracious and free," he said once. He paid the same way, magnanimously. He never thought the universe was niggardly or unresponsive. He gave freely of what he had, his strength to work, regardless of whether any return seemed possible. It was his pact with the universe.

When he took me to the crystal ridge, I had a holiday from backpacking: I carried only a knapsack with lunch and wraps. It was to be a day of wonder and disappointment.

I was taking stills of flowers blooming among the crystals when Cris stepped to me and said quietly, "I feel as if I had an appointment and if I rushed I could keep it."

I had seen too much of Cris's hunches about where animals were going to be to disregard this one. I rose at once. Timing is of the essence in a hunch. It is a cogent but diaphanous thing; if you quell its faint impulse you need never try to follow it out somewhat later. It won't work. But if you obey, you sense the timing: "Go a little faster. Not so fast. Steady."

Cris led where he had never been before as if he had a map of his destination. I followed him along a sharp cleaver of black-lichened rocks, some of them kicked tan by recent caribou hoofs. Nothing deterred me from pure enjoyment of easy going except cutting my rubber shoepacks on the sharp rocks. They were the only shoes I had to see me across the Range. I didn't want to wind up a few weeks hence with the soles roped to my feet.

Cris hesitated at a faint, zigzag caribou trail dropping down the side of the ridge; impulsively he followed it. It led us into the pleasantest little valley we had yet come to in the Arctic. Grassy, no hummocks, like a pasture of home except for the sponge of yellow moss under the greening grass. And away through the pass at the head of it coursed a startled wolf, going so fast you could hardly make him out.

Beyond the pleasant meadow we climbed another ridge and at its top paused in wonder. We were in a place we never saw except on this one day, but we could never forget it. We called it the Wolf Walk. It was a cleaver along whose crest ran a trail made not by humans—no human trails were in all this land—but by paws of wolves and hoofs of caribou. It was propped up oddly in places by two-foot slabs of rock. Along it lay white crunched caribou bones and bone-cluttered wolf scats.

When did caribou walk this trail? "How would you like to be up here at forty below and the wind blowing?" Cris speculated.

Wide and far on either side, before and behind us, spread the arctic land, unlike anything else we had ever seen. Cones, ridges, rounded rock outcroppings rose dark from the tan tundra below. All smooth-looking, all rounded. "Bland!" I thought in surprise. "That's the word for the Arctic." But the blandness was eerie, for it was one face of danger; one never quite forgot winter.

But we had wasted time. Now we jogged rapidly along the Wolf Walk. A storm was overtaking us. At the north end of the cleaver—a lower cleaver was ahead across a gulch—we stood still under the eave of a cloud breeding rain. Out ahead, twenty miles away, cumulus clouds floored with azure piled remote and calm over sunny lands.

"There they are!" Cris said quietly. "That's what I hurried up here for. And we're too late, it's too dark for color." The light was storm-darkened to f 2.

We watched but Cris never rolled a foot of film. Below us in the dark light on the wild land moved two bands of caribou, about a hundred in each. One band was already ascending the side of the ridge we had come down, beyond the meadow, weaving in files among the dark rock outcroppings.

The other caribou were just entering upon trails freshly dusted by the first band, and these trails laced the steep, impossible face of the lower ridge ahead of us. Cris spoke quietly.

"If we had been ten minutes sooner we'd have caught that first band moving on those trails and it would still have been sunlight."

I stood, feeling wretched. Cris spoke again and there was pleasure in his voice. I looked at him. The pleasure was real. "Aren't they beautiful!" he said. "They're a wonderful animal." He had cast away the moldy nut of failure and was reaching for good cheer as for good fruit.

There was the smell of rain on dry earth. We got into our old feather-weight, knee-length parkas—we cherished this apt equipment—as if in little tents and sat out the rain on rock slabs.

Cris eyed the slabs. He got a rock for maul, a rock for wedge and split rock boards, four feet long. "Wouldn't we have a camp, though, if these were near enough!"

The sun warmed honey-clover sweetness from all the white dots of candytuft bobbing on the bare rocks. We speeded back toward camp. Nearing it a few hours later we found ourselves suddenly in one of nature's wild, "personal-impersonal" moments.

We were hurrying along a ridge ahead of another rainstorm. The sun shone level in our faces over black mountains ahead. We glanced back to see if we could make it to camp without putting on rain parkas again, and stopped in our tracks.

Almost on our heels stood one leg of a wide, soft, intensely glowing rainbow; it had the deeper iris of mountain rainbows seen against darkness. The arch sprang low over the abyss beside us. Through it showed dimly the dark storm sky and darker peaks.

At camp Cris dived into the tent as the rain hit. I had donned my parka. It streamed with water as I gathered food and stove and thrust them through the door to Cris. Wet-faced and laughing, I followed. That is one of the world's unique pleasures—to lick a storm and make your bed warm in the teeth of the Great Powers.

Cris had rolled the down sleeping bag against the wall. Safe in the five-gallon Blazo can we had brought as windbreak for it sat the one-burner stove, boiling the lima beans I had started at breakfast that morning. Lima beans are my favorite backpacking dinner because they fill you up, yet you don't feel guilty about using up a lot of backpacked weight. We had crisp dried raw onion shreds and, for dessert, tea and walnuts. It was a good meal.

Afterward Cris leaned back against the roll of down and bragged with a straight face. "If I had five years' practice I could keep up with the caribou. I can keep up with them now, but I have to walk twice as far as they do because I have to come to camp to eat and sleep."

This was "cosmic gaiety." Not plain bragging but a special kind of wilderness bragging. The mountain men of the old West must have done it often. You get tired of smallness and hard work. You crave power as you crave a drink of water. Then some exultation of well-being and wild power around you, the great power of wilderness, catches you; you break into cosmic gaiety, pretend you control the uncontrollable. You defy the Great Powers and don't even need words to do so. In the tense gray air on a mountain ridge, as a thunderstorm strides toward you over the plains below, you can catch hands and run laughing as far from your rock over-hang as you dare. Farther. Unnoticed mice defying a cosmic Cat. Then flee for the rock and under it as lightning hits and thunder crashes like surf overhead.

The mists now were pulling off the black mountains against the north sun. It was eleven P.M. but the impression was invincible that it was seven of a fine June day.

Cris sunburned in bed that night.

I felt a faint tension about Cris on the days when I relayed and he camera-hunted alone. He would be unfindable if hurt. So I feared.

As I crossed the last ridge into sight of camp one evening and saw a black pencil stub far off on tawny tundra, Cris on his way to camp, I was glad. I had snow melted and supper started when I heard him say hello. I looked around from where I knelt by the stove, on a folded tarp to keep my knees dry. He waved gaily but I saw he was tired: it costs an effort to raise an arm when one's shoulders are bound by the straps of a heavy pack. As usual he carried camera and tripod over his shoulder.

I restrained myself from jumping at him with the main question, any pictures? He sat down in front of the tent, took off shoepacks and socks and asked what I had seen—two bands of bulls, as usual going westward. Then I inquired delicately, "Did you see anything?"

He grinned. "Yes, I got some pretty good pictures. But I walked for them."

We stood at the edge of the drop-off and on the map of the grand terrain, with the aid of field glasses, he showed me his course, confirming my belief that it would be futile to search for him if he ever failed to return. Around us in black shadow and sunlight marched twenty-three nameless peaks of the Range. Rock outcroppings and tundra valley rolled at their feet. One black dip on the skyline was the pass where next our camp would stand.

After supper Cris told me about his day's nugget.

"I set down my tripod and lay down at a creek to drink. When I raised myself I was kinda startled. A band of bulls was running straight down the hill toward me. Then I thought they were thirsty, traveling and no water, like cattle kept away from water on a hot day—forgetting they depended on snow.

"Instead of coming to the creek they stopped when they got to the foot-high willows along it and began nipping off pussywillows. Those pussywillows were what they were all after and what they all started eating. They didn't stand and eat on one bush at that. A nibble here and a nibble there, meanwhile walking on up the creek."

It sounded like a humble item to add to our growing hoard of caribou information but it had greatness in it. Invisible but beautiful as a fine equation is the interstructuring of the ways of these arctic deer and the fragile arctic flora.

"I think caribou must be the most considerate boarders nature ever set a table for," Cris concluded.

My days were monotonous—there is no monotony like that of toiling a step at a time with a load over vast treeless land where you can actually see your goal hours ahead of you. But daily there was some new kind of flower in bloom, once the small wonder I never forgot, of knee-high plants in bud in the shelter of the very crest of a pass in this high land where most plant life crouched low.

I had fun with the caribou. I supposed this was how it was on the tundra—you always found bands of bulls going westward. In a band of say a dozen big bulls there would be a couple of year-old fawns. These fawns amused me. When the band lay down, the fawns lay heads high, calm and stately like the big bulls.

More and more "teen-agers" were coming along with the bands of bulls and a custom of theirs amused me too. The big bulls would run from me, but always they paused for that one more look back at what had scared them. It is the famous "caribou vacillation." The teen-agers instantly seized this chance to hurry back toward me and stand watching me intently. Was I the first of my deadly species they had seen in their young travels? Never could they quite satisfy their curiosity. When the big bulls turned to flee, follow they must; they dared not linger.

It gave me a scary amusement when I broke over a ridge and found a band of bulls right below me. They vacillated and veered, generating what Quakers call "the sense of the meeting" about how best to save themselves from my small silent figure. Then they lined out and ran, hoofs thudding, long noses lifted level with backs so that the great antlers sank to their shoulders. The palms of the re-curves floated over their heads like helicopter rotors.

It is quite possible that the most beautiful antlers in the world are the antlers of a bull caribou in black velvet. The velvet sometimes is tawny but it is black that is dramatic. The antlers of a feeding bull soar in a steep black V across his white chest, its tip to the tundra, palms spreading wide above his head. In spite of the re-curve, the antlers ascend higher above the bull than his legs go down below, provided he stands ankle-deep in grass.

I observed details. Cris noted something else. Almost absently one evening he brought it forth, a generalization. "About five or six hundred caribou a day, mostly bulls, have been going west and northwest on a ten-mile front for a week now."

I realized this was true. We were in the midst of some great movement of the caribou.

BELLE HERBERT

Belle Herbert was born sometime in the 1850s in the Gwich'in Atha-paskan village of Chalkyitsik, fifty miles east of Fort Yukon. At the time of her death in 1982, she was the oldest living citizen of Alaska, having lived through much of the state's recorded history. Belle Herbert's words were recorded and edited by Bill Pfisterer, assisted by Alice Moses. The text was translated by Katherine Peter, and the English text was edited by Jane McGary.

Skin-Tanning, Rabbit-Snaring, and Old-Time Cooking
Aii ch'adhaa giitii shrigwilik giyahtthaii
aiitł'ee t'ee ch'anghwaa haa zhrii.
Ch'agahdzii kwaa shrii choo kwaa
    nats'aa dee.
Ch'anghwah haa
jyaa digii'in ts'a' vadzaih dhaa
aii zhyaa jeiinchy'aa dazhoo ts'a'
giyahkii.
Shant'ee googaa dazhoo ałkhii
    t'oonchy'aa roo.
Kwat jyaa digii'in aiits'a' shrii choo goodlit
    gwats'an t'ee ch'adhaa tr'ahdzii ts'a'
jyaa ree digwii'in
ts'a' vitii googaa chan ree jyaa daragwah'in
    haa vitįį tthak shririgwilii roo.
Gwehkįį t'ee ch'angwal ree
nehtthaa tr'ahtsii aii zhrii.

Akwat ts'a'
jidii shrii
varahnyaa ree izhik gwanaa gwanlįį.
Deeddhoo gwich'in t'agahnyaa.
Khagayahtrak ts'a' it'ee ree ch'anghwah
    tsal oo'ok giyahtan ts'a' ree
jyaa digiyah'in.

Aii t'ee
ch'ookwat zhee googaa tr'ookwat
ch'adhah.
Ch'ookwat zhee goodlit gwats'an.
Aaa! shitseii gwintł'oo
ch'adhaa
ich'idiidhan aii t'arahnyaa.
Dazhoo
thal dazhoo ik haa
t'agąąhchy'aa roo
nivyaa chan.
Gwintł'oo niivyaa nitsii t'agahnyaa.
Aii tthak dazhoo nilįį tthak giyahkhii ree.
Łi'haa zhehk'aa gwintsii roo.
Geetak hee jyaa
dagwąhtsii lęįį nąįį googaa nihk'ehdak
    googaa tr'igwich'įį t'oonchy'aa roo.
Zhyaa łyaa gwintsal t'igwinyaa
gwiindhan dǫhlįį.
Zhyaa ree zhehk'aa gwachoo ree zhyaa
    changoo'ee.
Akoo
geetak hee vits'ii tr'igwich'įį kwaa oodit
    k'iinii jyaa dinchy'aa
dazhoo
kak jii kwaii zhyaa t'agąąhchy'aa ooduk
    ohts'ąįį.
Dachan
tik jyaa digilik giik'at zhaatak ts'a'
aii vitih ree yeedee k'iidak ree
khagwiin'ee k'iidak ree
lat haa ree jyaa dii'in.
Oondaa vatł'an
nihts'įį dachan diin'ee vit'įį gwa'an ch'iilkit
jeiinchy'aa.

Aiits'a'
jii dachan
ts'ii
vii nitsii
aii gwintsal ehdee jyaa doonchy'aa ts'a' ree
dzaa gwatł'an ree gwaak'a'.
Akwat shitseii
izhik hee t'ee
oodak
dich'intł'ii nąįį
aii nąįį chan
tl'eevi' gahtsii roo.
Tł'eevi' gahtsii
aii
aaa! shitseii gwintł'oo
tł'eevi' gahtsii
vakwai' khehłee ach'ahochaa ts'a' k'iizhak
   neets'aii khaiinji' adach'aadhat aii oo'ęę
   neegaazhik.
Giitsin tthak khagwilik tł'ęę
gał tsal haa deedoogiyiitsak tł'ęę oondaa luu
jyaa digilik
zhak a'ee ts'a' jyaa digiyilik.
Aiits'a' giik'at neeluutak ts'a' giikak
   neegwaahtłak.
Ninghuk kwaa kheet'eegivaatthak ts'a'
luu ghat nizįį giyahtsik tł'ęę traa
kak deegiyahchik ts'a' giidhaa
   giyeełeehahchaa.
Akwat zhyaa
geh dhivir gwich'in t'oo
ak'ii hee zhyaa ree neethaagahtłii.
Aaa! shitseii gwintł'oo aakin ch'igwiidlii
   dinjii gwiindaii jaghaii.
Aiits'a' t'ee gwiteegiyahtsit.

Akwat ts'a'
kharil'aii ts'a' gwilii tr'adal kwaa ts'a'
vadzaih gwanlįį dąį' chan viki' neets'aii
　　yeendaa gwaak'a gwinyaa hee ree
　　neets'aii.
Joł gahtsit
aii
k'eiich'ii yeendaandaa hee tanch'igįįł'ee
lihts'eeradąąhdaa.
Aaa! zhyaa ree vikeedhich'ii zu' dhaa zhyaa
　　ree nji' neegaadal roo.

Old-Time Household Furnishings and the Coming of Cloth; Muskrat Hunting and the Coming of Guns

Ąąhą'
vadzaih dhaa khaii
gizhiłchųų aii zhyaa vaghai' khajii ts'a'
　　ditr'uu
ditsuu zhyaa vakak haa'ee veelin zhyaa
　　tthak
lihts'eehotthak
aii zhit giłchųų t'oonchy'aa.
Jyaa gwizhrii goo'ąįį.
Veegogwantrii naii geh dhaa ahotl'ii
aii chan khajii dąį ree
khehłaa t'inchy'aa kwaa t'inchy'aa.
Aii k'it t'inch'ii tsal haa zhrii aii ree
　　kak digilzhii.
Vit'ee chyaa ts'a' oozhak iltsuu ah kak
jyaa gwizhrii.
Tsuu chan googaa kwaa.
Dagogwach'aa tlik
aii digikįį giłtsuu gwizhrii.
Jeiinchy'aa
vakwai' vitsįį . . .
jyaa dinchy'aa ts'a' gilchuu.

Shandaa t'arah'in aii gwach'aa googaa
  kwaii haa tthak nał'yą' eegįįhkhii
t'iihnyaa.

Aaa!
łyaa lagwadoo
kwaa t'igwinyaa.
Akwat it'ee ihtsii gwiizhik at'oohju' hee ree
  geetak ree
Inglis ts'an ik
naraatsuu gwaał'in.
Ch'eetak nąįį zhrii.
Geetak chan k'ooneiit'aii ki'
narooljik nał'in jyaa
gwizhrįį.
Ninghit kwaa gwanaa gwats'an
yeeduk ts'ąįį vaanoodlit
nąįį zhik gwa'an Dawson,
Circle,
yeedit
Neets'it Gwich'in nahkak gwats'an tik ts'a'
  ch'aragwah'ąįį, gwats'an steamboat
  goodlit
ts'a' at'oohju' hee jeiinch'ii kwat goodlit
  t'oonchy'aa.

Izhik gwanaa googaa
zheegwadhah tr'iilee iltsąįį gwanłįį kwaa.
Ik tr'iilee iltsąįį gwanlįį kwaa
zhyaa jyaa t'inch'ii ky'oot'aii
akwat ts'a'
zheegwadhaa tr'ahahtsyaa
daagąįį
aii ch'aghwah
aii chan goodlit
k'iighai' dinjii

jyaa shandaa
digwiizhik t'oonchy'aa.
Aaa! shitseii, neeshreegwąąhchy'a'
t'oonchy'aa
neeshreegwaahchy'a' t'oonchy'aa.
Mahsį' gwinyaa ts'ąįį gwinzįį t'oonchy'aa.
Duuyee dachan zhee chan ree gaagwiindaii
    kwaa nats'aa.

Aii t'agwaihnyaa
laraa kwaii aragwah'ąįį k'iighai' vaanoodlit
    nąįį goodlit t'oonchy'aa.
Aii gwik'iighai' t'ee zhyaa jyaa digwii'in
    chan gik'iranjik t'oonchy'aa.
Łi'haa
hee gwanaa
aii vijuu gwanaa hee
chan dzan
khyąą haa dzan keerii'in gik'igwanjik
    t'oonchy'aa roo.
Akǫǫ aii jyahts'a' digwii'in k'iighai'
nan kak tthak chan zhyaa ree dzan
    keerii'in nagwaanąįį t'oonchy'aa.
Jidii ghoo tsal diky'aatł'įį haa
zhyaa van vęę hee jyaa digii'in.

Aii
van
dzan tr'ihiltaii hee goghoh gwanłįį nahąą.
Aii ihtreech'aratthak vats'a' ahtr'aii
    k'it t'injik
it'ee dzan tr'ihiltąįį.

Aaa!
shitseii jyaa darah'in
gohch'it dee tan tr'igok.
Oodok ts'iivii

kharikyaa
jyaa dąhjyaa tr'ahtsii ts'a' aii
jidii k'aii ch'ilsaii haa oondak
vatąįį neechiridiitthak.
Yi'eendaa chan it'ee łyaa tr'ihiltąįį
   vik'igwaandak.

Aiits'a't'ee
nihts'ąą
dachan jyaa darah'in
ts'a' k'iinaa tr'ihiltąįį gwizhrii ts'a'
dzan ah chan.
Aii deetły'ah
jyaa dąhtsii
aiits'a' aii ahotł'ii jyaa dahjyaa
dzaa hee vadąįį.

Akwat ts'a'
k'iinaa tr'ihiltąįį oondee
k'aii gwiniriitthak
akwat ts'a'
dzaa ree dzan aa chiheechyaa.
Dzaa chan k'aii gwiniriitthak akwat ts'a'
   t'ee dzan aa chirichik.
Zhik k'aii it'ee ree dzaa tr'ahaghal
k'aii ree jyaa dii'in.

Akwat ts'a'
it'ee dzan aa zhihak ts'a'
yeenjit chan jyaa dii'in jyaa dirlik
deiinchy'aa
vizhit ree dzan dhidii.
Jyaa darah'in ts'a' dzan lęįį kharilii.
Jyahts'a' gwizhrįį giyunkee'in t'inchy'aa.

Akwat ts'a'
shin hee duuyee.

Jidii haa t'igiihah'yaa gǫǫ aii chan k'i' haa
giyaahkhok gwizhrįį
jyaa dinchy'aa t'inchy'aa.
Dats'an googaa tthak k'i' haa zhrii.
Twenty-two chan kwaa dink'ee kwaa
    t'oonchy'aa nats'aa.
Ch'antsįh dink'ee giyahnyaa
ree shandaa goodlit.
Forty-four chan
aii haa neekwąįį ree shandaa goodlit
    t'oonchy'aa.
Gwanlii gwats'an ihlįį.
Akwat ts'a' it'ee dink'ee goodlit.

The Arrival of White People

Yeedit Koyukuk gwinyaa it'ee
    gaakhwandaii
izhik ch'aragwah'ąįį izhik it'ee shigii
    neehidik t'oonchy'aa.

Akwat ts'a'
vaanoodlit zhyaa
Yukon di' zhyaa tly'aa ch'aganąąht'aii.
Izhik
gwitsįį googaa vaanoodlit
gwanlįį kwaa t'agwaihnyaa.
It'ee izhik
zhat kwat ts'a' yeenjit Dawson
Circle haa ch'aragwah'ąįį ginyaa izhik
    gwehkii hee vaanoodlit dǫhłii.
Gwee'an aii akwaa jeiinchy'aa googaa
    kwaa t'iihnyaa.
Yeedit
ts'aii ch'arągwah'ąįį aii chan k'iidi'
tly'aa ch'aranaaht'aii.
Geetak hee chan vaa neerahąąhtr'il haa.
Geetak hee chan ganiisak

vakwaiitryaa kwaa ts'a'
ganiisak
dakwai' k'oołchaa haa.
Jidii vaa neerahąątr'il
chan ch'eeghwaa kwaa chan ree jeiinchy'aa
    valaii chan ree zhyaa
neehaahtr'il chan ree tąįį gwinjik di' ahaa
    ree tr'agwąąh'in.

Akwat ts'a' aiitł'ee
gwiizhik it'ee steamboat goodlit roo.
Aii ree yeenji' nahkak geenjit t'ii'in akwat
    łąą dzat gwee'an chan store gwakwaa
    kwat
t'ee nats' aa k'eiich'ii kwaii gwiheelyaa gǫǫ.
Akwat it'ee ree
store gwakwaa akwat ree
zhyaa ree steamboat zhrii ree.
Akwat ts'at gohch'it ree
zhyaa ree ch'ookwat zhee gwiltsąįį.

Akwat
yeedit Koyukuk ch'aragwąh'ąįį
ts'a' izhik ree tł'ee ree oonduk nahkak
dinjii li'haa laraa
choo zhya di'įį aii ree.
Aii ree
dinjii vitsyaa yinlįį chan
nivee t'ah'in tr'injaa choo chan gavaa.
Captain Ray ree.
Aii ree zhat indi'.
Izhik it'ee ch'ookwat zhee gwiltsąįį.

Izhik
yeendok khaiinjii dinjii teech'ehdli'
yeenii tr'iindii
ch'adąį' jihnyaa ijii

izhik aii gwats'at t'ee store goodlit
t'oonchy'aa.
Yeedit N. C. ree t'igwiizhik gwich'in gaa
tth'aii hee chan
gohch'it t'ee shin shaaghwąįį k'iindaa
tth'aii hee store gwanlįį roo.
Akwat ts'a' store ch'ihłak zhrii ree gwanlįį.
Akwat aii steamboat t'ii'in aii kwaii haa
zhyaa ree
shih lęįį teeraadlii dǫhłii.
Aak'ii łąįį choo haa
zhyaa jyaa digwiizhik aii geedan.

Akwat ts'a'
it'ee ree geelee heedyaa it'ee aak'ii
tr'inghan t'ee.
Aii łąįį choo aii geełee giihaadlii gwats'an
vijuu gwanaa hee chan łąįį choo k'ąąhtii
ree gwanlįį aii nik'ee giky'aanjik.
Ąąha' izhik gwats'an t'ee t'iginchy'aa
t'inchy'aa.
Akwat ts'a' aii aak'ii aii ginghan roo.
Akwat ts'a' aii
Captain Ray vaihnyaa aii
zhik store
shih lęįį steamboat k'ilik
zhat t'iheechy'aa ts'a'
zhyaa teeragoodlii aii kwan dinjii
dzat nirinlii aii nąįį tthak gokwaa
t'oonchy'aa.
Oonjuk gwich'in nąįį łyaa
aiits'a' zhyaa tthak nigiinjik t'iginchy'aa.

Ąąha'
Gwichyaa Zhee izhik.
Izhik zhyaa yi'eendaa zhyaa

tąįh choo nin'ee chy'aa zhyaa tthak
  vihtł'eech'ąąhtlik.
Aaa! shitseii
gwintł'oo neeshreegwąąhchy'aa
  naagwaah'ąį' neenjik zhyaa vaanoodlit
  goodlit t'oonchy'aa.
Aii googaa
łąą dinjii kwaa ts'a'
gohch'it zhyaa gweendaa shriit'agwąhtsii
  ree
yeeduk hee ree gaanigwigwii'aii roo.
Akwat jyaa
doonchy'aa t'oonchy'aa.
Zhyaa nehshrit zhyaa vaanoodlit nąįį
  goodlit t'oonchy'aa.

Skin-Tanning, Rabbit Snaring, and Old-Time Cooking

They cleaned the flesh side of the skin
  with a bone scraper, and after that just with an iron scraper.
They didn't scrape it with a knife — they
  didn't have one.
With an iron scraper
they did it, and they tanned
the caribou skin
just as it was, fur and all.
Even I myself have tanned hides with the
  fur on that way.
Now, since we have had big knives, we
  scrape the flesh side
in that way,
we take the dark layer off and make it
  real clean.
Before that they used to use
a bone flesher to clean the skin.

At that time
they had a knife

made like this.
They called this skin scraper a *deeddhoo*.
They cut the hair off the skin, then put it
    outside to freeze,
then they used the iron scraper on it.
Later
we even bought skins
at the store.
Since the store was established.
Ah! grandchild, it was very easy
to work on a skin
with those tools.
Fur
pants and fur parkas
were all they used, and
also skin tents.
They mean a really big skin tent.
All of that was fur, and they tanned it all.
The household was very big.
Sometimes
it was so big that several families lived in
    it, one here, another there.
I'll bet you think
it was really small.
But actually it was big enough for a
    family, with an entrance to the outside.
And then
sometimes there was another house opposite,
    and sometimes not.
The fur
side they put on the outside of
    the tent.
They put three
sticks, and over them they put snow, and
up at its peak
there was an opening
through which the smoke went.

Out in the middle
two logs lay side by side, with a fireplace between them and
stakes pounded behind them this way.

And then
in between
those
big logs
there was a little space, and
here in the middle they built the fire.
Well, grandchild,
in those days
people who snared rabbits,
they
caught them by the foot.
They caught them by the foot,
and,
ah! grandchild, they just
hung there by one foot up in the air, and
    they really suffered a lot when people
used that kind of snare.
After they cleaned the guts out,
they trussed it up with sticks, and then
put it under the ashes,
lying on its back.
And then they covered it with dirt and
    started a fire on top of it.
After a little while they took it out, and
after they dusted off the ashes,
they threw it on a log and peeled off
    the skin.

And then
the rabbit was as white as if it were
    boiled,
when they tore the skin off.

Ah! grandchild, how interesting it is, the
    way people used to live, isn't it?
And then they gave part of it to everyone.

And then
sometimes we spit-roasted meat
when there was a lot of caribou, turning
    each side now and again to the fire.
They made a roasting stick
and
thrust it through the meat
and roasted it before the fire.
Ah! when it was cooked they took it off
    and ate it, nice and warm.

Old-Time Household Furnishings and the Coming of Cloth; Muskrat Hunting and the Coming of Guns

Yes,
in the winter they slept
on caribou skins so worn the hair was
    falling off them,
there was just a little hair on them around
    the edges,
and in patches,
and that was what they slept in.
That's the way it was.
People who had hard times wove rabbit
    skins together;
when those lose their hair,
they are no good at all.
They would cover themselves with things
    like those.
On the floor they spread skins on a
    mat of spruce boughs,
that's all they had.
There wasn't even a pillow.
They bundled up their old clothes

and used that for a pillow.
Just like that,
in their skin pants with feet attached,
was the way they slept.
I'm talking about things that happened
    during my lifetime, I've seen these
    clothes and things.

Ah!
there was not any
cloth then.
After I grew up, I sometimes saw
people wearing
clothes they got from the Canadians.
Only some people.
Sometimes I saw women
wearing kerchiefs on their heads,
that's all.
Not very long ago
white people struck gold over on that side,
around Dawson
and in Circle
down in
Neets'it Gwich'in territory, and
    from then on the steamboat started,
and that's when trade goods started
    to come in.

Even at that time
there were no ready-made tents.
There were no ready-made dresses,
only lengths of material,
and then material for tents,
white,
in a bolt;
that also first came
because of those men;

during my lifetime
it happened.
Ah! grandchild, we were poor,
that's so,
we were really poor.
So we should say thank you now.
We didn't even know about log cabins.

But as I said,
they struck gold, and so the white people
    came.
That was how we learned about those
    things.
Really
not long ago,
just recently,
we also learned
about trapping for muskrats.
So we started to do that,
everybody in the country started to
    trap for muskrats.
There was a round thing tied to a pole,
and they went around the lakeshore with
    that.

In that
lake
were muskrat tunnels—you know by the
    bubbles.
They cast the pole at them, and the wind
    carried it
to where the tunnel was.

Ah!
grandchild, that's what we did;
finally we poked through the ice.
In the woods we cut

spruce poles,
we made them this long, and
there was a bend at one end with which
we poked down into the channel.
Then we knew for sure where it came out.

Then
we put the poles
close together on each side,
and where it came out,
we also used the muskrat dipnet.
That dipnet
was about so big,
woven like a fishnet, about so long,
and it went into the channel.

Then
at the outlet of the channel
they poked two sticks
and then
the muskrat net was tied to them.
They poked two willow sticks down there
    and put the net in the water between
them.
The willow stick shook a little here,
since it was made of flexible willow.

Then,
when the rat went into it,
we would pull it out,
and there it was
with the muskrat sitting in it.
We took a lot of muskrat out that way.
This was the only way we hunted them.

But
not in the summertime.

How else could they hunt them — sometimes
they killed them with arrows,
but that's all.
Even ducks were only killed with arrows.
There were no twenty-twos or rifles then.
What they called a nose gun,
that first came during my lifetime.
And the forty-four,
those two first came during my lifetime.
I was alive at that time.
So then there began to be guns.

The Arrival of White People
Down there at Koyukuk, the very first time
they struck gold there, my child was
    walking then.

And
the white people
strung down the Yukon one after another.
After that
there were
no white people, however.
From then on,
when they struck gold at Dawson
and Circle, maybe there were white people
    before then.
Not around here, not even one.
When they struck gold down that way,
they just strung out down that way,
    that's all.
Sometimes with skis.
Sometimes just a gunny sack,
he didn't have any moccasins,
and he tied a gunny sack
around his feet to walk with.
Or just with skis,

he just slid along without even any pack
   on his back,
I saw them sliding down the trail like that.

After that
the steamboat started to come around.
The steamboat even started going up that
   way, though there was no store around
   here then;
how could there be any goods around here?
And then
there was no store here,
there was only the steamboat.
But finally
a store was built.

Since
they struck gold down at Koyukuk,
after that somebody from Outside,
a really
rich man just did that.
That
man had someone working for him,
and there was a big soldier woman with
   them.
His name was Captain Ray.
He was there.
That's when the store was built.
That time,
when people almost starved to death
back here,
that time I talked about before,
the store was established down at
   Fort Yukon.
The N. C. [Northern Commercial] Company was downriver there,
   I think, and still is,

now I'm really old and that same store
    is still there.
There was only one store.
And they brought freight with the
    steamboat,
a lot of food, I guess.
There were cows and horses,
they brought those in.

Well,
he was going to leave, so they killed all
    the cows.
They took those horses away somewhere,
    there was a man who took care of them,
    did you hear about that?
Yes, that's when they [the horses] arrived.
And they killed all those cows.
That
Captain Ray I'm talking about, he
built that store
and brought a lot of food with the
    steamboat;
he was going to stay there, and
those people who were going to stay there
all died.
They were Outside people,
and they all died off.

Yes,
in Fort Yukon.
At that time out in the middle of the river
there used to be a big hill and it's all
    worn away now.
Ah, grandchild!
It was very poor at that time, and finally
    little by little the white people came.

Even so
there were not very many people, but
here and there, from time to time,
they sometimes came around.
That's
the way it was.
The white people just came gradually.

EDWARD HOAGLAND

Edward Hoagland was born in 1932 and was educated at Harvard. His collections of essays include *The Courage of Turtles*, *Walking the Dead Diamond River*, *Red Wolves and Black Bears*, *The Tugman's Passage*, *Balancing Acts*, and *Heart's Desire*. He is also the author of four novels and two travel books, *Notes from the Century Before* and *African Calliope: A Journey to the Sudan*, which was nominated for a National Book Critics Circle Award and an American Book Award. A member of the American Academy of Arts and Letters, Mr. Hoagland has taught at Columbia University, Sarah Lawrence College, and the Universities of Iowa and California. He lives in Bennington, Vermont.

Up the Black to Chalkyitsik

Wilderness has a good many meanings. Bitter cold or uncommon danger can make of any patch of the outdoors a "wilderness," but nothing precludes balmy weather from the equation; nor are snakebite and quicksand essential ingredients. My happiest experiences in wilderness landscapes happen to have been in Alaska, and my favorite town there is Fort Yukon, a dot of a place thrown down near the junction of the Yukon and Porcupine rivers, one mile north of the Arctic Circle, eight hundred seventy-five river miles from the Yukon's Canadian headwaters, and a thousand winding miles from its debouchment into the Bering Sea. Canadian traders of the Hudson's Bay Company established the fort in 1847, not so much to protect themselves from the Gwich'in Indians of the region as to fly the flag and fend off the Russian traders operating from a station five hundred miles downstream. (Russians had discovered the mouth of the Yukon in 1834.)

This was the first English-language community in Alaska, but after Alaska was sold by Russia to the United States in 1867 for a price of $7.2 million, the Hudson's Bay Company was forced to move its operations eastward to British territory. Fort Yukon continued to be a fur-buying center under American auspices, however, and then it became a gold-rush way point for the riverboats headed for the Klondike frenzy near Dawson City at the turn of the century, and finally the site of a small radar base after World War II, as well as an administrative sub-hub for six or eight Indian villages in the surrounding fifty or sixty thousand square miles, a huge terrain, abutting the Brooks Range from the south, that is equivalent in size to two Irelands and includes the so-called Yukon Flats, which is an area of forty thousand lakes and one of the richest breeding grounds for waterfowl in the world.

Though the radar base has closed, Fort Yukon (pop. 650) is still fairly busy, a jumping-off point for winter trapping trips and summer jaunts up the Coleen, Chandalar, Christian, Porcupine, Sheenjek, and other pristine rivers that feed this portion of the Yukon. Thirty-year-old flying boxcars roar off the airstrip to bomb forest fires in the outback in July and August, till it sounds like a war zone. Surveyors for the Bureau of Land Management, or the Fish and Wildlife Service, federal and state social workers, construction crews, oil geologists, and health and sanitation experts bunk at the Sourdough Inn while they attempt to carry out various Sisyphean projects. Alaska is the land of the dubious contract, as one gradually discovers, and, besides the more drawn-out scams, is full of white people who are angry about whatever they were doing down in the Lower Forty-eight before they came up here, how long they kept doing it, and who they were doing it with. They lend a frenetic or malcontent air to a mainly Indian village like Fort Yuk (as they sometimes call Fort Yukon when they're in Fairbanks). Other whites, with better intentions, may feel they are being defeated as they struggle against intractable problems like fetal alcohol syndrome and a rising suicide rate and, like the first group, ask the perpetual questions, "Shall we stay in this crazy state?" and "Where are we going on vacation?"

Baja, Belize, Bangkok, or London over the Pole may be where they go, on the high salaries paid. Paris, New York, and Tokyo are about equidistant from Fairbanks by airplane, so one has the feeling one can go anywhere in a matter of hours—to the edge of the earth on the coastal plain of the Arctic Ocean, over the Brooks Range, where polar bears cross scent lines with grizzlies and wolverines, as maybe two hundred thousand caribou sift through; or to the Champs Élysées and Trafalgar Square.

This can be exhilarating but, if you've gone off the deep end over the long lightless winter, demoralizing too; freedom becomes vertigo. Of course, the complicated skies above Fort Yukon aren't really lightless even then. The sun flirts with the horizon, the moon rises, stars spangle the firmament, and the northern lights flicker, shoot up, and glow. You see what you look for—a collapsing conclave of "neo-Indians, salt-and-pepper Indians," as they were described to me by a flipped-out social worker, whose wretched and dangerous job was to take abused children away from violent mothers and drunken fathers; or a lively, self-reliant,

age-old, resilient subsistence society still holding its own with at least
some degree of élan beneath the drumfire of soap-opera television
and do-gooding welfare programs, beer-hall bravura and bathos, and
satellite-powered telephones. At the Sourdough Inn, one tilts back in a
barber's chair at the pay phone to talk to New York. There's a daily mail
plane and other amenities: the Alaska Commercial Company general
store; the community hall, with shower baths and washing machines.
The University of Alaska has put up a million-dollar log building for
extension classes. The town has three churches; a Lions Club for bingo
and Budweiser and a two-dollar cup of moose stew, if you're hungry;
a new little historical museum established in the hope that tourists will
come; a Wycliffe Society Bible translator, putting psalms into Gwich'in
(though English has swamped Gwich'in by now); and Fort Yukon's
federally funded psychologist, who estimates that a fourth of the citi-
zenry shows up every year in her office, which is situated between the
town-owned, tin-walled liquor store and the bootlegger's green plywood house, which opens for business when the liquor store closes.

The river itself, spraddled out with its islands to a width of three miles
at this point, imparts importance to every settlement alongside, and its
armies of salmon—kings, silvers, and chum—churn by invisibly from
July through September, heading for Canada to spawn but at hand for
the netting meanwhile. In the winter, frozen, it's a causeway for sled
dogs, and during the summer, if you camp on its banks, you can lie
at midnight watching a thousand swallows whirl in the wind, and the
giddy sun loop like a rolling lasso along the rim of the forest, while
the town's chained packs of dogs bay jubilantly at each other from several backyards. Although the Bureau of Indian Affairs has built rows of
pastel prefab housing in a newer quarter, many residents prefer to live
in the old log cabins close to the river and venture out in snowtime
to run snare lines and trap lines. Six to ten thousand mink and two or
three thousand marten skins are marketed through Fort Yukon's "A.C."
store in the winter.

I fell in love in Alaska, with the person in charge of tracking tuberculosis all over the state, and therefore have visited Eskimo villages
like Point Hope and Kotzebue and Crooked Creek, Indian villages like
Angoon and Tanana and Sleetmute, Anglo towns like Dillingham and
Tenakee Springs, while she tested and chatted with patients. I've seen

the Copper River, the Susitna River, the Koyukuk River, and the Killik River, hundreds of miles apart, going from south to north. I've barged on the Yukon, summered in Fairbanks, wintered in Anchorage, and twice, when I've been in the north on other business, have dropped in by mail plane with a pack and a tent to walk Fort Yukon's dirt streets — streets refurbished with gravel after an ice jam during spring breakup in May 1982 floated six-foot bergs into town.

If I walk half a mile from the airstrip, I reach Fred Thomas's cabin, and he greets me with emphasis. (Everything he says is with emphasis.) And if it's lunchtime, Charlotte, his wife, will take out some beaver meat to feed us, knowing that, coming straight from the city, I will enjoy that. She is fifty-six, comely, husky, reddish-skinned, smooth-complexioned, aging gracefully, and, in the manner of Indian wives in these villages, does not talk to white strays such as me unless her husband is present, but has many visitors of her own sex and race, with whom she is warmly responsive.

Fred is sixty-four, compact and wiry, built smaller than Charlotte, with a beardless, keen, concentrated, round, predator's face, bristly short hair that is turning white, and a relaxed but peripatetic look. As a family man, he did maintenance work for seventeen years at the radar base in order to raise his six children well, and only trapped and hunted in his spare time, though still managing to average about fifty foxes and two or three wolves a year. But now he has resumed the calling of woodsmanship that he loves.

Fred's mother was a Gwich'in from a band that lived on the upper Porcupine (the Dagoo Gwich'in), and his father, Jacob Thomas, born around 1880 in Wisconsin, had worked on a Mississippi riverboat for a little while before joining the 1898 gold rush. He'd arrived late and mostly trapped mink and moose-hunted in the Klondike for meat to sell to the miners at a dollar a pound to keep things going while his partners dug holes. Nothing panned out for them, but as "Tommy the Mate," Fred's father worked on the Yukon boats for fifteen or twenty years, before settling down to have Fred and six more children and to carve out a life for himself far from other white men.

It was July 1919 in Fort Yukon when Fred's parents put him and most of their belongings in a boat and paddled twenty-five miles up the Porcupine River to the mouth of the Big Black River, and paddled, poled, and lined their laborious way up the midsummer shallows of the Black for two hundred more miles in the course of a month to its Grayling Fork, where they built a trapping camp, which has remained the heart of Fred's own family's activities ever since. They would stay out from August—when they already needed to begin laying in wild foods for the winter—till the following June, when the muskrats, last of the fur animals to lose the lush nap on their coats, finally did so, and the river was high and yet safe enough to travel upon with boats stuffed with furs, dogs, and youngsters.

Fred has a vaguely "Irish" look, which is darkened and blurred with the admixture of Athapascan Indian, so that he reminds me of several of the Cajun trappers I have traveled and camped with in southwestern Louisiana, and like them, he speaks the elided English of someone not so much bilingual as caught between two languages and master of neither. His two sons, however, live within yards of his house and trap and collaborate with him in the old-fashioned way (seen also in Cajun country, or any tribal region I've known) by which an older man becomes simply as strong as the number of his grown sons. And two of his brothers go out from Fort Yukon every fall to trap from cabins of their own on the upper Black. Flying in with the winter's supplies, they don't have to start as early as in the old days.

Fred spent so much time on the Black when he was a boy that he had only three years of schooling, but he is a sophisticated man, nevertheless, partly from watching hundreds of servicemen from all over the United States matriculate through a tour of duty at the little base at the edge of town, and partly because he contracted tuberculosis as a young man. After trying the local boneyard of a hospital and realizing he would die like the other Indians and métis there, he lived for three years alone in a tent to clear his lungs, never spending a night indoors. That, too, frighteningly, was of no avail, and so his father at last, pulling strings as only a white man—even a "squaw man"—could do, persuaded the government to send Fred to a sanatorium in Tucson, Arizona, to recover. So he's seen orange trees, though never an apple tree, he says.

His mother's father, Ab Shaefer, was also a white man, a whaler from Nova Scotia who had jumped ship in the Arctic with three other sailors about two decades prior to the gold rush by pretending to go on a caribou hunt. The ship's officers pursued them and shot one man, but the rest escaped and, it being summertime, passed safely through the Eskimo country of the Arctic Slope and crossed up over the British Mountains, which in the Yukon Territory correspond to the Brooks Range, and then were saved from the terrors of winter in the interior by the Indians at Crow Flats, the Vunta Gwich'in. Anyhow, on his way home from Tucson in 1945, Fred stopped off in Chicago to get acquainted with a few of his Shaefer relatives and saw a big city.

Ab Shaefer and one of his companions had married two sisters at Crow Flats village, near the head of the Porcupine. (The third of these surviving whalers floated down the Porcupine to Gwicha Gwich'in country at the village of Beaver on the Yukon River, thirty miles below Fort Yukon, and married a woman there.) And Shaefer, living at Crow Flats and Old Crow and trapping with his in-laws along the upper Porcupine's tributaries, like the Bell River and the Eagle River, sizable in their own right, which run to the Northwest Territories, went so happily native that he simply ignored the gold rush when it occurred, almost next door; did not participate. Fred has not many memories of Shaefer—except that he said, "Well, I'll be damned!" a lot—but remembers his own surprise, as a small boy visiting with his mother and father at his grandfather's winter camp on the Bell, where some of the vegetation was new to him, when he was sent out of the cabin to get dry firewood and chopped at a leafless tamarack, thinking it was a dead spruce, but found that because tamaracks drop their needles in the fall, it looked dead yet was alive. The other whaler who lived in Old Crow drowned in the currents of the Porcupine around that same year, and Fred last saw Shaefer in 1943, during his own scary siege with TB, when the old man came down the Porcupine on a riverboat to Fort Yukon to change boats and go up the Yukon to Dawson City (in this age before ubiquitous planes) to live in an old-age home.

Now it was Charlotte's father, a Tranji Gwich'in named Henry William, from Chalkyitsik, the one village that exists on the Big Black River, who, Fred told me, was sick. He suggested as we had lunch that we might make a trip of it and bring Henry William some fresh salmon. The Indian Health service doctors at the hospital in Fairbanks had discharged him after an operation for what they'd described as "an intestinal infection." Presumably, he had been sent home to die in familiar surroundings of bowel cancer. In Fairbanks, Henry had got sick of store meat — what he called "meat with no blood in it" — and the doctors and everyone felt that it was a shame he wasn't enjoying his meals these last weeks.

I said sure. A New Yorker born, I come to Alaska's high wilds like Alice diving down her rabbit's hole, and that great city, as I gaze back at it from the Northwest Orient Airlines Boeing, smokes like heartburn personified or a multiple smashup of racing cars. But in a dozen hours I can be smelling wood smoke, tending a supper fire in front of my tent, camped in Fred's yard, or with my friends Beri and Mary Morris (who manage the Alaska Commercial Company store), whose spare cabin lies close by, or else in the Anglican churchyard. Its veteran minister was on sabbatical on the occasion of this visit but had told me before to camp there, to cut down my chances of being robbed. Wilderness buffs sometimes raft or canoe for five or six hundred miles down the Yukon, surviving mazes of rapids and sloughs, though still less than halfway to the river's mouth, and then beach their craft on a sand spit within hooting distance of the Sourdough Inn, make camp on the beach with exultant relief, and rush to tuck in to a huge, candlelit, tablecloth meal and chat long-distance on the telephone, only to return to the spit and find everything gone.

Fort Yukon is full of violence — one of the worst posts to be a state trooper in the whole state — and stories abound of white people who commute to marriages elsewhere, while grinning meanwhile, come dusk, when an Indian mother on welfare shows up at the kitchen door wanting grocery money, beer money — a town of gunfire by night but considerable sweetness by day. I was camped, in fact, on the riverbank inside the fenced yard of another couple, the wife a retired schoolteacher here, the husband the man who installed satellite dishes and suchlike necessities. They may raise the northernmost tomatoes in the United States, and probably the northernmost honeybees. They were out, when I heard a knocking at their door and the voice of an English lady calling them. My tent was up, but my sleeping-bag zipper was stuck, so I went to introduce myself, tell her they were out, and try to persuade her to unstick it for me.

She did, although she exclaimed, "Oh, what an impossible nuisance you are! You're like my son when he goes on a trip with the Scouts.

You've come all the way from New York, and you don't know how to zip your own sleeping bag? I suppose you're a world traveler too — we get those. How do you function?"

"There's always somebody to do it," I said.

In her forties, blond, younger than I, she turned out to be Fred's sister-in-law, Mrs. Johnnie Thomas.

For a novel that I was writing, I had become curious to learn more about Bigfoot, or "Brush Man," as the Gwich'in call the phenomenon, translating from their own word, *Naainn*, for Bigfoot. Sure, Bigfoot had lived in these river valleys, a number of people told me. Some had seen him or knew of circumstantial evidence of his existence. All had heard the stories, as well as others, about an odder, perhaps still more intriguing humanoid wild being: the Little People. These tiny, aggressive, quite talky inhabitants of the taiga and tundra had prodigious strength and cryptic personalities, living mostly underneath the earth and snow but contacting human beings more confidently than Bigfoot. They were self-sufficient, for one thing. They didn't need to steal food from a campsite, as Bigfoot would, and didn't hunger for the companionship of women either, like Bigfoot occasionally. They played quirky and raffish — or sinister and heartless — pranks, yet also were capable, when the spirit moved, of doing a good turn: saving a lone traveler's life or extricating him from great danger, if he pleaded with them. Whenever they proved troublesome, the only way to quiet them was to build bonfires over their burrows, boil pots of water, and threaten to pour that down their holes.

Bigfoot was a kind of howling fugitive, by comparison, an outcast figure apparently in need of fellowship with man at the same time as — glimpsed at the end of a trail or across a frozen lake — he fled from him. So I asked my new English friend, who had already heard about me from Fred, who I should seek out to talk about Bigfoot.

"And *Vanity Fair* magazine in New York City sent you to Fort Yukon to find this stuff out?" She laughed.

"No, *Vanity Fair* is sending me to Anchorage to find out about 'Alaska's Millionaires.' But that gets me to the state, and I come here. Or *House & Garden*, or another one, sends me."

Having fixed my zipper, she felt it improper to chat much longer, saying Fort Yukon wasn't Britain and she hardly ever missed Britain, much less went back. "I'm certain you'll manage. Ask on Front Street and ask Fred and Johnnie."

Front Street, a dirt track alongside the river, is where the row of old-timers' log cabins is—white prospectors', traders', and trappers' cabins at the turn of the century that now belong to their descendants, of mixed race but in solid-looking housing unmessed with by the Bureau of Indian Affairs. In no time, asking along, I met a middle-aged Indian woman, married here but originally from the village of Beaver, whose sister had been abducted by a Bigfoot, she said. All one summer her brother had tracked the two of them through the mountains, hearing the girl's cries receding in front of him wherever he followed, and had never caught up. A very sad thing. On the other hand, as kids they used to go out and shout down a Little People's hole that they knew about—not really afraid, as their parents would have been—for the fun of hearing words come back, she said.

"What words?"

"I forget. But you knew what they meant. Grouchy."

Getting interested, she led me into her house, which was a jumble of river and trapping equipment and furniture and cartons of food, with several kids, and two other women, who had dropped in. Her husband was heavy, paleish, drunk, sixtyish, reclining in the slatted sunlight in a broken easy chair, and unfriendly, assuming I worked for the government or a social agency.

"Why don't *you* go?" he told me, rousing slightly.

"He just wants to know about Brush Man," the lady explained.

"Brush Man!" he said, with a dim smile. "You're talking about olden days—my father's days, my days. My friend fed a Brush Man one time. Is that what you want to hear about?"

"Yes," I said.

"A whole family of them, three babies and the two big ones, came to his fire hungry, in the winter. He was a hundred miles from nowhere, camped in the snow. And he had half a moose left that he had shot, so he let them eat that. Just watched them eat, and they didn't say nuthin to him. Only he said you could tell what they thought without speaking. Why don't you go now?" he repeated.

Back at Fred Thomas's, I asked what *he* thought.

"Sometimes they're a downed airman," he said.

"A Bigfoot is?"

"I don't know. You see what you're looking for. It could be a pilot that's scared shitless, running around in the woods, gone off his rocker, after a crash."

"And how about before there were planes?"

"Well, then it might be an Eskimo," he said. "Or a family of Eskimos."

"Yes? How?"

Fred explained that before the whites arrived and instituted jails and asylums and so forth for crazy people and murderers, they were likely to be expelled from their settlements, or they ran away before they got killed. "And where would they go?" He pointed north toward the handful of Eskimo villages spotted along the Arctic Ocean and Arctic Slope north of the Brooks Range, six hundred miles or more above where we were. "They'd come down here, if they survived. All crazy and shaggy, mumbling Eskimo."

"There was a war on, anyway, with the Eskimos," Charlotte added.

"So he'd stay in the woods and be crazy there? Steal fish, steal food, look at the women from a hiding place?" I asked. This was an explanation, if not an answer.

Charlotte said when she was a girl she knew people who used to leave sugar, tea and salt for a Bigfoot at a certain rock on the riverbank, where he'd come down and pick the stuff up. And he learned to leave a few furs there, in return, for them to sell.

We went to check Fred's fishnet, which was set on a fifty-foot line, buoyed by empty ammonia bottles, out at the point of a midchannel sandbar two miles south of town and a mile from shore. The net seemed ludicrously short and small, in the scale of the vast yellow river, but three king salmon were tangled individually in its monofilament—a red forty-five-pound male, a reddish twenty-five-pound female, and a paler twenty-pound male. As Fred very carefully landed each of these, I sat holding the previous one under my feet in the little skiff to keep it from leaping back into the water. They filled the boat with their anxious and strangled despair, and if we had tipped over they could have lived, while we would have drowned very quickly, not just because of the water's hand-numbing temperature, but because its immense freighting of silt soon fills your clothes like a crushing weight and drags you down.

Yet such an easy catch of flesh exhilarated Fred and me, rather like a windfall of money. It suddenly made life seem more secure and, day after sun-swept midsummer day, is a commonplace coup on the Yukon. Besides providing for his father-in-law, Henry William, in Chalkyitsik (frontier Indians often chose two first names for their "white" name, because they would name themselves after several new friends, though sometimes an unscrupulous white man might "charge" them for his), Fred wanted to send a salmon or two on the mail plane to the Natsit Gwich'in of Arctic Village, on the Chandalar River, in the Brooks Range, the most remote and self-sufficient of these Gwich'in communities. In exchange, his friends there would mail him a caribou next winter. Even out in his bush camp, he seldom has a chance to eat caribou. Small bands of the Porcupine Herd straggle as far south as his Black River country only about once in every five years.

At home, Charlotte filleted the three fish, dropping the organs and roe into a jug to rot for trap bait and cutting the backbones into sections, which Fred would stick into punctured tin cans and hang close to his traps and snares. His practice is to set out literally hundreds of these in November and just leave them be until March. In his smokehouse, he also has strings of goose wings stored, which, when dipped in beaver castor, he will tie in low spruce branches to attract lynx. He laughed and told me he'd once caught thirteen two-hundred-fifty-dollar lynx in a single night, when they were moving through his trapping territory in one of their strange, periodic migrations, and how he had remembered then that his father, in hard Depression times, had wished he could catch even two thousand dollars' worth of fur in a season to feed his family of nine.

Charlotte showed me their photograph album, which, like other Fort Yukon photo albums, consisted, apart from its wedding and graduation memorabilia, of numerous pictures of dead bears and moose, in toto, then the same moose and bears being skinned; and of trap-line cabins and stilted caches on chutelike rivers, or trap-line catches pinned in a row on a clothesline rope in front of one of the cabins for the camera. The meat represented a winter's food and the line of wolf, fox, otter, mink, beaver, marten, and fisher skins a year's worth of money; so what else ought to be in an album of memories?

Jimmy Ward, the son of another old-time white settler, turned up for supper. We ate a snow goose, which Fred had shot last spring, and some pickled strips of dried salmon and left-over beaver, with store-bought spinach and rice. Jimmy Ward is a white-haired, black-bearded mischief-maker of whom it is no exaggeration to say that he is frequently drunk. He had been besieged in his cabin by gunfire one night a few months before and been carted away for a night in jail after the shoot-out, and while he was gone, his cabin had somehow caught fire and burned to a shell. Now the government had placed him and his Gwich'in wife in a ninety-cents-a-day government prefab for the rest of his life and, he announced cockily, he was sitting pretty.

"It was an active winter in Dodge City," he said. U.S. Representative Don Young's cabin — summer home to Alaska's perennial congressman — had also been set afire; and so had the Fish and Wildlife Service's cabin, from which the eight-and-a-half-million-acre Yukon Flats National Wildlife Refuge (itself as large as Massachusetts and Connecticut combined) is managed. So he didn't know whether to be insulted or flattered to be in such company. Tomorrow he and his wife were going out to camp in a favorite slough up the Yukon a couple of dozen miles and put out their fishnets and rabbit snares and lean back and enjoy themselves. After you'd split, smoked, and sun-dried a few hundred salmon, with those smells on the wind, you'd soon have a young black bear to cure too.

This is his summer camp, of course. In the winter Jimmy's trapping camp — like Fred's, it was his father's before him — is not on the Yukon but one hundred sixty miles up the Porcupine, between two of the Porcupine's principal tributaries, the Coleen and Sheenjek rivers, a less traveled territory, although as fall gets in the air in Fort Yukon, one hears people telling each other, "I'll see you on the Sheenjek," "I'll see you on the Coleen."

Jimmy said he wanted to die on his trap line, not shrink to skin and bones in a hospital bed, as several friends had. "I'd rather fall down in a rat tunnel and die."

Fred said that one spring he and his brothers had caught thirteen hundred muskrats on the Black. Last winter he and his sons had trapped about eighty lynx, forty marten, forty mink, fifteen red foxes, two wolverines, and seventy-five beavers. No wolves, but his brother Albert, who is based seven miles upstream from them, had gotten six.

Jimmy argued with him about how high a lynx snare should be set.

But they agreed that the most fearsome creature in the bush is a "winter grizzly," a bear that is too hungry to hibernate and has woken up desperate and on the hunt for a quick meal. Jimmy mentioned, however, that he had once shot at a Brush Man. It had been standing on the ice of a lake, and he'd fired at it twice, but it wouldn't fall and didn't drop down on all fours to run from him either, as a bear would have done; instead it ran into the trees on its hind legs. So he ran, and was too scared to come back the next day to check on the tracks; instead had cleared out of that valley entirely.

I said Fred had said that Brush Man could be a downed airman instead of a Bigfoot, or else an Eskimo exiled from the North Slope villages, or maybe (I wondered) a Koyukon Indian, from the next tribal group, down toward Galena on the Yukon, where I'd also been visiting and where I'd seen snares set around a homestead cabin for Bigfoot—or Woods Man, as the Koyukon Indians called him, because their slightly milder climate on the Koyukuk River grows more woods, less brush.

"I don't see why you have to limit your options," Jimmy answered. "If you see a Brush Man, he could be a pilot that's crashed, or he could be an Eskimo that's lost his marbles, or he could be a Bigfoot. Couldn't he? When I first saw you, I thought you were James Watt, because you wore glasses and you asked too many questions and you smiled too much."

We laughed. It was not impossible that the horrendous secretary of the interior would turn up. Worse folks did. Later on that first trip, Jimmy had decided I was really a fur buyer who was scouting around from cabin to cabin to see everybody's catch by pretending to be a writer asking questions. At the end of my stay, he had swung around to believing my story about what I was, but then, just on my last day in town, I'd walked over to Fred's house and paid him two hundred fifty dollars for two little wolfskins. So Jimmy didn't know what to think. Gleefully, now, he informed me that I looked older. And he asked if I owned one of those tube-shaped tents and mummy-style sleeping bags that all of the river floaters and mountain climbers and trail hikers who passed through town had.

Because one of my annual pleasures is to be put down by Jimmy Ward, I said yes.

"You zip yourself inside that, and it's like a grocery sack for the old grizzly bear. You're all wrapped up for him. He can just drag you anywhere, and you'll never get to see who he even is. You'll be zipped inside, where he can hold you nice and still."

Fred said Jimmy shouldn't have shot at that figure on the lake if he didn't know what it was. When he was fourteen, he, Fred, had almost shot his own father. It wasn't a simple case of buck fever, because he had killed his first moose three years earlier, but he was hunting moose and saw something brown through the brush across an opening, and because his father was supposed to be out overnight on the trap line, he took aim. But what had happened was that his father's lead dog had broken loose from the sled and gotten snagged in one of the traps. So his father was returning early to mend the dog's foot. Fred didn't fire, and within a few years he had his own nine-day trap line, with six overnight cabins on it.

Darkless summers are a jubilant time. I've been spoiled for some of my usual Vermont haunts by summering in Alaska, where, for instance, the daylight is continuous in Fort Yukon from May 13 through August 4. The sun's manic ball never dips below the edge of the sky. Instead it revolves incessantly, looping to different levels like the motorcyclist who rides around and around inside a giant barrel at a carnival, while the swallows dive after bugs and packs of sled dogs halloo to each other back and forth across town. Like the dogs, I found depression impossible. People, birds, bugs, dogs, didn't sleep much, and the sun, as if bleary from overwork, turned orange and red within the halo of its yellows.

That evening, before our departure for Chalkyitsik, I sat at the Sourdough Inn with some smoke jumpers from Montana, a fisheries expert from Anchorage, two mining men from Fairbanks, and a helicopter pilot from California, originally, by way of Vietnam. One of the "millionaires" I had interviewed in Anchorage for the magazine in New York in exchange for my air fare had made his money developing a shopping mall but had arrived in the state as a bulldozer driver. Had got off the plane drunk, he said, because of the breakup of his marriage; had rented a car and weaved toward the friend's house where he would be staying and immediately was impressed with Alaskan hospitality because the trooper who stopped him didn't arrest him, merely led him to his destination and wished him good luck. In the same spirit, he offered to introduce me to a woman friend of his and to take me sport fishing. But what was most special, he said, was that people here, whatever they did, were the best. Pipe fitter, electrician, dozer operator, geologist, bush pilot—they could work at thirty below or go round-the-clock in the summer and maintain quality. That trooper who had stopped him stood six foot five and "could have stopped the gunfight at the O.K. Corral."

I'd found the same thing. The pilot from New Jersey with whom you flew to lost little villages through snowstorms, fog, mountain ranges, either could cut it or pretty soon quit and went home—or died. The riverboat captain who ferried you to Yukon River settlements either could pick out the braiding of hundreds of channels that led him past hidden sandbars to his destination in the course of a week or grounded at a cost of ten thousand dollars. Mostly, I'd traveled with my tuberculosis supervisor, who flew to Eskimo and Indian villages, doing skin tests to discover latent cases of this antique disease, examining active or former patients, talking to the district nurse or a local health aide and occasionally speaking to the populace in the school gymnasium. We slept on the floor of the health clinic or a first-grade classroom or maybe the gym, staying a couple of days in a town of a hundred and twenty souls before moving on.

The district nurse, living in a center such as Bethel or Nome and flying out to a half-dozen individual villages, seventy or a hundred seventy miles away, which were under her own supervision, had life-and-death power. Not just in the sense that she quickly developed emergency-room skills; but there was no doctor on these scarce visits—a few days per village every six or eight weeks. She determined who got plastic surgery after a fire, or special prenatal care, or a timely cancer exam, or plentiful painkillers. With a limited budget, she authorized a mercy flight or a seat on the mail plane for somebody who wanted to see a doctor—or else she said no. I—whose eyelids froze shut in about five minutes in Arctic villages at forty below—had been much impressed by the stamina and panache of these women, sheltering humbly under their wings.

I napped on a cot in Fred's smokehouse for a few hours, till breakfast time, when we ate bacon and eggs. Fred's neighbor, a wide-cheeked, husky man who lives in a blue house across the road and takes phone calls for him, came over to help truck our gear to the riverbank. Fred had me store my valuables behind his daughter's picture on the mantel, which was the safest place there was, he said: his daughter who's working to be a lawyer in Massachusetts.

"There's no give-up in this guy. Good man for a trip," the neighbor told me. He drank a cup of Yukon-yellow river water. "Well, there's my coffee this morning."

Fred was zipped into a black windsuit, with a snazzy white life belt buckled to his hips. It was August 1, and as we got out on the water he remarked that it must be the first day of fall, because the thousands of bank swallows that nest in catacomb colonies in the river's cutbanks had begun vanishing, to get a good start on their flight to South America. So had the smaller flocks of white Arctic terns, which go nearly to Antarctica for another darkless summer at our antipode: true light-loving birds. Because Fort Yukon lies within the wide bowl of the Brooks Range and the more southerly White Mountains and Crazy Mountains, summer temperatures can go to one hundred degrees, but the first killing frost occurs around the third week of August. Our boat, flat-bottomed, square-bowed, thirty-two feet long, four feet wide, and powered by a forty-horse Evinrude, had been built for Fred by the local fur buyer to fit the chop of the Yukon's currents and the Porcupine's surge, plus for shallow-draft marsh running—a salmon boat, a muskrat boat.

In such a boat I'd crossed the Mississippi's mouth after muskrats and garfish, armored prehistoric-looking creatures as big as king salmon. On the Mississippi, dodging the high wakes of supertankers and containerships, our skiff had seemed like an anachronism. But on the Yukon, whose silent roar is bridged only once between Dawson City and salt water—a stretch equivalent to the Mississippi between Minneapolis and New Orleans—I felt natural.

After three breezy, down-slipping miles, we turned up into the Porcupine, which at its mouth looked to be about a third of a mile wide. The Porcupine is itself a major river, more than five hundred fifty miles long. Its waters are a rich shade of gray in the sunshine, not Yukon yellow, but just as cold and fast when you dip your hand into it. Less thickly silt-laden than the Yukon, it wouldn't cram sand into every interstice of your clothing if you found yourself unexpectedly swimming in it, but like any Arctic river, it has *gravitas*.

With the Porcupine's constant turns, and the sun's vagrant positioning over us, the water constantly changed color. It turned black and mirrored the sky, or shifted into a spectrum of handsome grays. Loons were flying determinedly every which way with breathless speed, propelling themselves in a goose's posture except that they held their heads lower. Snags in the current porpoised rhythmically, with their roots or stumps stuck down in the tangle of driftwood along the bottom, but their free ends poked out so much like whiskery heads that it remained a surprise to pass them and look back and notice that they really were stationary, and to watch gulls land on them even as they bobbed. Seals, farther toward the Yukon's great debouchment, do swim upriver for two hundred miles to feast on its salmon.

We slid by the mouth of the Sucker River, and then that of Eight Mile Slough, which looked just like the Sucker's mouth, though the Sucker in fact is a fairly intriguing river. Sloughlike in its sluggish currents, it is named for the bottom-feeding species of fish that thrives here, and it is a fine territory for beaver. A man used to live right here and make a good living from them (though he had to pay a price, with the nickname "Sucker"). Fred himself trapped along the Sucker River a good deal during the years when he was a wage slave for the air force because he could reach it easily from town—from foxes, he made a gold mine of the radar-base dump—and he had his two scariest experiences with grizzly bears here. Thousands of animals must have watched him from hiding places over the years, he says, but only twice has he realized it telepathically, and each time it was a grizzly, flattened down close to the ground, "with its nose going like crazy," along the Sucker, in springtime. He thinks an animal that large and formidable may be required to "register" on him; that the brain waves of slighter wildlife slip past. On each occasion, he made cautious haste to clear out, and then the grizzly cleared out. He is live-and-let-live with grizzlies, and he has prevented his sons, too, from shooting them when it was not necessary for self-protection and when the carcasses were too far out from home to be dragged back to feed to the dogs.

At Seventeen Mile (a location measured from Fort Yukon), the Porcupine looks about a hundred fifty yards wide, and there is one cabin left from what was once a small Indian settlement. Then we glided by the modest-looking outlet of the Grass River, where, as in the Sucker, whitefish can be netted in great numbers and the pike that congregate to devour them can be jigged for. The Grass River is a couple of hundred miles long, counting its tributary, the Little Black River, which curves in a parallel course through the same country that is drained by Fred's Big Black River. Only one trapper works the Little Black River nowadays, and as with all of the other rivers around, this relative emptiness of what is very familiar country to Fred, full of a hubbub of memories of dozens of families who worked the vast drainage of the Porcupine for furs, depresses him. It's not like the changes afflicting woodsmen in the Lower Forty-eight, where development is consuming everybody's old haunts. In much of Alaska, though perhaps temporarily, the land is emptier. Old-timers who went everywhere as a matter of course die off, and young people stay in their villages in the winter, drinking their government checks.

At Twenty-five Mile, chunks of ebony water appeared in the swift gray roil of the Porcupine. Then blocks of obsidian water. A sand spit split the river from the entrance of its tributary, the Big Black, on the right-hand side. We entered it. Two hundred miles up was where Fred's home was, but we were going only seventy-five, to Chalkyitsik, where Charlotte had come from. The Black, at first about sixty yards wide, narrowed to fifty, spread to seventy-five, shrunk again, and swelled, mirroring meanwhile the tiers of white clouds. The current was slower than the Porcupine's, with cherry-colored gravel visible on the shallow bottom and frequent grassy banks that were vividly green. Chattering kingfishers scolded us from both banks, darting between their roosting trees. Plentiful loons of three different species flew by in speedball haste, with giggles, and raffish large flappy ravens, croaking, and little mew gulls that nest on the tundra, and sizable herring seagulls. We saw five pintails and a family of goldeneyes, several mallards and a number of mergansers, or "sawbills," which dive and catch fish and therefore, like a fish-eating grizzly, are considered too "fishy" to be good eating.

At Steamboat Slough there used to be a cabin shaped like a steamboat—five-sided, and pointed at the bow end—which had been built for fun by some cheechako prospectors after the gold rush. "And then it fell down. And then it burnt up," Fred said.

Abundant dark-green spruce trees grew twenty to fifty feet high for miles. But a few lightning burns are interspersed through this forest, with dead black spars remaining that have refused to fall over, and alder thickets and willow woods that are gradually growing up in place of the burned spruce. Since these burns are of different ages, the new vegetation is accordingly lower or higher, but other patches have burned in one wholesale sweep, except where the wind's whimsy has spared odd vibrant clumps of waving spruce trees.

Besides fire, permafrost is the other tyrant here—Fort Yukon in winter is one of the coldest inhabited places on earth—and creates what is called "the drunken forest." Where lightning spares a stand of trees long enough for them to begin to grow big, their roots meet the barrier of the permafrost and are stymied until, top-heavy, they reel, they slant like cartoon sailors, surviving for years at desperate angles.

Mostly, though, the spruces and willow-poplar woods alternated with a rhythmic pleasantry, often facing one another across the river, and on the mud flats in front of the willows, moose, in feeding, had left their tracks. By the banks where poplars grew, we saw beaver workings; and on the grassy swales above the gravel beaches, bear paths. Black bears were the best meat legally available now, so Fred kept his .30-.06 at the ready. Moose weren't supposed to be hunted for a few more weeks, but he was mentally noting each location where he saw tracks to tell his two sons and five brothers about in Fort Yukon, as well as some of his in-laws in Chalkyitsik. He pointed out the signs of beaver to me with a more detached, merely professional interest, because they were in someone else's trapping territory.

"Goddamn, it's falltime! They're getting their food piles ready already."

The Yukon Flats stretch for nearly three hundred miles and host perhaps two million ducks during the summer. The Wildlife Refuge proper, which we were within (and within which trapping and hunting are permitted), is four times as large as Yellowstone National Park, and it serves as a sort of duck factory from the standpoint of the Fish and Wildlife Service, producing, as the birds fan south over the continent from California to Maryland, an estimated four hundred thousand "hunter days" of recreation. Rounding the many bends, maneuvering between the frequent sandbars, we saw wigeons and scaup and canvasbacks and startled up a golden eagle, which had been eating a dead duck on a beach. As it flapped in a circle to gain altitude, the trees almost forced it to graze our heads. Both white-fronted and Canada geese appeared, and later a bald eagle; then an osprey's nest. And we saw a number of sandhill cranes, tall gawky birds who seem to shift and balance themselves as edgily on their legs as on their wings. And a great number of hectic loons, intent upon getting rapidly from one place to another and then back again, as if they knew they were already rare in the Lower Forty-eight.

The copses of willows and spruces changed sides too, from left bank to right bank, or right bank to left bank. The water was seldom deeper than three feet, and so clear that the salmon that run up the Big Black cannot be netted in any quantity because they can easily see the strands even during the summer's night. The cherry-colored pebbles on the bottom, and the clarity of the clouds reflected upside down ahead of us, and the black and silver riffles just ahead of them, were very beautiful, with the constant bending of the river's course revealing new vistas of trees, new beaches of sand or stones that we were coming to, or a little oxbow that had filled up with earth in the spring floods and grown up with grass, where animals came.

When I could hear him above the water's rush, Fred was telling me of trips like this up the river in falltime, with as many as thirty people transporting themselves to trapping camps above Chalkyitsik—camps at Red Bluff, Doghouse Slough, Salmon Fork, Grayling Fork, and the topmost tributaries of the Big Black—and how they'd sometimes get stranded in inadequate water and have to live on just the fish that they angled for and the ducks that they shot. The worst year, it was a month before a rain at last released them and they got off the river's "high bottom" in their slow, old, deep-draft inboard motorboats. And when they did, they poled around just three bends and saw two moose on the bank and shot them and camped right there and—between the thirty of them—ate all eight legs in a couple of days.

After four hours and maybe forty miles, we stopped at Englishoe Bend for lunch. It's a campsite where Fred regularly stops, next to a muddy slough where nets for whitefish can be set, in grassy waters that are aswarm with pike, and opposite a long gravel bar where he said the women used to collect hundreds of tern eggs in June and then go back a week or two later to gather a hundred more, that the robbed parents had relaid. Board tables and butchering racks had been nailed between the poplar trees. We saw the fresh tracks of a three-year-old-size bear, which had wandered around in search of relict scraps, and heard the chirp-chuk of a ground squirrel, a delicious animal that Fred kept a watch for thereafter, to shoot for Henry William if he could, while we boiled salmon and potatoes for lunch and laid the salmon skins on a stump for the magpies to pick. "Chuk, chuk, chuk." With cupped hands, he tried to call the ground squirrel out of its den.

Only seven government staffers are assigned to care for these eight and a half million government acres, and they live and work in Fairbanks, more than an hour away by plane. So the original Gwich'in caretakers pretty much still have it, insofar as they go out, plus the fly-in white hunters and fishermen, who are not numerous enough to put undue pressure on the animals but can unnerve and infuriate an on-the-ground trapper by landing at his muskrat lake and making waves that throw both rats and sets out of kilter for a week, or by landing and shooting a particular moose that was slated for his winter larder. Only an average of six and a half inches of precipitation falls in a year—a desert's quota—but the fact that so much stays as snow for so long and is underlain by permafrost makes it a duck factory anyway.

Fred said the Indian families had acquired their "white" names when passing whites would bestow a first name such as William or John on a man and eventually his sons and daughters got another first name tacked on ahead of that one. Fred himself, being three-fourths Caucasian, is another story, but he always chose the Athapascan life—and indeed, with the provisions of the 1971 Alaska Native Claims Settlement Act, passed under the gun of lawsuits by native groups that were holding up construction of the Alaskan oil pipeline, it became financially desirable to be classified as a "Native." In hindsight, he realizes that his own and other families probably could have, and certainly should have, founded their own statutory village on the upper Big Black River at its Salmon Fork, where there is an abandoned ancestral Gwich'in village site, at which his brother Harry still traps, fifty miles below Fred's cabin. If the proposal had worked, the government would have built them a school, brought in a generator, mail service, and other courtesies, and they could have set up a store, passed a restrictive liquor ordinance, and otherwise established a quiet place to live for themselves, with opportunities for going into business, if they wanted to. Chalkyitsik has survived into the post–World War II era because it's at the head of navigation on the Big Black. The little tug Brainstorm, pushing a barge with barrels of fuel oil, stacks of lumber, and heavy items of replacement machinery, still makes it that far up the Black once every year at high-water time in June. But some other villages are supplied solely by air.

With my friend Linda, I'd been to several of these, on the Kuskok-wim River or the Chukchi Sea. It had become unusual for me to travel alone. I was spoiled, in fact; never in a tent without being in her arms; never in an isolated settlement without sleeping in the warmth of the health clinic, surrounded by the appurtenances of first-aid gear and medicines supplied to these places, or else in the womb of the school, in which all these communities focus their assets: the one sure oil furnace and hot-water heater; showers and laundry machines; and a commu-nal kitchen stacked with cases of government-surplus peanut butter, canned peaches and peas, macaroni, and jack cheese. When I had insom-nia, I'd wake in the middle of the night on a wrestling mat on the gym floor and shoot baskets—an ace at sinking three-point baskets at 3:00 A.M., being so utterly relaxed at that hour, my wrists loose as flippers, my fingers a pianist's, my eyes a deadeye's. I don't believe a man should travel far without a woman's company; it's unnatural; and even when the war between the sexes comes to the fore, man is born of woman, spends nine months inside her, and depends upon her for long suste-nance. Nor can I imagine dying with any degree of resignation, even of old age, anywhere but in a woman's arms. That women are taking over the Western world is no surprise; I've expected they would. They're awesome. The only protection from the power of women is a woman, and the best are the feminists, because they have all the virtues of men.

Fred tried to call the ground squirrel out of its burrow for Henry William's supper before we started again. "Chuk, chuk, chuk." But it wasn't fooled. The afternoon sky already looked cold, but autumn holds no ter-rors for a ground squirrel: as from Fred's rifle, it just goes underground. There were still plenty of dragonflies and many mosquitoes. "Where do they get all their food?" I asked. "There aren't that many of us around." Goldeneyes were running on the water, leaving patterns of footsteps like skipping stones as they took off, and we saw a mother merganser with twenty flightless though fast-swimming babies in tow. Four fledg-ling red-tailed hawks were awkwardly testing their wings between spar trees, and periodically we slid past a watchful, affronted owl.

The so-called mew gull, which mews, is a seacoast gull that nests along interior lakes and rivers and is so versatile that it feeds on swarms of flying insects like a swallow, but also upon bugs in a field, and on fish, crustaceans, and mollusks. It likes the gravel bars of the Black River to lay its three olive-colored eggs on. The babies, by now a month old and almost full-grown, still couldn't fly, but wore as camouflage a mottled brown, like the bars where they stood, ungainly, uneasy, as we went by.

More kingfishers agitatedly flew up and down between bankside sweepers — uprooted trees leaning over the current — and spar trees. At Agnes Bar (named for a local woman named Agnes Druck), Fred told of sneaking back here one time on a gaggle of honkers who thought they had seen the last of him and bagging nine of them with three shotgun shells. "This is my supermarket, this nice river."

On another occasion along through this stretch, during a spring flood just after breakup, he had lost control of his canoe and was swept violently under a sweeper and nearly flattened and swamped. "Whoa!" he'd yelled, forgetting he wasn't still behind his dog team — which had been part of his problem: he'd been sledding for so many months.

Then we spotted a moose in the water, which had been drinking. It wheeled and ran up out of the river and onto a high bank, where it stopped and stood surveying us, like a wild horse with horns, just the way that a hunter would want it to do.

"Lots of hamburger!" Fred laughed and said that it had "a three-year-old's palm." Shortly before freeze-up, he said, when he's hunting hard, he sometimes likes to sleep in his canoe, to be well placed at dusk and at dawn. But the warmest part of the day is also a good time to hunt, when moose and bears may wake from their noon naps and want a drink. Nowadays, when he hasn't strong arms for hard paddling, he hunts from this noisy skiff, but once he missed a shot at a moose when he'd just cut his motor and his own wake caught up with him and rocked his boat as he was firing.

We watched the riffles, watched for smooth but quick currents, following the cutbanks but avoiding disturbed water. Past bend after bend after bend, we watched the taiga and willow scenery unfold — the "drunken forest" of leaning spruces narrating where the permafrost rose momentarily underground; then placid tree lines again — until, three hours from Englishoe Bend, we rounded yet another bend in the river and suddenly sighted a bluff in front of us with several log buildings on top, a dozen beached skiffs at the base, and a sandy path leading up. Some kids were playing on the beach, and a couple of fishermen were flapping and tossing their short nets about to dry them in the wind. The Black River fishhooks around the bluff, past the mouth of a good fishing creek that faces the town, and so for both reasons Chalkyitsik is named Chalkyitsik, "Fishhook Town."

Walking up the path, we met John William, Fred's brother-in-law, a shambling but big-built, handsome, Indian-looking, young-looking forty-nine-year-old and born-again Christian, who promptly began lavishing elaborately scatological invective upon Fred, pausing only to introduce me as an honored visitor to the Reverend David Salmon, the Gwich'in minister of St. Timothy's Episcopal Church in town. It's said of the Yukon Athapascans that they're born into and die in the Episcopal Church but "shop around a lot in between." Just so, an evangelical family of fundamentalist preachers with Tennessee accents had dropped into town, and John enthusiastically let us know that he had fallen under their spell. Also, the state trooper whom I knew from Fort Yukon was here to deal with three teenage kids who had smashed up the town's pickup truck. Chalkyitsik, with only a little off-again, on-again general store, has a mere handful of teenagers and a single truck and perhaps one mile of road, which runs from the school to the dump. But they had snatched the keys and driven that far and come to grief on the way home.

"Sure feels like falltime. A few leaves turning yellow," John William said. He borrowed enough money from Fred to buy some sugar for our tea at the store, and he knocked on a friend's door and borrowed a small slab of moose meat to give us a good supper that evening.

"Going to make an Indian out of him yet. I already gave him some beaver meat and some snow goose and salmon, and he's only been here two days," Fred said.

John's house was as old as he was, John told me. The leaky sod roof was covered with plastic sheeting, and the walls were lined with flattened cardboard cartons for insulation. It stood next to the store and was hooked into the store's generator for electricity. He had a deep couch for me to sink into, two *Newsweeks* and a *Real West Yearbook* on the table, a wood stove fashioned from a steel barrel, and a Coleman white-gas burner for cooking. John took out his old violin and horsehair bow

and played "Be Nobody's Darlin' but Mine," as Fred told me later he
had been doing for visitors for thirty years. He'd been the storekeeper
for a while and now was village council president. He had had eleven
years of schooling, including stints at Bureau of Indian Affairs boarding
schools in Sitka on Baranof Island, in southeast Alaska, and in Phoenix,
Arizona, because he had impressed his teachers as being promising.

"But still it was just a glimpse," as he told me, of the immensity and
complexity of the outside world and the wealth of cultivation beyond
the watershed of the Yukon. Unlike a lot of the Indians and Eskimos I
had been talking to around Alaska, who felt that they'd been unfitted
for life in both worlds by the experience of being partially immersed in
each, he wasn't sorry to have gone Outside. Liquor had been his weak-
ness, he suggested, and Newsweek, he said, remained his link. In Alaska
opinions tend to be strong and unambiguous, and many Eskimos and
Indians are consumed by a rankling bitterness toward white rule, white
society—and even a death threat whispered or yelled at a strolling white
man who is transient in the community isn't uncommon, especially
in Eskimo towns such as Barrow. But John wasn't angry. He had come
back to Chalkyitsik to settle, not with the sort of ringing and emphatic
choice of how he wanted to live that Fred had made. He was divided.
He knew that there were other ways of living—with music, books,
and bustle—that appealed to him. For Fred, the deeply drastic changes
in Fort Yukon—like the "wine scramble" on the Fourth of July, when
grown men scrabble in the middle of School Street to grab a bottle of
wine; the crime wave, including a double fratricide last year; the rising
rate of drownings and outright suicides all along the Yukon—were not
cause for personal alarm but simply confirmed that the old life in the
bush, with his brother Harry fifty miles below him and his brother
Albert trapping seven miles above him on the Black River, was best.

There are many young men with a mocking bitterness toward everything they can identify as "white." They drink bottled beer, drive snowmobiles and "big-horse" outboards, and envy their fellows who fly off
to be educated elsewhere, yet with a full dose of self-flagellation as well
as a rancid, vituperative resentment of an outlander walking by. Then
maybe, alas, you hear they've shot themselves while cleaning a rifle or
have taken their boat out and rolled it over within sight of shore—a
favorite sister possibly witnessing this in horror as the river effortlessly

seized them and pulled them down. But it's not the fiftyish people who do this, or even share the fury, as a rule. Several times I met men or women of late middle age who said wistfully that the happiest years they'd ever known were when they'd left their native villages and gone and lived with a white friend in Seattle or Salt Lake City, removing themselves from Indian life altogether. It wasn't politically popular to say so, but sitting in an ancestral cabin isolated on a reach of riverbank no longer inhabited by others, they might confide.

Old people, however, had no such memories of a romance with a lonely Anglo schoolteacher, perhaps; no williwaw of doubts assailing them as they remembered a sojourn ten years before in Santa Cruz, where a summer lover had spirited them after a tryst on the Yukon and where they had worked on the amusement-park boardwalk, running a kiddie ride, until the lady in question — an anthropology professor on sabbatical, a social worker on furlough, a federal accountant, or whatever she was — after one drunken binge too many, bought them an Alaska Airlines ticket home. In these villages you may meet an Indian woman who at one point was carried off too — by a white barge worker, a store manager, a bush pilot, a firefighter, a hydrologist — and then gently sent home because, in Juneau or Los Angeles or Tulsa, she no longer looked so good. It was not that her hair was less black and lush or that the measurements of her bust had shrunk, but that she didn't know what to do; she had to be led by the hand everywhere. She became meek and confused, too easily bossed around and too tempted by liquor, or frightened of it, and couldn't pull down a healthy paycheck, and sat by the TV all day if left alone.

But the women somehow survive this kind of experience better. More flexible or philosophical, they go to work in the village post office and grocery store, or the village or tribal office, with enhanced skill. There seems to be a mrked difference in how "Native" women bear up under the stress of demoralizing social change. They can remember the big-legged oil-field guy carrying them off to Houston when his contract expired and his wife, by letter, had informed him that he shouldn't expect to move back in the house. So instead he brings his Fort Yukon girlfriend to roost in a condo by the Ship Canal or Chocolate Bayou, and they lie in bed in a luscious X late every morning and drink shooters late into the night, living off his Prudhoe Bay earnings, while he phones divorce lawyers or tries to get through to his kids on the phone—him climbing her body half the night, in between bouts of snoring like a walrus—until one day he begins shaking his head and says, "Oh, no, no, it's no good. I'll drive you to the airport."

No, she protests, and he "kindly" gives her another chance. But he begins joking about "firewater" when they drink, and the fun goes out of so much of it. She feels foreign, inadequate, a dumbhead. She sneaks off to try to make it on her own in Houston, but finally her family sends her a little money, and a barmaid takes pity and deposits her on a plane for Minneapolis, where the stewardesses can steer her to the gate for Fairbanks—where the ancestral, rapacious cold itself is as steadying as a hand on her elbow.

"The hawk almost got you?" they say in the Arctic when you've just survived a close call.

But we didn't talk of these things in John William's log cabin in Chalkyitsik. Nor did I ask about his personal history. Instead John and Fred agreed that it was too bad the Englishoe Bend ground squirrel hadn't come out of its burrow, because John's rabbit snares were turning up empty and it was animals like these, cooked in their skins, that the old man found most palatable in his last illness. He was tired of eating pike, which were the easiest fish to catch in midsummer. Salmon swam by the town all the time but would not bite a hook, because when spawning they don't like to eat and the Black is as clear as glass in August anyway.

We went to look at John's new cabin, of which only the deck had been laid in quite some while.

"You better finish it," Fred said. "Your rafters look like deadfalls from lying there on the ground."

"I'm going to build a Log Cabin Syrup–type cabin," he said.

They talked more about wild foods. Fred said his mother used to bake hoot owls and that if you first boil and then bake a loon, it's pretty good too, though most people don't know that. We walked for a mile or two around John's snare line to see if Fred had any suggestions for improving it. Fred has been snaring rabbits in a serious way for half a century, in town and out of town, for a garnish for a meal or living off them when he had to, and never gets on a plane without a roll of picture wire in his pocket, in case the plane goes down and he has to set snares to survive—gave me some wire, for safety's sake, when I left him—and he said it was harder in the summer, without tracks in the snow to read like a newspaper.

John observed that a shot rabbit tastes better than a snared rabbit, because it hasn't strangled slowly in the snare, while its juices soured. He pulled an imaginary bowstring back close to his eye and sighted along his outstretched arm. But we weren't seeing rabbits that you could shoot at, either.

We went up on Marten Hill, where the old man was going to be buried and where Fred said he himself hoped to lie. Cranes were calling from the sky, and we also heard a ground squirrel's *chuk*, which made us all grin but was frustrating to the two men trying to tempt Henry William to eat. The view was low-lying but splendid—to the northeast, Frozen Calf Mountain; to the southwest, Bear Nose Mountain. Immediately beneath us lay Marten Lake, a modest dab of water that the "black ducks" (as they call white-winged scoters here) arrive at in legions on Memorial Day, even more concentrated than the mallards, which need less open water and arrive two weeks earlier. The Chalkyitsik hunters lie on this sunny cemetery hill and blast away as the exuberant, amorous scoters, which have wintered down the Pacific coast, swoop up again off the level of the water in wavering lines, sometimes without having landed, and skim up the slant of Marten Hill past them to have a look-see at the other lakes all around.

Fred talked bolt-action versus lever-action versus pump-action guns and showed me where they lay and how they fired. Probably more hunting fun is had here in this week or two, he said, than anywhere else around the village, so he'd like to have his grave dug where he can hear the guns and laughter and remember how it was. In their gleeful, flirtatious courtship activities on his own hunting ponds, farther up the Black, the ducks are so very unwary that, alone and paddling quietly after them, he can get close enough to shoot several, and then go home when they fly off, but come back and do the same thing again before dusk.

Before we returned to the village, he and John showed me two sites where arrowheads have recently been found that indicate raids that were staged upon these Chalkyitsik Gwich'in more than a hundred years ago by Indians of the Koyukon group, living hundreds of miles to the west, and by Gwich'in Athapascans from northeast on the Porcupine, who almost within living memory had attacked an outlying encampment by surprise one night, thinking it was the main one, with such force that they might have wiped out everybody if they'd got their target right. All these Athapascans, living south of the Brooks Range, also warred intermittently with the Eskimos, whose territory lay only two hundred fifty miles north of Fort Yukon. The animosity lingers in muted form at Native American rights conferences and the like, and in Fairbanks bars. But Fred told me the story of the last Gwich'in who had died at Eskimo hands. He had come home very sick after a long hunting trip in the northern mountains and simply took to his bed, saying nothing about what might be the matter with him. He asked that he be buried with the regular ritual (which in those days meant being placed in a tree), except for one special stipulation: that nobody examine his body closely for three years, but then to do so. And when the period was finally up and his sons carried out these filial instructions, they discovered an Eskimo lance head — serrated like a harpoon head that holds sea animals — at the center of his bones. And they realized that by remaining silent, he had succeeded in bringing the long cycle of vengeance, countervengeance, and counter-countervengeance at last to an end.

Not just the local Indians and Eskimos tend to take a leery view of each other, but the whites who work with Native American Alaskans often choose sides. Alaskan Eskimos, if one can generalize, were more innocent until recently of whites' duplicity and brutality than the various Indian and Aleut bands. Because of the climate and remote locations in which they lived, they had been "discovered" later, and perhaps protected a bit better by the missionaries who interceded with the whalers, adventurers, and officials who visited their villages during the summer. The "Red Power" political movement and the rage accompanying it were slower to reach the Inupiat Eskimos of the North Slope than the Indians of southeast and central Alaska. Consequently, a traveler is more likely to be threatened with a beating or with getting shot in an Eskimo village nowadays — Indian activism having reached a more political, sophisticated stage. Thus traveling much there takes a bit more intrepidness (not counting the fact that my eyelids freeze shut). And I am a stutterer, and Eskimos will make fun of a handicap more readily. Their culture, pummeled by the exigencies of the Arctic, makes less allowance for handicaps; their religion itself seems simpler.

But with my nursing friend, I had an entrée and a protected status. Sometimes people even took me for a doctor at first, because I was accompanying a nurse. I would go with her as she visited patients: not just kids, but old men and women dying of liver cancer—to which Eskimos are particularly susceptible because they are subject to hepatitis B, a precursor disease. The bed would be by the window of the back room of the small, slapped-together, government-built house. The man lying there looking out would glance up, politics and Red rage being far from his mind, if indeed he didn't disagree with its premises from the different perspective of his own generation. Linda would feel his pulse, take his blood pressure, and do the mildly painful business of drawing blood, unless perhaps he was so close to terminal that she had the option of not doing so. She would ask if he was where he wanted to be—would he rather be in town at the hospital? No, no, he said, with his eyes fastened on the landscape again. Did he know that he could have a sedative or an anesthetic shot anytime he needed one—had the village health aide made that clear to him, and did he trust her to do it? Yes, he said. Linda explained with tenderness that she herself was from Anchorage and would not be back, but she would talk to the district nurse and that if he told her of any way she could help him from now on, she would. Resigned, his gaze outdoors, he smiled no.

At John's cabin, John showed me the moose shoulder blade he hunts with during rutting season in the early fall. The Gwich'in will gently brush a moose scapula across the bushes and branches as they walk through the woods or canoe a small creek, imitating the sound of a bull's antlers in order to provoke the approach of other bulls. At this time of year, a hunter doesn't necessarily try to walk softly. He may deliberately break a few sticks underfoot to mimic the noise of a bold bull that is looking for trouble. People who have hacking coughs, people chopping firewood—even drunks vomiting their breakfast at the edge of the village—have unwittingly attracted a rutting moose. Because moose don't eat much during their rut but drink lots of water, you hear the water slosh in their bellies as they come. A 1964 vocabulary listing gives eleven different Gwich'in words for "moose."

Fred and John talked about hunting in the old days, when if you met a cow and a bull, you shot the cow once, and then the bull once, and then the cow, and then the bull, swinging your rifle back and forth so that neither escaped, but husbanding your shots because each bullet ruined at least a couple of pounds of decent meat. Fred's father apologized if he needed more than two shots to immobilize a moose, but then would patiently let it die in its own time. With moose, you try for a heart shot —under the shoulder and from the side—but in hitting a bear, you place your shots not so much for a quick kill as to break the bear down so that it can't charge, with shots into its shoulder bones and chest, or the face and eyes. After a moose died, the Gwich'in immediately cut off its ears, for reasons of piety which Fred has forgotten, just as they would cut the muzzle off a wolf and tack it to a tree, or put a piece of moose meat into the campfire at night if wolves howled, to share their kill in this manner with them. Bears, as they died and afterward, were treated with special respect and gentle solemnity, befitting a manlike creature whose spirit would go back into the pool of bear spirits and help to determine how much luck the hunter would have at hunting bears again. But except for putting meat on the fire when wolves howled, Fred's riverboatman father didn't allow "superstitious" practices in his household.

Fred and I ate moose for supper, while John preferred to boil the heads of the two salmon we had brought. Henry William, John's and Charlotte's father, came over to share a bite and to meet me. Gaunt-chinned, pale, and crumpled over, leaning on his cane even after he was sitting down, Henry William wanted to tell me his story but was too tired to say more than a very little.

With John's and Fred's assistance, he said that the first time he had ever seen a white man was early in this century, when his own father had taken their family cross-country from the Big Black River to the Little Black River, and down the Little Black to where it meets Big Creek to form what is thereafter called the Grass River. But instead of con- tinuing down the Grass to the Porcupine and to Fort Yukon, they went up Big Creek to its headwaters, at a rise that on its other side overlooks the Yukon River opposite Circle City, which is now the village of Circle, pop. 81. At the turn of the century Circle City was a small trading me- tropolis, two hundred ninety-two river miles below the larger hubbub of Dawson City, and by sled, about a hundred sixty miles northeast of Fairbanks. In fact, in 1896, just before the Klondike strike, Circle City had boasted twelve hundred citizens, a million dollars in gold extrac- tion a year, two theaters, an opera house, twenty-eight saloons, eight dance halls, and the sobriquet, "The Paris of Alaska." The Klondike rush, much richer, had partly depopulated it, but even in 1906, fourteen years after the first Circle City strike, a quarter of a million dollars' worth of gold was taken out of there.

Although the William family was a bit late to see Circle City in its glory, the buildings did remain, and everything was new to them, he said—even flour. They bought some flour and stirred it into water with some newly acquired white sugar and poured this white white-man's gravy on their moose meat, not knowing any other use for it. After the meal, he, Henry, had carefully felt his face and looked at his hands to see whether he might not be turning white, too.

"Right down here in America we get a square deal," said Henry. "But in Canada, no. Shoot him! Shoot him! In 1919, natives scared of police. Grab a guy and smell his breath and maybe shoot him. Take a girl to the station and all screw her before they let her go."

After their initiation in Circle, the family had gone to Canada, but ended that unpleasant sojourn after World War I and came back to the Big Black River to set up a homesite at Doghouse Slough, upriver about twenty miles from Chalkyitsik. John, who consequently has some land rights at Doghouse, said he wants to open a "Doghouse Restaurant" when the tourists come, and that although he doesn't know how it used to be with those Canadian Gwich'in up the Porcupine and Yukon, now (on the grass-is-greener theory) "The girls are friendlier up there in Old Crow. They're more relaxed."

"But I'm sure glad that goddamn Seward bought this country from Russia," Henry told me—as if I, as a white American, could somehow share in the credit.

"Beautiful mornings, with the mallards and the laughing geese talking. On the Salmon Fork it's like Marlboro Country. Fast river. White mountains." John laughed, teasing Fred because it was Fred's brother Harry who actually trapped the Salmon Fork, whereas Fred's Grayling Fork, named for its grayling, a troutlike fish, was fifty miles farther up the Black, and "dark like a dungeon," and too shallow and slow-moving for salmon to choose to spawn. With no salmon holes, it had no salmon—"except for a few strays that missed the turn," as Fred himself admitted with a grin. Even the otters that wandered into his Grayling Fork got starved out by winter or else would put their feet into his mink traps simply "to get a scrap to eat."

Henry William let them kid each other without comment. Now that Belle Herbert had died—supposedly the oldest person in the United States, at 129—he was Chalkyitsik's senior citizen. Belle had lived so long that she outlived her family and dwelled alone, though comfortably, with a string that ran from her house to a bell in the next house, which she could ring if she had to.

Fred and I went back to the riverbank and put up separate tents, I with my air mattress to sleep on and Fred with a bearskin. We stood watching the river's ripples and fish surfacing and muskrats making V's as they swam about. Fred called the muskrats closer to us with squeaking sounds—saying his father "couldn't call a muskrat to save his life"—just as he does from his canoe when he is hunting them with a .22 after the ice goes off the lakes in the spring and they have so much freedom to swim anywhere that you can't trap them, but the fur's still good. Then the days have lengthened like mad, and the males think he's a male and the females also think he's a squeaking male, and both come for him. Between pursuing the muskrats and the gleeful ducks, it's such a happy time of year that he once tried to tape-record the sounds of May, to play back for himself in midwinter, but wound up mostly with his own voice cussing the recorder.

We built a smudge fire to fend off the mosquitoes, and John and Fred talked ducks, fish, and mosquitoes. But John said he was tired of fooling around alone in the woods. He wanted to get married now, "either to a white woman or to a red woman." Fred, being an old married man, said it wasn't so bad being alone. He regularly had only two lonely moments on the trap line, both in the early fall. The first was when his kids went back to go to school, and the other, right afterward, was when the geese went headlong overhead, which they did just as soon as their young ones had grown wings that could fly. Sometimes the geese's heading south seemed a little lonelier, maybe because his kids, but not the geese, were sorry to go.

A cousin of John's stopped by and, when I brought up the subject of Brush Man, said he thought he'd spotted one once but now doesn't believe it, because he was a kid. His father had told him they'd traveled

overland from the Lower Forty-eight, just as the miners did, but, unlike the Klondikers, they couldn't go home again.

John said, "A guy here shot one a few years ago, but they paid him
back—he blew his head off a little later." And expressing his impatience
with white-style "proof," he added that "If they aren't still on the Yukon,
they used to be, that's for sure. *Used* to be. Now you might have to go up
north, up where the big bears are. They don't like the helicopters and
all the stuff around Fort Yukon. Everybody's got a finger in the pie."

"But you mean they're in the mountains?" I asked him.

"And farther away than that. Way up north; what's that place called
where it's so wild?"

"The Arctic National Wildlife Refuge?" I said.

"Empty place. Yes, that's it. You don't know what you'd find."

In broad daylight, we slept awhile, grateful that our tents were dark.
Then we breakfasted at John's with the state trooper, Dan Hickman,
whom I knew from Fort Yukon and whom John seemed quite interested in courting, both in the manner of a local politico and as someone who was fascinated by people who had found their niche in life.
The trooper, in his turn, was curious to get to know Fred, because
Fred had been the foreman on a local jury that recently acquitted a Fort
Yukon Indian of the charge of threatening a policeman with his chain
saw. A certain electricity flowed between them, therefore. Alaska has
two varieties of trooper—the giant macho guys who look prepared for
rifle duels, icy shootouts, treks by snowmobile, and bush-plane chases;
and these more limber and amenable officers, who can tactfully adju-
dicate racial or domestic disputes. The tough troopers used to be sent
to Native villages, but now that the Natives have organized and acquired collective wealth and clout, one meets the tougher troopers in
the white cities and towns, whereas the skillful negotiators go out to
Eskimo and Indian communities—men like Hickman, who say "Caucasian" instead of "white" and "Athapascan" for "Indian," even though
the locals themselves happily use the informal terms. Our man, besides
being less massively built than your stock-in-trade Alaskan trooper,
was the son of a trooper and probably from birth had been free of the
compulsion to vaunt his manhood.

We talked about a pending case where two trappers on the Black
were said to have shot fourteen moose last winter to feed their sled

dogs, instead of feeding them fish and rabbits the way everybody else does now that fly-in hunters from Fairbanks compete for moose. John kidded Hickman about the Mad Trapper of Rat River, a famous mystery figure who fifty years ago in Gwich'in country among the tributaries of the upper Porcupine River in the Yukon Territory led the Royal Canadian Mounted Police on a forty-eight-day midwinter steeplechase and shooting match. The Mad Trapper was a canny Swede named Albert Johnson, not a Gwich'in, and his stamina was superhuman, but even so, Alaskan troopers, as well as the Mounties, have to take some kidding in these Native villages about him, the trooper's job, meanwhile, being to cultivate contacts for solving a crime later on.

In the two weeks, altogether, that I spent around Fred, I never heard him speak of the bush as menacing or unmanageable. But from childhood on he has heard stories about berserk white men coming to grief in the drainage of the Yukon and the Porcupine: "Old Man Rice," for instance, a Southerner who did not like Indians because their skins were dark. He and a German immigrant, known on the Black River as Smitty, had had adjoining trapping territories along a rich beaver slough near the headwaters of the Salmon Fork. When Fred was young, they'd quarreled over who the slough belonged to, and shot each other one April. At least this was the theory. April is the season when trappers shoot beavers on the thawing ice, as their trap sets become less effective and the hungry animals emerge to forage through newly melted holes. Because the German's three dogs were discovered dead on their chain in front of his cabin later, the police, the Thomas family, and other neighbors drew the conclusion that Smitty had expected to come back. Apparently Old Man Rice was whipsawing lumber out on the ice for a boat he was building, when Smitty bushwhacked him. But presumably he played dead, when shot, to get his revenge. Then, at breakup, both bodies, as well as the boat, floated away. Neither individual had any friends—the one because of the language problem, the other because of his prejudices about Indians—so nobody cared very much, but it was the kind of insolubly enigmatic murder in the wilds-beyond that can provoke rumors of crazy-bad Injuns, or maybe a Bigfoot.

There is still a yearly toll of migrants into the Alaskan bush who come to a bad end. On a lovely, pristine river like the Coleen, a famished body will be found, twisted inside its muddy sleeping bag in a little tent that the rains have pounded askew, with its plaintive diary, the entries growing incredulous, frantic, pinched, sliding toward incoherence. The man may have made his way into the wilderness on his own, or been dropped off by a bush pilot who forgot about him, or else when the pilot did return, as scheduled, the wanderer was dead. No licensing procedures, no training requirements exist for people who wish to immerse themselves in frontier conditions. The plane, needless to say, just drops them off, and in an hour — as I've heard tell — the person may find himself wet to the waist in the spring thaw, with his pack soaked through, and no dry ground to stand on. The temperature is 33 degrees, and although he may not know the word for hypothermia, he is suffering from it. He has dry matches, he thinks, but where to build a fire? The expensive pilot has been told not to come back for three months.

Calamitous adventures are commonplace in Alaska. You can struggle for your very life for days in the muck and muskeg across Cook Inlet from Anchorage, within sight of its silvery skyscrapers. The same sort of dithery idealism that sends young people off to become hippies in Vermont and Oregon, or to demonstrate in front of a government building, propels them to risk their good health in a quick study of wilderness skills — a oneness with nature you can't back out of. The plane flies off and leaves you, and you build a hut, shoot meat and throw it up on the roof, and maybe learn enough about trapping to feed yourself that way too. You learn the intricacies of meats in balancing a diet; your woodpile is an object of high labor and devotion. But your candles run out; the night extends for eighteen, twenty, twenty-two hours. Will the pilot ever remember? One meets people in Alaska who have literally frozen their buttocks off, wading for many miles through deep snow, though it may be that this ordeal began as a lark.

Pilots are heroes in the state, and one soon grows keenly fond of them — an unrequited fondness, as a rule, because once they have delivered you deep into the tortuous chaos of the Brooks Range, for example, they will drop you off and fly away to risk their lives alongside somebody else, dropping onto a dot-sized landing strip along another river, and then by day's end maybe five other parties as well. In the summer, pilots make lots of money and the sky doesn't darken to crimp their fun. Geologists, prospectors, surveyors, kayakers, hikers, mountain climbers, Native people visiting around (or pregnant, undergoing contractions, or schoolchildren going to a basketball game with a rival town), government experts of a dozen stripes with doctoral degrees or axes to grind or a sudden furlough—the complete cosmology of contemporary humankind in Alaska hops in and out of their aircraft. In many villages they are the sole reminder of the stopwatch tempo of the outside world, roaring in and out with insulin and bread and beer, housing specialists and sanitary engineers, wolf hunters, glaciologists, archaeologists, and behavioral scientists who intend to study bighorn sheep. The roar, the preliminary passage overhead to scout the runway, is followed by the abrupt, whooshing landing, a quick palaver, exchange of passengers and heaving of baggage onto the ground, possibly a cup of coffee, a ham sandwich, and up again, with that frenetic sangfroid.

A pilot is the one white man an angry Indian can't make fun of, because he covers ground, sees game, does good, carries the mail, and earns money putting his life in jeopardy. But the roar punctuates the static life of his sinking culture with news of its cruel eclipse. One of my social worker friends spoke of these Indian villages as becoming like "fox farms," which, during the boom of the twenties, when furs were in vogue, sprang up all over. People would pick a small island isolated enough so that foxes would drown if they tried to swim off, and breed and feed them till they overran the place, killing a crop when prices were right. But when the stock market fell and prices crashed, the people stopped bothering to catch and deliver fish to their fox-farm islands, just abandoned the places. The foxes turned into living skeletons, cannibalized one another or tried to survive for a little while on sea wrack and injured birds. And this, he thought, was about what would happen to these settlements, nurtured with hothouse oil-fed welfare programs, when the Prudhoe Bay fields run out.

The pilots, who teethed in Teterboro, New Jersey, or Huntsville, Arkansas, and who may go on to fly airliners someday pretty soon, are not overly interested in the deterioration of Indian culture and the morale of these villages, or in the private survival dramas of young hippies on a tiny quilt patch of ground sliding under the plane. Life was passing those guys by, too. You dropped them off and picked them up five months later, and they'd eaten some ducks and porcupines, masturbated to beat the band, fished a little, scratched in the riffles of their creekbed for signs of gold (of which they knew next to nothing any-

how), taken a fuzzy picture of a wolf that had surprised them by visiting, and gut-shot a moose that then got away. This is not really what life
is all about. Of course, the white hippie may have originated in Teterboro himself and have his own perspective on things, but the pilot is a
vivid reproach to younger Indians, who have no way of remembering
how their society is supposed to work and see only its present decay,
into which the plane plunges with groceries, hospital services, and so
on; then darts off to cover ten other villages, carries native leaders to
their lobbying meetings and kids to the dentist—living refutation of
some Red Power arguments about the self-sufficiency of Native culture
now. Old people, accustomed to living by the fishnet and snare and a
few well-placed bullets a year, hardly care except when they look at
their daughters and sons.

White sufferers, on the other hand, have come from home, are not at
home, and are an entirely different breed. They can leave, if they want
to, and go back where they came from, but in unusual cases, when
they don't, they get into still steeper trouble, not just pulling a trigger
on themselves or suddenly drowning, but a kinkier, lengthier unhappy
ending. We have in America "The Big Two-Hearted River" tradition:
taking your wounds to the wilderness for a cure, a conversion, a rest,
or whatever. And as in the Hemingway story, if your wounds aren't too
bad, it works. But this isn't Michigan (or Faulkner's Big Woods in Mississippi, for that matter). This is Alaska. You get into trouble here and it's
not a cold spell, it's eight months of cold; whereupon if finally the ice
goes out on the river and you're on the wrong side, how are you going
to get back?—for days, floes splitting around you. And Fred, though
he recognized that people from my world often went into the bush to
get away from the ailments of what they called civilization (so did he,
partly, from Fort Yukon's tensions), had no idea what a crazy constel-
lation of distresses these migrants sometimes brought with them. Nor,
in the serenity of his duck lakes and stick forests, did he quite realize
there were ills that might never be healed.

Alaskans take for granted, but then tend to conveniently forget, the
round of psychodramas of a good many migrants and newcomers, who
may arrive with the fervor of born-agains, with furniture piled on the
car, with infants in tow and maybe a master's degree, riding their last
dollar and gallon of gasoline into Fairbanks to throw themselves on the

mercy of the first working-class family that smiles at them and has a lawn to mow—a meal for a mow—but may not last half the year. It's a tradition that you grubstake newcomers and hope they work out. That's how the state grows. Nor should anyone arrive too auspiciously. People who have managed their lives well elsewhere wouldn't be here.

In the towns of McCarthy and Manley Hot Springs, however, while I was living in the state, mad gunmen shot multiple sets of victims dead in fathomless rampages—the McCarthy murderer a short-term resident in this white community reachable only by air, the individual in Manley Hot Springs, a man who had driven as far west of Fairbanks as you can go. And so drifters on the Yukon receive less of a welcome than they used to, even from whites, and in the towns at the end of the last road you can't be sure of a grubstake now. Reversing the fundamentalists' old view of the wilderness as satanic, people thought it was Eden for just a while, and satanic souls may head straight for Eden if they can, to see if their madness abates.

After the thick, frantic dramas of the gold rush, from 1885 through 1906—a hundred million dollars in gold; the Northern Navigation Co. ran thirty-two stern-wheel river steamers at once on the Yukon alone— veterans of World War I arrived, not simply for healing purposes but with the zest of the twenties too. What better place to roar? And in the Great Depression, hungry men came on a shoestring, needing grub-stakes.

(These, mostly, were the pool of men whom I knew during my wan-derings in the Stikine and Skeena and Cassiar and Omineca districts of British Columbia during the 1960s, men in their fifties and sixties by then but still able to get about pretty well if they needed to, though I met a few who had preceded them by twenty or thirty years, now going blind and lantern-jawed. When you walked to their cabins, usually by a river that they could fish in, a creek that they could pan in, if you wanted to stay over, the general etiquette was that you split wood for your helping of moose meat and a night's lodging, like in the thirties. Not just the supper's kindling and a summer night's firelight, but wood for the pile—"to remember you by when I'm all by my lonesome," as one guy said. He panned enough to buy his boat gas and groceries. Gold was hourly wages to him—so many hours put in: so many rice-sized grains or hangnail-sized flakes wound up in the bottle he kept. "There never comes a time when there's no gold in a place that has gold." That and his woodpile was all he needed. My book *Notes from the Century Before* was about such as him.)

Then World War II vets migrated to Alaska; then sixties hippies; then Vietnam vets: each group with its quota of nuts and hard cases. You read any old-timer's memoir of Alaska and you'll find some paranoid soul marching from the village of Dillingham, on the Bering Sea, over stupendous country to the village of Sleetmute, on the Kuskokwim River, in rags and burned black by the sun and the frosts. Or from the Kuskokwim, over another hump of the Alaska Range, to the Yukon River. Or from the Yukon over the Brooks Range to the Arctic Ocean, raving and muttering, mad as a hatter. These are the iron men, who survive. But others just go out and camp, get cold, wet, and hungry, shiver, and die.

In 1981, shortly before my first visit to Fort Yukon, a Texan starved to death near the Coleen River, only about thirty miles off the thoroughfare of the Porcupine River, and because his death needn't have happened and he kept a poignantly detailed, frightened diary, discovered by a newspaper reporter, it made headlines. But another such death, in 1975, affected Fred more personally, because it was on his own Big Black River. He and his son Jimmy may have been the last people to see this man alive.

Fred was working at the Fort Yukon radar base during those years and so on September 24 was on his way back "downtown" with Jimmy after a vacation at his trapping camp on Grayling Fork. The first night he stopped at his brother Harry's cabin, fifty miles down the Black, at its Salmon Fork. He could easily have made Chalkyitsik, seventy miles farther down, by the next night but he became curious, seeing a new cabin going up on the bank at a bend halfway there, and stopped to say hello. The fellow, who looked to be in his late twenties, told Fred he had served in the Vietnam War and "wanted to get away from people." Yet he was pleasant, and although they were hurrying to get their skiff downriver before freeze-up, Fred and Jimmy stopped to camp and get acquainted with their new neighbor.

He'd made good workmanlike progress with his carpentry, but Fred remembers being surprised at how little exploring he'd done roundabout. He had paid a Chalkyitsik Indian named Paul Ben to ferry him out there with six five-gallon cans of gasoline (half of which had been burned on the trip), five gallons of kerosene for his lamp, and a rubber raft, which of course would be useless within a couple of days, when the river froze up.

"He had no calendar or radio or watch, because he was trying to get away from everything, and he had three or four sacks of oatmeal — that was his long suit for food — but I didn't see no rice or macaroni or stuff like that," Fred said. Fred's brother Harry, on a visit, had given him a hunk of moose meat to help him get started, and it was hanging in a tree where the bears couldn't get at it. But the "camp robbers" (gray jays) were pecking away at this at a great rate. He claimed he didn't begrudge them what they could eat, but didn't seem to realize that they would eat lots, just peck and peck and peck and fly away to store what they got for a rainy day. "They can do an awful job on your store of meat."

He had brought a fishnet, but it was lying on the beach, not in the water, where it should have been right now during the fall whitefish run, and he said he didn't know how to set it under the ice, a skill he would need in less than a week. Fred tried to tell him that freeze-up is the time to be working like hell laying in food for the winter while you still can. First whitefish and then the suckers are running past on their way back from their summer hangouts in ponds and creeks to deep holes in the river bottom, where they can get below where the ice will reach. Setting his nets in these few weeks, Fred fills a couple of washtubs with fish each day to throw up on top of his cache to freeze. And this is also the time when young rabbits born during the summer are foraging hungrily as the green things die off and the first snows begin hemming them in, before predators have caught large numbers of them. Before the fur bearers get prime, a trapper will devote days to stringing a regular maze of rabbit snares, laying up meat for himself and his dogs. Fred and his brothers caught sixteen hundred rabbits one very fine fall and threw them up onto the cache along with the whitefish. Their twenty dogs ate twelve pounds of cornmeal boiled with twelve pounds of these (or of moose fat) a day. By October it's a matter of grabbing all the flesh you possibly can, so, in the bitter weather, you can devote your energy to trapping.

Also, now that the willows alongside the river had lost their leaves, the moose would be leaving the valley for higher ground and wouldn't be back till the snows drove them down. So, quite apart from the legali-

ties of the hunting season, it was crucial to bag one first. Yet it was
easy for me to imagine this newcomer's sense of peace and relief. In
the late summer he had built a sound cabin, and he felt that after surviving combat in Vietnam he could survive anything. He had a .30-06
for big game, but no .22 for rabbits and grouse. Rabbits, indeed, were
all about, feeding on the tops of the trees he had cut for his house, but
he said he'd seen enough killing; he was enjoying watching them.

"You talk about a man digging his own grave! He wouldn't let Jimmy
shoot a few of them for him," Fred said. The ducks were already
gone—Fred ordinarily goes into winter with forty ducks hanging in
his cabin—but he'd had no shotgun to shoot them when they'd been
around, and said he didn't know how to set snares for additional meat
at the beaver house that Fred had seen half a bend upstream; nor was he
interested in learning. He seemed reluctant to kill anything. Two days
before, he had watched a bull moose across the river but hadn't shot
it, wanting, he said, to wait till it crossed to his side—he didn't realize the dark, hungry time was almost upon him and he should paddle
like hell to get meat when he could. His few gallons of kerosene would
quickly burn up. Fred uses nine-hour candles, thinly wicked, fat with
wax—three of them set on spikes inside his cabin, so he can see while
he skins, and one outside, sheltered in a punctured tin can hung by a
wire under his snow roof to welcome him home from the trap line.

Paul Ben had gotten this poor fellow started, and undoubtedly Paul
Ben would have looked in on him again to check on his progress after
a while, or at least have come back to invite him down to the village for
Christmastime. But what neither Paul Ben nor the man had anticipated
was that Paul Ben would go to Fairbanks and get shot in a barroom
brawl and not be in a position to take care of him again. Perhaps Fred
is nagged by guilty regret that he himself, down in Fort Yukon, hadn't
made inquiries. Paul Ben's Chalkyitsik friends may be too. Apparently
the stranger, as Fred speculates, having watched the late-summer traffic
of skiffs (such as Fred's) going by, was fooled into thinking there would
always be people passing and had not been told that the winter trail the
dog teams and snowmobiles used did not follow the Big Black River's
endless windings, but cut cross-country considerably back in the bush
from where he was. If he'd explored at all, he would have found it, and
certainly would have discovered, too, that a Fort Yukon trapper named

Harry Carroll, who winters in Chalkyitsik, had a trap-line cabin only two bends, or three river miles, down the Black from him. Harry Carroll didn't actually stop in more than once a week, but when the poor guy was starving in January he could have got his mitts on a whole stack of mink, marten, and lynx carcasses there to subsist on till the next time Harry came by. In fact, if he hadn't waited until his strength gave out, he could have hiked down the river to town in two hard days. Tracks showed that, late in the game, suffering hunger pangs, he had left his cabin in desperation and struck through the woods for a mile or two, but had missed both Harry Carroll's cabin and the winter trail.

The sad story, which in its particulars was like the dithering behavior of the man who had starved to death near the Coleen, except that this man was so close to help, puzzled Fred—unless you took it to be simply a story of suicide. He didn't think his having been in a war might have had much to do with it. The idea of people retreating here to lick their wounds, wool-gather, and recruit themselves seems odd to someone at home in the place, with a year-round raft of breadwinning skills, amid brutal extremes—Fort Yukon's recorded temperature range is −78 to +105. You can craft a snowhouse around willow boughs, or sleep on the boughs where coals have warmed the ground, with maybe a moose skin propped up to cut the wind and a leeward fire—and on and on, if you know these things—but it's not the best site in the world for eremitic experiments or peace-love theatrics.

In Alaska you meet people who are still boiling mad at what they were doing before they got here, and it sticks in their craw that they have children growing up five thousand miles off, under another man's auspices, and their money from whatever project they failed at is gone. Children, money, time, love—what isn't lost? Such a honcho stands next to another in a bar (or next to an Eskimo who under different circumstances would be ranging behind a dogsled after caribou), and you may see the fur fly. The younger ones build nomad-type houses out of scrap wood, with cupolas and whatnot, and provisional marriages—one couple I knew "married" each other on a heart-shaped bed of purple fireweed—and hybrid careers. A bit of oil-rig wrestling at Prudhoe Bay, a bit of gold smuggling to Mexico City, or buying emeralds in Bangkok and hustling them back. "Gone to Goa," said a hand-lettered sign on the door of the jerry-built house of my fireweed friends, when I stopped in. Next time, Lethe-land; same people zonked out. Another man, a loner, has constructed bottle-shaped refuges dug into the ground in the deep bush that he can parachute to if he feels the need to, each with supplies and a plug.

Lassitude or pugnacity: if these are two of the stock reactions outsiders have to their awe or distress engendered in Alaska, I'm subject to lassitude. Fred was, I think, politely astonished, if not irritated, by how little advantage I took of my overnight stay in Chalkyitsik. He'd brought me so far in his boat, introduced me around, charged me a sum, and I had disappointed him by not venturing on my own into the cabins of older Indians who spoke English as a second language, at best, and might tell me Bigfoot or battle stories or lore even he didn't know. And of course he was right. He had watched me barge into old-timers' houses in Fort Yukon often enough, but here I sat engulfed in John William's broken-springed sofa, reading an out-of-date *Newsweek*, unless he led me out to meet people. Perhaps he wasn't reminded of the young veteran who'd got himself all the way to the upper Black River and then starved to death because he had ceased to exert himself, but I made the connection. My gush of energy in just getting to Chalkyitsik had exhausted me, which naturally puzzled Fred, for whom it was a boat trip between his and his wife's hometowns.

I'd first had to leave New York, entailing a fight with my wife—our marriage then being in its waning-fireball stage, her boyfriend calling her every day and spinning the dial on his phone to produce a Bronx cheer of clicks if I was the one who picked it up at our end. The flight to Seattle was an ordinary red-eye, with sleepy yuppies loosening their ties, the tempo of business breakfasts ahead. But the Alaska-bound passengers in the Seattle terminal are a breed apart. Headlong young men with grandfather beards and bristly mustaches; hectic but more ill-assorted souls, middling in age, who had fouled their nests and were banking on better luck in the "Last Frontier," hoping its rigors could swallow their bile. The profile airport clerks use to distinguish potential hijackers is presumably not applied to Alaska flights, or a third of the passengers would be pulled out of line to be questioned discreetly.

Then, on the Boeing, "Man Mountain," as he introduces himself, is your seatmate, an acidulous presence, obese as a bear, with a part interest in "the third creekbed down" in a nameless wing of the east

Wrangell Range: that is to say, a Pleistocene creekbed, under another prehistoric creekbed, under one of the myriad present creekbeds in this almost roadless region of rock, ice, and snow. "The western end of this country has been ruined by the eastern end of this country," he says, with which I cannot entirely disagree.

Or the man next to you, in a "halibut jacket," with big hands, may be a Cessna pilot who earns up to twelve thousand dollars per long frenzied day during the brief herring season, spotting schools of fish for the boat he is contracted to, in highly hairy dogfight maneuvers over the ocean, competing with other spotter planes.

Or he owns a chain of California gas stations and has just opened a new one on the Glenn Highway for a tax loss and for fun and games, where he can let his hair down, hunt moose with an Uzi, hang out with mechanics who look like the Confederate general staff, and talk about "necktie parties" with them.

Alaska is also a place where people like big shaggy dogs. At the Anchorage end of the flight, with a bizarrely frozen musk-ox, mountain goat, and polar bear, all glass-encased, looking on, one sees them rassling a crate with a husky in it off the conveyor belt—"Going to count salmon!"—while kindred burly spirits with U-shaped beards yank at huge backpacks, at hundred-pound cardboard cartons wrapped in masking tape, and at reinforced trunks, as if aiming for a winter "assault" on Mount McKinley, as perhaps they are.

In Anchorage, there'd been my reunion, delicious but tense, with the friend who had taken me on TB investigations all over and who I had hoped would go to Fort Yukon too. She couldn't and so resented my going, and inevitably the division of allegiance and memories between New York and Anchorage caused stomachache, heartache, split-screen images of what was going on in one place at the same time that I was busy elsewhere. Infidelities are chickens to eggs, until it's hard to remember who started what; and my dark-haired Anchorage friend had turned me down when I wanted to transfer my home here, so the wrongs at issue had become a cat's cradle, indeed.

Some Alaskans like to call Anchorage "Los Anchorage" because of its temperate climate and nondescript sprawl, but the glass skyscrapers reflect a most muscular, lovely cloud action, as well as the big Chugach Range of grassy white mountains very closely crowding the city. You can hear wood frogs croak, see a pet caribou penned in a family's front yard directly across the street from the Atlantic Richfield oil company's headquarters, eat splendid king crab and other seafood that's fit for a king, and admire a couple of volcanoes across Cook Inlet, a glistening wide arm of the sea.

Fairbanks, more bleak and extreme in winter and summer, has a giddy, ad-libbed quality, being a long way from succor if the roof falls in. When I'm not exhilarated, I get lonely in Fairbanks; I get like a dog hearing thunder, after a while, and rush about seeking company, which in Fairbanks means people with breaking-up marriages as often as not. More hair of the dog.

I'd spent a couple of days there, visiting trailers, walking the tunnely corridors of the state university, huddled in an igloo of a hotel at a downtown crossroads where people have hunkered through a lot of tough winters. There's a great government store for buying maps in Fairbanks, and one or two riverfront restaurants overlooking the muddy Tanana River, and a bare-bones airport which is freight train, ambulance, and grocery store to that world.

Fort Yukon, where I had come next, is a more precarious place than Fairbanks by common standards: e.g., more gunfire, farther from a newspaper, a boiled shrimp, a Cat scan. In Fort Yukon the river is still primeval, and the stars, like the permafrost, hump close. The sky, where the weather god lives, is one story up. But as a consequence, if you don't panic, there's a dignity, even a gravity, to the spot; you could find worse spots to die.

Anyway, here I was in Chalkyitsik, on the roof of the world, irritating Fred Thomas by sitting on my ass on the morning of our departure reading month-old news of Manhattan in Newsweek. I should have gone to the camp meeting the night before. I'd liked Jerry Falwell in Anchorage, and this would have been better. The village was emotionally hung over, but as we undertook a final tour of his in-laws' cabins, something stronger seemed to be laced in their tea. Though Chalkyitsik had voted itself dry recently, the state trooper told me that, with a telescope at the end of Fort Yukon's runway, he had watched bootleg liquor being loaded for the flight here. I was finally feeling peppier, coming out of my shell and getting in shape for talking with people with dark skins, "Native"-looking faces, and heavy accents—which, alas, takes

extra energy for me because, like most of us, I am a prisoner of my upbringing—but our time was up. John, who wanted to keep us around
for another night, said the highbush cranberries were ripe and that the
three of us should go pick a bunch. Or go fishing, maybe—wouldn't
we like to stay? My middle name is Ambivalence, so much of my life,
it seems, has been accidental, and I was willing to, but Fred got us into
the boat about 4:00 P.M.

The bluff, with its tall view of swift water, is a congregating point for
the villagers, who have rolled several logs there to sit on. Just watching the river makes you feel you are accomplishing something, and a
clever eye can read news upstream and down from the wrack and the
roil, the shadows of salmon, the impetus of quick birds, fat fish, inches
of current. Two kids were poking a stick in a muskrat's hole, and we
had half a dozen other people to wave us off.

A muskrat, too, would have been a treat for old Henry William.
Fred's one regret was that we hadn't procured him any wild meat. Even
I knew how good muskrat or squirrel can be. But it wasn't more than
two or three bends down the river that I felt the boat rock silently, as
Fred was wont to do to alert me. Looking a hundred yards in front of
us, I saw two swimming heads close to the left bank.

"Bears," he snapped in a low voice, while reaching for his gun, because with only the tops of the heads showing, I didn't know. They
turned, watching us, not sure what we were or what they ought to do.
Fred revved the outboard motor so that they wouldn't reach shore soon
enough to get away. Then he cut it and drifted down because of their
reluctance to leave the shelter of the water. He didn't want to shoot one
of them there and have to haul its carcass onto the beach. They were
yearlings, he muttered, born the winter before last—he could tell from
seeing only their heads, while their bodies were still underwater, as we
waited for them to scramble up onto the mud. The mother had probably kept them with her until about a month before, when she would
have driven them away in order to mate again, in accordance with her
bearish two-year cycle. If we had not intercepted them, they would
presumably have stuck together through another winter, hibernating
as a pair and bolstering each other in the meantime.

At last we were so fearfully close, they did swim into the shallows,
crouch for a hesitant moment, then dash out of the water in that ado-

lescent spirit of *Oh, we've done it now! We better run!* As wilderness bears, they may never have seen a person before and did not really try to tear away until Fred's first bullet hit the smaller, plumper, blacker cub. Each weighed perhaps a hundred pounds, but one was larger, rangier, and browner.

Obviously they had never seen an animal shot. The black one stumbled, glanced at us, flopped down, got up. Fred fired four more times in slow succession as our skiff drifted past, although he deliberately did not turn his gun on the brown cub as well as it fled.

Shocked, seeming to sorrow like a human figure at what was happening, the black cub kept looking our way as it fell again and struggled up, swaying, gazing at its wounds and sniffing them, trying to absorb the separate calamity and mystery of each shot. Finally it fell and rolled up on one shoulder but could go no farther and began to kick reflexively, bled at the throat, began a wholesale jactitation, and died.

"Meat for the old man," Fred said.

We pulled ashore, checked that the little bear was dead, and recapitulated its story as told in the prints. Fred said that the two of them had just started out from this beach for a cooling swim, probably not intending to cross—had been eating highbush cranberries back in the brush but came to the river because the day was hot. Two sets of footprints entered the water, and two emerged. The larger bear had then paused at the first explosion of Fred's gun and its impact on his stumbling sister before bounding into the willows, where the mud became sand. The other set of prints meanwhile milled and bumbled about, were sometimes blotted by having been sat or fallen on, staggered slackly, and ended with the limp body of the bear herself. Fred, who is not afraid to make fun of himself, said he had aimed at the shoulder the first time, the way he does with bears—"to stop 'em, break 'em down"—but had hit her in the loin. He had then aimed at the shoulder again and had hit her there—he showed me—but too high. Next, he had aimed at the side of her head but had hit her jugular vein. Like tracks, the bullet holes were tactile evidence.

When I asked if he had spared the other yearling because of me, he shook his head. But the people back in Chalkyitsik (and later his wife, Charlotte) were so surprised at his restraint that I didn't quite believe him. He is known as a man who never shoots animals he can't eat, however, and as a conservative trapper who always leaves his trap lines with a breeding stock to repopulate them, even letting a creek valley "lie fallow" for a year, his fur buyer in Fort Yukon told me afterward.

After buzzing back to Chalkyitsik to tell John William about the meat, we returned to the mud bar, where Fred cut off the little bear's right shoulder and arm for his own family's use. The browner, humpier twin was poised on his hind legs, wraithlike, back in the willows, trying to figure out why his sister wasn't getting up. If John William really wanted him, all John had to do was hide on the far bank come evening, Fred said.

Sliding downriver, we saw horned owls and sparrow hawks crying killy-killy-killy. A couple of bald eagles swerved away from us in the air, sailing up a tributary. We saw many loons; many, many ducks. On flat stretches, the river meandered practically in 6's and 8's, marvelously slow going on a brightly cool day with the world afresh. A whole loop would bring you just about back where you'd started, and climbing the bank, you could see that the next loop would do almost the same. The geese feeding there would simply move over again.

We stopped at a Fort Yukon family's new cabin, chinked with sphagnum moss and overlaid with a sod roof; also boasting a seven-dog log doghouse. Tracks showed that both a mink and a fox had been foraging in the yard. "First sign of fur I've seen," Fred remarked happily.

Arriving at Englishoe Bend, we moored the boat and horsed two two-pound pike out of the slough by leaning over the stern and wiggling a trolling spoon past them on a broken fishing pole. They struck in five seconds. One spring, Fred caught fifty pike in two hours in the slough grass here. Another day, he shot a hundred thirty-nine muskrats on the ponds nearby. The point in a wilderness is that when you do this sort of thing, the slough or pond fills up quickly again with pike or muskrats from the virgin sloughs and ponds all around.

Pike are ferocious predators—eat baby waterfowl and muskrats as well as fish—and so their livers taste extremely rich, like the top of the food chain in these waters, which is what they are. We also fried a bear steak with bacon. Our bear had fed on salmon, leaves, and roots as well as berries, so she tasted complicated, munificent, protean, like the mistress of a larger realm, and Fred claimed that sometimes when you're eating a blueberry-fed bear you would swear she's had sugar sprinkled on her. One June, going upriver, he and four brothers lived on a bear cub the entire way, roasting it whole all during the first night, then boiling parts of it each successive night.

"Damn, sounds like springtime!" he said when the sandhill cranes started calling on the two river bars in front of our camp. *Garrrooo. Garrrooo.* Wide-winged, five feet tall, and yet small-headed, they seemed exuberant that their summer's householder duties were done. A wedge of what he called "laughing geese" (white-fronted geese) skimmed overhead, crying *Kla-ha! Kow-lyow! Ka-la-ha! Glee-glee!* And the various loons that we had heard before were howling up a storm, a regular hootenanny. The geese tootled. The cranes said *tuk-tuk*. The loons yodeled and wailed in falsetto.

Fred slung a mosquito net over four posts that were set in the ground and cut spruce boughs to serve as his mattress and laid them inside, with his bearskin on top, and his three-hundred-dollar Arctic sleeping bag and his .30-.06 rifle. He'd fed the magpies our scraps and put the remaining wrapped food on a bench twenty yards off, with some tin cans piled on top to give warning if a bear scrounged by. It was bait, so he made sure my tent was out of his field of fire.

In the lambent dusk we fed sticks to our supper fire, building it bigger than was proper for cooking, and watched the endless unfathomable tales the flames told. Fred talked about trap lines, which might be ten to thirty or forty miles long. Your main line followed a river, and "side lines" five to fifteen miles long would weave up each sizable creek. He talked strategy for catching marten, lynx, beaver, and mink, and about how he puts out hundreds of steel leg-hold traps and wire neck snares in November, leaving them in place into March, because "no matter how many animals come through the country, you can't catch them if you've got no traps out." Around now, he said, the ducks on the lakes are all moulting—when the young can swim well but can't yet fly. This is when the whole village of Chalkyitsik used to turn out and paddle slowly in a fleet of canoes down Ohtig Lake, which lies only about five miles behind town, driving the total year's crop of young and grown-ups into the narrow end, where nets were strung for them, and other people waited on shore with clubs, if they tried to climb out. That one lake could fill Chalkyitsik's needs, give up all its babies before they flew, yet be as good as new the next year, replenished by ducks from the dozens of undisturbed lakes round about.

He told me about the most recent gold rush in this area, during the 1940s, when small nuggets were found on the axle of a fish wheel twenty-four miles above Fort Yukon, on the Yukon, and a couple of thousand people poured in and put up a tent city. But it amounted to nothing more than that. If it wasn't somebody's hoax to bring in business, they figured that an old-time prospector coming downriver on a stern-wheeler must have lost his pokeful of gold overboard, or a Klondike barge had turned over.

He also told me about one fluke winter when a wing of the Porcupine Herd of caribou had migrated right through his Grayling Fork country and he'd shot ten of them. Fed a lot of people. Another year, however—this was before World War II—at around this same point during the summer, thirty people, including his dad's whole family, had started from Fort Yukon for their trapping camp at Grayling Fork, but the water in the Black was so low that they got stranded at about where we were now. For that month they couldn't budge, waiting for rain. They just jigged for pike and stalked ducks and shot small game in order to survive. Finally enough rain fell that they reached Salmon Village, at Harry's Salmon Fork, in about two more weeks of struggling. There at last somebody shot a moose.

"Everywhere you went, people had a pot on the fire and were offering you a piece." But then the skies rained so hard that the river went half over its banks and choked up with new driftwood that they had to dodge as they went on, hugging the banks.

He told me about a "magic" war between two shamans of rival villages, in which good old-fashioned poison, supplied by a miner, won the day.

And Fred said that in the Eskimo-Indian wars, which were fought across the valleys of the Brooks Range before the white men interfered, the Indians would try to wipe out the Eskimos, whereas the Eskimos would try to adopt any Indian children they captured—"because maybe Indians are smarter." He laughed.

He said the Eskimos hold more of a grudge against the Indians for the old feuds than vice versa; and that on the Kobuk and Noatak rivers, the inland Eskimos will still camp on islands overnight, instead of going up on the heights to sleep—which would be a better place for a hunter—because of the defensive habits they formed when they were scared of Indian attacks. (Of course, in Eskimo towns, you hear accounts of these campaigns that are quite the reverse.)

He said a moss-chinked house is the healthiest place to raise a baby, because the moss "breathes." And again he talked of hunting muskrats in his canoe with his .22 in May, his favorite time of year, quietly calling them to him one by one but paddling clear of the grizzly bears, down from their winter dens on the mountainside and hungrily digging out roots and muskrats from the edge of the pond.

On this short, bright night, the cranes and loons whooped, trumpeted, and hollered, above the river's continuous rustle: a party babble—hilarious voices—and young ones being schooled. I'm not accustomed to wildlife sounding loud when humans are around—short of Africa anyhow; and that, too, is being silenced. I told Fred that at home I was a person who would take in animals that were unwanted or had been "outgrown," such as South American parrots and African pythons, so that I ran a refugee center at times, sort of end-of-the-world or end-of-the-line. Hobbyists who went in for exotic animals in larger ways were willing to pay three times as much for a "liger" as for a lion. A "liger" is a cross between a tiger and lion. "And then what do they do with them? It's crazy," I said. "I took care of some circus elephants when I was younger, and now I take care of parrots, and I see that parrots use their beaks for the same purposes—reaching, pulling, prying, tasting—as elephants use their trunks. But they're both disappearing. It's like archaeology to know these things."

Fred smiled to show he understood, and we went to bed.

"Goddamn high bottom, I'll tell you!" he shouted next morning, as we traversed the river's numerous shallows. The river had fallen a few inches overnight and brought the bed closer. In the strong wind Fred steered for high waves instead of avoiding them, because where the waves were, the water would be deeper. At second sight, the river's course already seemed homey to me with its landmarks of gravel bars, winter-skinned knolls, and leaning trees. Bird heaven, just for the moment. Kingfishers, owls, diving ducks—the ducks gabblers and busy-bodies, the kingfishers florid, aggressive personalities, the owls buffa-loed by the sunlight, though velvet-glove killers. Actually, we'd heard several owls whooping it up during the night, but the gleeful-sounding loons had been so vociferous or argumentative as to overshadow them. Owls put out a lot of noise when on their own turf and not maintain-ing hunting silence, but not like a loon. Loons have a fish-eating gaiety, like a barking seal's, versus the meat-eating reserve of an owl or a wolf. All of them howl and all of them bark, but the fish eaters seem to enjoy doing it more, as if with freer spirits—like the yelling that gulls often do versus the subdued mewing of hawks. Maybe it's because the earth is three fourths covered by water and their ancestral experience of food hunting has been so bountiful. The confidence of loons, seals, por-poises, and gulls reflects the amplitude and ubiquity of the sea. Our gulls of course were tracking the spawning salmon, skimming above their shapes underwater, certain that such a riot of fish would provide a feast.

Eventually the Porcupine's sea-green, sea-gray waves, triple-sized, swallowed the Black River's dark ropes of water, and in the wind there we had a deep-water chop, a new lilt and velocity. Then after twenty-five brisk, breezy miles of tangled low forest that seemed like a narrative I'd just come in on—it had started more than five hundred miles earlier, in the Mackenzie Mountains—the Porcupine's gray-green currents met the great yellow Yukon. This was no contest at all. Like motes among the forested islands, two other skiffs were busy on tiny errands, check-ing fishnets or carrying vegetables to families in fishing cabins down-stream. We were scooped into the massive, monumental flow like a motorized wood chip wiggling upstream, and duly arrived in the sunny and slightly truculent town of Fort Yukon, where most of the kids were swimming in Joe Ward Slough, named for old Jimmy Ward's father, who was more of a public figure than Fred's father, Jacob Thomas, though Jacob was maybe a better father than Joe Ward had been.

I went to the Sourdough Inn and sat in the swiveling barber chair next to the pay phone and placed some long-distance calls. A party of floaters who had rafted down the Porcupine from Old Crow were cele-brating their safe arrival with a kitchen-cooked dinner in the dining room and joking about "catching the subway home." On the windowsill sat an ant the size of a cat, constructed of wires, facing a poster on the opposite wall, which showed a rat that seemed to be tunneling through, with the legend: *I gotta get outa this hotel!*

I ate mashed potatoes, beet-and-cottage-cheese salad, and chicken-fried steak with the floaters and joined them for a look at the town's new stockaded museum. We saw a Gwich'in awl made from a loon's bill; a moose's stomach displayed as a cooking utensil into which hot stones would be put; a three-pronged fishing spear; and a whistling swan's leg bone, such as Gwich'in girls had to drink through during their first menstrual spell. In the "white" graveyard next to the museum is a plaque:

In Memory of the People
Of the Hudson's Bay Company
Who Died Near Fort Yukon
Between the Years 1840 and 1870
Many of Them Being
Pioneers and Discoverers and
Explorers of Various Portions
Of the Yukon and Alaska.

I went back to Fred's in the bright dusk. He was still up and took me to see the log cache on stilts where he and his brother Albert store furs. By now everything was sold except miscellany, but he looked for a silver fox I wanted to see. Found a cross fox, instead, whose yellow, black, and red shadings were probably even prettier. In another gunny-sack was a "bum lynx" Charlotte was going to sew a hat from, and a small wolf she wanted for parka ruffs.

"You never know what you'll find when you tip a sack upside down," he said. We discovered, indeed, six wolves in another bag, two of them black wolves seven feet tall.

I sat on a case of shotgun shells as we talked some more. Flying box-cars were taking off to bomb a forest fire, and Fred remembered he'd wanted to give me a bottle of matches and a roll of No. 3 picture wire for rabbit snares for my flight south, in case the plane went down and I needed to live off the land. He showed me how to tie and set the loops, having just made two hundred forty beaver snares for the winter, and the same number for lynx. Dry and chatty, he said he goes to Fairbanks every couple of years for a medical checkup and doesn't mind the flight as long as he's prepared.

I put up my tent by the river and the next day heard of a grizzly bear that learned to mimic the bawl of a cow moose calling her calf, while lying in wait on the trail. And, again, of the man who had once fed a family of starving Brush Men who sat with him beside his campfire talking to him only by mental telepathy. Of how to set snares around one's cabin for a murderous Brush Man. And of the Little People, the trickster gnomes who live underground and are as strong as a dozen men — of the stealing but also the good turns they do. Probably the only way you can scare Little People into returning what they have stolen from you is by boiling pots of water and standing over their underground holes and threatening to pour. Brush Man you cannot speak to, but Little People will talk to you.

JOHN HAINES

For twenty-five years John Haines lived in seclusion in the Alaskan wilderness, homesteading, hunting, trapping, fishing, and writing. Born in Norfolk, Virginia, in 1924, Mr. Haines served in the U.S. Navy during World War II and studied at American University and at the Hans Hofmann School of Fine Art. His books include *Winter News; The Stone Harp; Leaves and Ashes; Cicada; In a Dusty Light; News From the Glacier: Selected Poems; Living Off the Country: Essays on Poetry and Place; The Stars, the Snow, the Fire: Twenty-Five Years in the Northern Wilderness*; and *New Poems*, which received the 1990 Western States Book Award and the Lenore Marshall/*Nation* Prize for Poetry. His other awards include two Guggenheim fellowships, a National Endowment for the Arts Fellowship, an Alaska State Council on the Arts Fellowship, and the Governor's Award in the Arts for his lifetime contributions to the arts in Alaska.

Leaving Alaska

Richardson Homestead, August 4, 1991

Once more I have closed up the house, locked a cable across the drive, and said goodbye to this place, to the familiar yard with its sawhorse and chopping block, and with the hillside above it closing in more and more with the growth of young aspens, poplars, and birches. It is never easy.

In recent years I have taken leave of this place many times and returned to find it, no matter the season, much the same. A few small changes: an older birch blown down by the wind, the drive blocked by a late snowdrift, the footpath to the creek in need of being cleared once more of brush; growth and decay. Yet, in ways not always easy to admit, everything has changed, changed as the country itself changes, and as the alterations of modern life intrude more and more on all places of a quiet and special nature.

Now I am leaving again, saying farewell to a locked house, to a system of sheds and footpaths, a mailbox, a comfortable writing studio hidden in the woods away from the highway. I am driving out, heading south, on the same road that brought me here, a road that has made possible my residence sixty-five miles from Fairbanks and which at the same time makes possible, even inevitable, the intrusions that have altered and seem likely to destroy what it was I came for.

And I wonder—as I have many times while driving back and forth between Richardson, Delta, and Fairbanks, avoiding the frost heaves, shifting gears on the hills—at this perennially restless activity of Americans, always saying goodbye and moving on to that something new which, in our present situation, and despite renewed illusions, seems no longer to exist. Or, we can say with increasing certainty, that the new turns out more and more to resemble the old and all too familiar.

In my own way, and without intending to, I seem to have entered some time ago on that accelerated American, or it may be simply human, predicament of arrival and departure. In 1947 I had come north for a set reason, one not clear to me at the time. I had come to find, and to know, some part of the American ground, and in that quest, to know myself. At age twenty-three, too young and idealistic, I had only begun.

In August 1948 I locked my new house and its one outbuilding and caught a ride into Fairbanks. I left by plane—my first flight—on August 19. There was ice in the rain puddles on First Avenue that morning. Three days later I was set down in Chicago in the middle of a late summer heat wave. I had run out of money and had to take a bus the rest of the way to Washington. I thought of my small house on the hillside overlooking the Tanana River and wondered, sweating and stricken, why I had left it. It was some weeks before the weather cooled and I was settled in Washington, absorbed once more in my art studies. Life, within as well as without, would never be the same.

I returned in 1954 to a house which, though still intact, lacked by then even a bed or a stove. Young trees had taken root in the yard, and everything of household value had been removed. But in a very short time, once more settled and at home, at work on all that needed urgently to be done, I thought I would never leave again.

Now, more than thirty-five years later and after many comings and goings, the hilltop view of this river country I have loved as well as anything in my life is much the same, though now in order to look down on the river itself I have to cross the highway and climb a guard-rail, where once, years ago, I looked directly from the house to see five wolves trotting downriver on the spring ice.

Islands, sandbars, and channels have shifted and reformed, and even there nothing is quite the same. But to the attentive eye, the distant and greater view across the river to the south, to the foothills of the Alaska Range, to the snowpeaks of Moffet, Hays, Hess, and Deborah, has not changed. Familiar as they have become, the names seem now to have been carelessly bestowed on those peaks, their syllables—except perhaps for Deborah, which has a dark classical tone—do not belong to the masses of snow and rock to which they have been attached.

Traffic on the highway this summer has been heavier and more in-trusive than ever. Watching the double-tankers and the holiday homes rolling by, one thinks of this mass of industrial and recreational metal propelled by an increasingly limited fuel supply, of all possible and necessary replacements, and wonders where the parade will end, in what desolated corner of an impoverished planet.

There is something at once inevitable and foreboding in the changes that have taken place here in my lifetime, and the more so in recent years: this relentless filling up of open spaces and the search for yet another space. And the question I have voiced many times repeats itself: What will happen when at last we understand that there is nowhere to go? No more Alaskas, no more Yukons, no more open and unsettled places on the continent or on the earth. Will we be able to face that and decide to make a suitable and habitable place where we are? Or, lacking that resolution, will we turn on each other in that ever more limited and constrictive space and destroy everything? No question seems to me more urgent and in need of an answer. To face one's history with insight and courage, admit mistakes, and decide to make the best of what remains of time and place—few things would seem easier to agree on, yet nothing has proved more difficult for humanity, as the history of civilization demonstrates over and over.

Of one thing we may be certain: Nature will cure everything, given sufficient time, and neither the earth nor the cosmos requires our presence to fulfill itself. One looks at the ceaseless activity of land, wind, and water, at the immense debris of the past, at the continued evidence of seasonal change and disruption, and observes how it all combines and reforms, how species fail or adapt, return and pursue their fates, and he knows that the worst we can do will not be enough to destroy life, neither here nor anywhere else. We can destroy ourselves, render obsolete and useless all of our mechanisms, but that is all. Our inflated claims and expectations amount to very little in the face of that primary perception.

Alaska, what I have known of it, has given me a great deal. I believe, in all honesty, that I have given something back to it and to the people who live here. This reciprocal activity of giving and receiving seems to me to be what our lives, in respect to the earth and to each other, ought mainly to be about. Yet there are many people—a majority, I fear—who believe, like our current governor in speaking of development in the Arctic, that there is "nothing there" and that that nothing should be made into a greater nothing, and that its wealth—potential or imaginary—should be made to serve a wholly limited and fleeting interest elsewhere.

Unavoidably, then, on leaving Alaska one feels at times that one is leaving behind a project that no longer has in it a great deal of promise, in that undefined, idealistic, and old-fashioned American sense. That unlimited character of land and distance so many of us have felt on first encountering Alaska, and which must have inspired the first Europeans to go and see the Far West, has for some time now been fenced and enclosed within corporate and jurisdictional limits. There is little reason to believe that the process can be halted.

It is all too easy to feel, too, on reading of the mounting difficulties of every society and nearly every major city, that the problems of humanity are insurmountable. Every solution, however innovative, brings with it new complications, and the prevailing mentality, despite all efforts to educate it, seems intent on confirming a prophecy voiced once by Jean Arp, that humanity would devote itself "more and furiously to the destruction of the earth."

But I will not attempt to be a prophet here, if only because it is essential to avoid despair while admitting that however we might wish it otherwise, nothing is likely to remain the same.

With that never-to-be-forgotten sweep of river, hills, and clouds held in mind, one says good-bye one more time, not knowing when or if he will return, nor which, the place or himself, will be the most changed.

JOSEPHINE SARAH MARCUS EARP

Between 1897 and 1901, Josephine Sarah Marcus Earp made three separate journeys to Alaska with her husband, Wyatt, living at various times in Rampart, St. Michael, and Nome, in the hopes of striking it rich in the goldfields. Her husband, one of America's most enduring frontier legends, was deputy marshall of Wrangell for a brief period in 1897. Mrs. Earp died in 1944.

FROM *I Married Wyatt Earp:*
The Recollections of
Josephine Sarah Marcus Earp

Anyone who has not heard the ice go out of the Yukon in the spring could never imagine the racket. Long cracks are visible in the river for several days. Then comes the shocking event.

The year we were there, at the instigation of Al Mayo, almost everyone guessed a date and hour for the ice to actually break up. We wrote our guesses on slips of paper and dropped them into a large crock at the Alaska Commercial Company store.

Suddenly one day the ice lurched forward and began to upend. A few moments after the first forward motion, the floes began to climb on top of each other. The grinding, booming roar was almost deafening. It sounded like huge explosions of some kind. Some of the pieces were a dozen feet thick and as large as a big city block. As they climbed over each other, they pounded up onto the bank, shattering. The year before, several greenhorns who had built cabins too close to the banks had seen them swept away. No one had repeated this mistake.

The break-up went on all day and night, then something seemed to give way downstream, and the whole mass began moving at once. For several days large ice floes slid past, then the last of them were gone. It was mid-May. Spring was with us in a day.

The money wagered on the ice break-up was won by the Indian girl, Babe. Wyatt and several others had each wagered a dollar and a guess on her behalf. She got around a thousand dollars, more money than she had seen in her life. Al Mayo took care of the fund for her. Almost the first thing it brought her was several offers of marriage. Philosophically she accepted what she considered to be her best bet. They disappeared upriver in a canoe with a load of supplies purchased from Babe's money. I never saw her again. I hope she has lived a long, happy life.

As the spring advanced Wyatt planted a garden; not in the ground, since that was still frozen, but on top of the house, for our cabin roof was covered with a thick layer of earth. The sun warmed up our little roof-top garden, and it wasn't long until the young lettuce, radish and onion plants were sprouting up.

Wyatt watched and tended the young plants like a nurse. One brilliant moonlit night I found him up on the ladder watching his garden. "What are you doing up there this time of night, Wyatt?" I asked. "Can't you watch those vegetables enough in the day time?"

"Why, honey," he said, "I'm just watching them grow! I do believe they grow as fast in the moonlight as they do in the sun. You can just see them shoot up!"

Wyatt was as elated over our first meal of tiny green onions and radishes from his garden as a miner over a new strike. I must admit that I have never seen anything grow as fast as those vegetables of Wyatt's did. There is an exceedingly short growing season in that section of Alaska, but it's offset by how fast things ripen.

Before I end the story of our stay in Rampart, I've got to tell about one more happening that shows the sly sense of humor so few suspected in Wyatt. The Yukon was a great lane of traffic during the summer. At Rampart it swept around a wide bend above the town, then was soon lost to view behind a wooded point. Thus we were unable to see the approaching steamers until they were close to town. We could hear their distant whistles, but the dogs always heard them before us. Those animals were as interested in the steamer's arrival as we were, since there was a very good prospect of scraps of food the cook had saved for them. For us there were the possibilities of friends, of mail, of new faces to see.

It was on such an arrival that I first met Wilson Mizner, one of the famous "many Mizners" who later became the writer of such successful plays as *Alias Jimmy Valentine*. Wyatt had known him before, and we were to see more of him later in our lives. He and Wyatt recognized each other before the boat had tied up, and they were shouting back and forth across the water.

Wilson stayed with us for several days, which led to the incident I remember best about Rampart. It started with Wilson's offer to hunt up some game for the larder. "Let me use your shotgun, Wyatt," he said, "I'll get us a bag of ptarmigan!"

"Can you hit anything with a shotgun?" Wyatt wanted to know. "Shells are scarce up here, and you should make every shot count."

"Of course I will," Wilson told him. "Why don't you try me and see?"

The upshot was that Wyatt trusted his favorite shotgun and several precious shells to Wilson's unproven hands. We heard him shooting on the slope back of the cabin off and on during the next hour or so. Some time later Wilson returned with half a dozen birds, dumping them proudly before Wyatt. "How many shells did you use?" my husband asked him.

"Only six!" Wilson stated with obvious self-congratulation.

"Where are the rest of the birds?" Wyatt inquired with a perfectly straight face.

"What rest of 'em?" Wilson asked indignantly. "I kicked up six birds —I used six shells, and I got six ptarmigan!"

"I see that," Wyatt agreed, "and I suppose that's O.K., being as you're new to the country. I guess I should have told you how to get the most from each shot before you ever went out."

Wilson looked puzzled. Sensing his confusion, Wyatt went dryly on, setting him up for the old one-two. "You know," he said, "the ptarmigan is a first cousin to the sage hen, or prairie chicken as we used to call them. They were so tame they could be killed with a club. That's why we also called them fool hens. The ptarmigan is the same proposition. We don't kick them up before we shoot them. Being a sport and wing-shooting them doesn't count up here, where shells are so scarce."

Wilson was set up ready for the final blow. He looked truly dismayed. "Howinthehell do you shoot them then?" he blurted.

"Well," Wyatt explained, "you herd no less than half a dozen together in a little bunch, then step back so the shot spreads good and get them all sitting, with one shot."

Wilson wasn't sure whether he was being kidded or not; Wyatt looked so solemn. "Why don't you go out and try it again, kid?" Wyatt suggested. "You'll get the hang of it!" Wilson trudged away for another try.

Sometime later a sourdough stopped by the cabin. He told Wyatt, "I just seen the damndest sight ever. Some feller is up the trail talking to a bunch of ptarmigan, tellin' 'em he has 'em herded together fair and square, so stay put, dammit! You don't know who he is, do you?"

"I expect I do," Wyatt admitted. Then he told the story. They roared. After the sourdough spread the tale around, the whole community started shouting out whenever they spied Wilson coming, "Stay put, dammit!" He was a good sport. He never visited us afterward in all the years we knew him without mentioning the incident and laughing, "And remember," he would add, "I got exactly twelve more with two shells!"

"And," Wyatt would confess, "you were the first and last man in the country I ever heard of who did!"

Shortly afterward we reluctantly concluded that we would leave Rampart City for Saint Michael on Norton Sound. Before the ice broke up, Wyatt had received a letter from Mr. Ling, who was the manager of the Alaska Commercial Company's store on the island of Saint Michael. Ling wanted him to come to the island and open a canteen. Charley Hoxie, who had been the United States customs officer there, had brought the letter. Eventually, since we weren't making much money in Rampart, Wyatt decided to take Ling up on his offer.

The prospects upriver at Dawson were not bright, with all the creeks already located and the commerce monopolized by the early comers of the year before. The other competition for our attention was on the north end of Norton Sound. There the previous fall (1898), gold had been discovered in Anvil Creek by the three "Lucky Swedes"—Jafet Lindeberg, Erik Lyndebloom and John Brynteson. The name first given to the settlement that sprung up was Anvil City. Later it was to be re-named Nome.

Claims were staked on the creeks and back into the hills. Then gold was discovered in the beach sand. No mining laws covered the finding of gold on such a strip of sand, so new laws had to be made on the spot. The miners got together and ruled that a man could have as much of the shore as he could reach with his shovel from the spot where he started digging. This was called "foot possession."

All this was developing while we were yet in Rampart. In July we left, making our way downstream with thousands returning from Dawson. The boat was jammed to the rails with sunburned, bearded men in prospector's garb—the mackinaw, boots and hat with fur earflaps.

Most of our Rampart friends were joining us on board the boat, or had already left upstream or down, so there were few on hand to see us off. I do remember that Al Mayo and his wife and children were there to wave and shout goodbye. The boat backed into the channel, then came forward, nosing downstream. We never saw Rampart again. There were tears in my eyes as we left. Wyatt himself looked sober and reflective. It had been a wonderful experience.

Mr. Ling was at the wharf in Saint Michael to welcome us as we landed. Wyatt was still somewhat on the fence regarding what to do. We were both thoroughly infected with "gold fever" and really wanted to go to Nome. However, the offer Mr. Ling made was just too attractive for Wyatt to pass up.

We unpacked our belongings in the Alaska Commercial Company Hotel, which was not far from the canteen Wyatt was to manage. The canteen sold two commodities—beer at a dollar a drink and cigars at fifty cents each. It was a poor day that didn't see two thousand dollars go into the till. Wyatt's share of this was ten percent off the top, generally two hundred dollars per day seven days a week.

Many shiploads of beer and cigars arrived from the states. From our hotel window some days I could see hundreds of barrels of beer rolling by on the boardwalk and as many cases of cigars. Sometimes the rows of beer barrels stretched for several hundred feet and were, in addition, stacked high behind the warehouse.

I was a little ashamed of Wyatt's business, though I can't say why. He'd been in it before and would be again. Perhaps it was seeing that monstrous volume of the brew that was universally condemned as a home-breaker and the ruination of many good men. I took some small comfort from the fact that at least no hard liquor was served—just beer and cigars, but three men were kept busy day and night selling these. I also was pleased that the rules required that the beer be consumed off the premises. This cut down on the need for bouncers, such as were required in Dodge City and Tombstone. I felt Wyatt, at the age of fifty-one, was getting beyond the time when he should engage in such a profession, though he remained in remarkably fine physical condition till only a few months before his death.

The bay town of Saint Michael had some things to be said in its favor over some of the inland settlements. For one, there were almost no mosquitos. For another, it was clean, orderly and law-abiding.

The Alaska Commercial Company had a compound forming one end of Saint Michael. A boardwalk joined it to the North American Trading and Transportation compound at the other end. In between, fronting the boardwalk on both sides, was the bulk of the rest of the town. Saint Michael was a lively place the summer of 1899. It was full of transients heading for Nome or the Klondike, or setting out for the states.

Wyatt stayed busy all day in the canteen, but I was free to roam about town. My most frequent companion was Mrs. Vawter, wife of the U.S. marshal. Sadly, the next year at Nome her husband became a member of the "Spoilers" crowd who tried to take over the town. Their criminal activities, when they were finally put out of business, not only made world headlines but were the subject of Rex Beach's novel, *The Spoilers*.

One of the fascinating scenes Mrs. Vawter and I used to watch regularly was the arrival of gold dust and nuggets from the Klondike. Bullion was shipped in small cases under the close guard of the red-coated Canadian police. They were allowed to operate on U.S. territory in the capacity of bullion guards between Dawson and Saint Michael. We saw hundreds of these cases piled up on small express trucks and rolled down to the waiting steamships.

That was the way our interesting and profitable life at Saint Michael went. But the possibilities at Nome always attracted us. We kept getting letters from both Tex Rickard and Charlie Hoxie urging us to come to the new discovery.

Finally one day when Wyatt was reading another letter from Tex, he looked up in a familiar tricky way and grinned at me. "Tex says we're making chicken feed here," he said. "He has an idea we could triple our take at Nome."

"Did you tell him we're clearing several hundred a day, rain or shine?"

Wyatt nodded. "Let's go over for a day or two and see what's going on. He has some idea for a business."

I had to make at least a gesture along the line of being practical. After all, we were making what came to almost seventy thousand a year, at the rate it was coming in then. When I pointed this out to Wyatt, he said, "That will taper off to nothing by winter. We won't make half that for a whole year."

"Well," I replied, "it's one thing to decide to go and something else again to get a boat."

Wyatt looked innocently toward the ceiling, tilted back in his chair, staring upward with his hands locked behind his head. The pose was pretty familiar.

"What pocket do you have the tickets in?" was all I asked. The old enthusiasm over a pending change of scenery was undoubtedly rising in my breast.

Wyatt pulled two slips of paper from his vest pocket and grinned like a small boy caught in some innocent mischief. "Better throw your trotting harness on, Mrs. Earp," he suggested. "I think we'll leave this evening on the *Saidie*." I threw my things together, as I had so often before.

The *Saidie* was a tubby little side-wheeler. Sometimes in heavy weather it took her three days to reach Nome. We were lucky. It took one night and one day. It was still fairly early in the season, and it never got fully dark all the way. We slept very little, staying up on deck and talking over the prospects.

The sea was glassy. Its color was silvery gold, as though an omen. We were headed toward making the second fortune of our lives, but we didn't know it.

TOM KIZZIA

Tom Kizzia grew up in New Jersey and graduated from Hampshire College. In 1975 he moved to Homer, Alaska, and worked as a journalist for the *Homer News* and the *Anchorage Daily News* and as a freelance writer. The author of *The Wake of the Unseen Object*, Mr. Kizzia presently covers the Kenai Peninsula for the *Anchorage Daily News*.

The Wake of the Unseen Object:
Black River

From the hills of Scammon Bay on the far coast of the Yukon — Kusko-kwim delta, the great physical bulk of Alaska appears as a low mountain horizon across lake-splattered tundra to the east. Alaska's two longest rivers have poured out of those mountains for centuries, one winding north of the Scammon Bay hills, the other south, silting in a shelf of the Bering Sea as broad and flat as Lake Superior. If the seas that once flooded the Bering land bridge were to rise another ten or twenty feet — as a re-sult of atmospheric warming, for example — the delta would disappear and the hills of Scammon Bay would be transformed into an island sixty miles offshore. Already the delta is half water, a shimmering, insubstan-tial landscape in spring when the snow melts. For the villagers leaving Scammon Bay in boats to go to their fish camps, the prominent hills are a comforting aid to navigation. All summer long the fishing fami-lies can look toward home and be assured of a return to firm ground.

Barely a generation ago, coastal Eskimo families in this part of Alaska were still scattered across the sloughs and lakes and dry mounds of the tundra. They lived in isolation and gathered at the coast during salmon runs, for society as well as for food. Today villages are well established, fewer, and larger, and the trip to fish camp has become a trip away from one kind of society and back to another. The people of Scammon Bay still go to that empty spot on the tundra forty miles up the coast where a tent city springs up overnight as soon as the salmon appear. At the mouth of the Black River, fish are cleaned and hung to dry along an eroding sod bank where children find tools carved in stone by their ancestors.

The mail plane to Scammon Bay dropped me at the airstrip at the foot of the hills. The village above was a jumble of old and new houses around a school and a small blue Catholic church. The houses run crowded up the hillside as in a poor Latin American barrio, with middens of cardboard and plastic trash lying in their midst, freshly exposed by disappearing snow.

By the door of each house was a hand-painted sign giving the occupant's name: Akerelrea, Amukon, Aguchak. These were legal family surnames, used for school enrollment and taxes. In the early census efforts, missionaries often assigned an Eskimo man's one-word name to his entire family, adding common English first names. Sometimes, because this struck people as an odd perversion of the personal and private Yup'ik name, which is not a family name, children adopted their father's first name instead: hence one finds families in the villages today with last names like John and Jimmy. The creation of official surnames did not put an end to the traditional Yup'ik names. Such names are still passed on to newborn children from someone recently deceased and may retain their sacred quality as well. Some aspect of the soul was traditionally believed to pass to a namesake. The names are therefore not written on signs and are seldom shared with outsiders or even used to a person's face—nicknames are used instead. The Yup'ik name's importance is recognized at birthdays and holidays such as Mother's Day, when a child who has been given the name of someone's deceased mother may receive a gift from the bereaved. People like to look for familiar traits in the behavior of a young namesake. The Yup'ik names, and the network of connections they create, are part of a separate world lying beneath the visible surface of a contemporary Eskimo village.

People moved among the houses with arms full of nets or boxes of food. I had never seen a village so busy. It was early June—*tengmiaret rinitiit*, I had seen one Yup'ik calendar call it, the month when birds are laying eggs. Another source gave the Yup'ik name *kaugun* and the translation "hit king salmon on the head." Life returns all at once in great migrations to this greening breast of the continent. Geese and ducks are everywhere. Subsistence nets had started to pick up salmon. A steady stream of wheelbarrows and three-wheelers moved to the tidal slough at the foot of the village as families loaded skiffs for the journey to fish camp. Small children caught rides up the hill on empty backhauls.

I came to a yellow house and knocked at a door beneath a sign that said Sundown. Myron Naneng sat at a crowded table in the dark interior, his mouth full of dried fish. He waved for me to take a seat that had cleared the instant my silhouette appeared in the door. The house was large and open and had the look of a place where people passed through constantly. Teddy and Mary Sundown were an elderly couple with many grown daughters. Myron was a son-in-law I had met in Bethel. He had read some of my stories and had told me I could come along to fish camp.

Children and grandchildren were gathered around the Sundown table for a lunch of black seal ribs and dried, papery ptarmigan. The adults dipped meat into a plastic bowl of clear seal oil and spoke among themselves in Yup'ik. Like most older people on the coast, the Sundowns spoke only a little English. The family surname had come from a riverboat captain in the gold-rush years, when Teddy Sundown's father had worked on a Yukon River steamboat and could always be found on deck at dusk, watching the sun sink over his native land.

Mary Sundown pushed a jar of peanut butter toward me and nodded encouragingly. Her face was dark tanned and creased by a life spent out of doors, but her throat was white where her parka's hood had shielded her. I gulped out one of my few Yup'ik words to thank her — qiana — and gnawed instead on a salty bit of seal, listening like a happy imbecile to the clucks and glottal stops and growls of the delta.

I reached across the table and dipped the meat in seal syrup. All talk stopped. They watched as I raised the black strip to my mouth and took a cautious nibble. I could well believe that homes were once heated with the stuff. Centuries of animal life were condensed in its powerful ripeness. The yua of all things sprang to life on the tundra outside the window.

"Good," I exhaled.

"Assirtuq," Myron translated.

They smiled.

Myron Naneng was a good-natured, moon-faced man in his thirties, an up-and-coming political leader on the delta. He came from Hooper Bay, down the coast, and had married a Sundown daughter. He'd attended the University of Alaska in Fairbanks, worked as a bush troubleshooter for the governor's office, and was currently vice-president of the Yup'ik association of fifty-five delta villages. His office was in Bethel, but he came to Scammon Bay every summer. The regional association, struggling to preserve the Yup'ik way of life, was not about to stand in their vice-president's way when he needed a few weeks off for fish camp.

Usually Myron went to Black River with his wife and family, but this year they were back in Bethel, and Myron was going mainly for the commercial fishing period at the height of the salmon run. He had a new twenty-five-foot aluminum skiff and a new forty-horse outboard, but he lacked a helper. The man with whom he'd expected to share the work of commercial fishing this season hadn't shown up. Myron smiled reassuringly when I asked if I could be of assistance and went off after lunch to talk to some people around the village.

With Myron gone I began to feel clumsy and in the way. The pack with my tent and sleeping bag was blocking the flow of traffic in and out of the Sundown home, so I moved it to the porch of a small house next door whose occupants were away. But while I was digging through my pack the door of the small house opened and an Eskimo man stood before me. He was middle-aged, sunburned, and bristle-haired. I explained, embarrassed, why I was on his porch. "They told me you were away," I said. He gazed out, quiet and expressionless. I could not tell whether he was annoyed or curious or what. Then he said, "You want tea?"

Francis Charlie and Myron were related through their wives. Theresa, Francis Charlie's wife, was another of the Sundown daughters, a friendly woman with a strong, tired face. She went to put a teakettle on the stove.

Francis did not speak much English. Theresa was more at ease in conversation. She had grown up in Scammon Bay, while Francis had been raised by grandparents on the tundra, in the years before Yup'ik Eskimos abandoned the last inland sites, leaving behind driftwood-and-scrap houses and the graves of tuberculosis victims.

Francis was forty-five and had been going to Black River since he was a boy. His family was among the first to go away to fish camp every year. In fact, they had already been away at Black River—not even Theresa's parents knew they had come back. With six children, Francis and Theresa had left Scammon Bay while snow still covered the tun-dra and creeks were frozen, when cross-country travel is easiest on the delta. The family rode in sleds behind two snowmachines. Along the way one son took a jump too fast and broke a snowmachine tread, so

Francis trailed both sleds behind the remaining machine and they continued several hours to their camp, where they set up for the summer and waited for the ice to go out on the river.

They had come back to Scammon Bay that afternoon in a boat for supplies before commercial fishing got underway. Their subsistence net at camp had been filling up, and they had brought down a king salmon for the Sundowns—a treat, since kings don't run close to the coast this far south. The trip was made in part out of respect for the old people. The Sundowns were too frail for the rigors of camp and would soon be left behind in a nearly deserted village.

That night Mary Sundown and her daughters cut the king salmon into chunks and boiled it on the stove in a wide galvanized pan. Dinner was a bilingual, multigenerational affair staged in shifts at the Sundown table and on the nearby couch. Francis Charlie spoke to his children in Yup'ik, and they answered in English that the Sundown elders had to call on their daughters to interpret when they spoke to some of their grandchildren. The six children of Francis and Theresa ranged in age from six to the early teens. For them the trip home to Scammon Bay was like shore leave, and after dinner they fanned out across the village.

Myron went off again in search of a fishing partner, and after some halting attempts at conversation with the Sundowns, I went off in search of the Charlie kids. I caught up with them at the Royal Igloo, a dusty-blue teen hall with a single pool table and a wall of video games, half of which were out of order. Later we stopped by the new gym, where two men's teams were playing full-court sprint-and-shoot basketball. The gym was a shiny wooden palace several stories high, the most imposing building in the village. Basketball is such a passion in Scammon Bay, especially in the long, dark winter, that construction of a full-sized gym had been the village's top capital priority in the era of Alaska's oil wealth. The village council spent more than $800,000 in state funds on the project. Not everyone was happy about the expenditure; there were those in Scammon Bay who would have preferred to build a washeteria like the one in Chevak. The Chevak washeteria was so popular that people from Hooper Bay had been known to travel twenty miles across the tundra by snowmachine with a load of dirty clothes. When sudden winds across the delta blew down the walls twice during construction of the gym, opponents of the project began to whisper that God did not mean for Scammon Bay to have a full-sized gym with a wood-tile floor and a balcony for crowds. But the basketball players, retaining a comfortable majority on the village council, persevered, and now they boasted the largest gym on the delta outside of Bethel.

Francis Charlie's children missed basketball and nights at the Royal Igloo when they went away to fish camp, but after a few hours on the town, Glenn Charlie was getting bored. Glenn was eleven years old, a slight boy with shaggy black hair who, like his father, preferred the Black River camp to village life. He was less talkative than his brothers — more like his father that way, too. It was understandable that his older brothers would appreciate the night in the village, for they had worked in the commercial fishery and knew about the hard hours ahead. For Glenn, Black River had always meant the carefree life of summer camp: swimming and hunting and playing with his cousins. He wandered listlessly back across the village late that evening, past smoking steam baths and windows lighted from inside with the colors of the sunset. When he got home, he watched television.

It had been weeks since Glenn had slept in his own bunk in the Charlies' small living room. He was sound asleep when his Uncle Myron shook him the next morning and asked if he wanted to go commercial fishing. The invitation came as a surprise. He hadn't been sure if this was to be his summer to join the men in fishing. Of course he would go. But even as he muttered a sleepy yes, Glenn said later he had felt a little sadness. Black River would never be the same.

Glenn and I joined the stream of traffic that day, carrying armloads of gear down to the boat landing. An amphibian culture was preparing for travel. Men in their early thirties, some of them Glenn's uncles and cousins, worked fiercely, then stopped for long conversations. They spoke in Yup'ik, switching to English to discuss the performance of Danny Ainge in the recent basketball championships, which they'd seen on satellite television. Ainge was a local favorite because he had the short, powerful physique of an Eskimo ballplayer.

Glenn helped Myron maneuver his new forty-horse out of a trailer. The gleaming engine caught the attention of the other young men, who crowded around for a look. Glenn's lessons had begun. He saw that while the owner of an old mud-caked kicker may have to struggle alone to lift it into his boat, there is never a shortage of volunteers willing to help set a new outboard motor in a stern for the first time.

In tall, bent-over grass near the slough, Glenn's grandmother and his aunts were stringing herring to dry. Shoals of herring had moved up the coast the week before, and the slender fish were now stored in piles under grass to keep them cool. One aunt worked with an uluaq, the gibbous-moon knife used by Eskimo women, splaying fish along the spine. The knife blade had been shaped and sharpened from the steel of a rotary-saw blade and was set in a hand-carved wooden handle. The knife looked stronger and more serviceable than the souvenir ulus I'd seen at airport shops in Anchorage, the ones with maps of Alaska etched into the blades.

While her daughter split fish, Mary Sundown sat sprawled on a leaf of cardboard, a scarf over her head. She was one of the accomplished basketmakers of Scammon Bay, whose pieces of tightly woven beach rye had come to be prized by art collectors, but today her expert fingers were weaving split herring into eight-foot strands of twined grass that would be thrown away in winter as the fish were peeled off and eaten. The strands were hung for drying over venerable-looking driftwood racks, and they stirred as the wind grew stronger.

A storm was moving in and I climbed the hill to watch. Gusts ruffled whitecaps on the sewage lagoon behind the gym. A rush of low clouds trailed rain across the tundra.

After supper the clouds were shot through with white light and the wind let up. As the evening tide crept into the slough, Myron and Francis Charlie filled their gas tanks from a blue oil drum. Once Francis's boat was floating, Glenn climbed over several other skiffs and handed across Wiggles, the family's white muskrat-sized house dog. Francis settled Wiggles in his lap and said to me, "He's my lead dog." His face crinkled with laughter.

Francis pushed off with his son Richard, who was two years older than Glenn. Myron's roomy aluminum skiff boomed beneath my feet as I jumped in. We used oars to pry the boat free from others and poled along the slough's curves until Myron had enough water to drop the new outboard. As we passed the driftwood fish racks, the dried herring swayed and crackled in the breeze, crisp garlands with a thousand eyes. The slough dumped us in the mouth of a river, and we accelerated into the gray evening across a growing chop. I snapped up my down vest and rain jacket.

The Bering Sea coast is so silty and shallow that the rip could only be made at high tide, and even now Myron had to keep the boat far offshore. Tall blue icebergs stood exposed in the shallows where they'd been stranded by the retreating ice pack.

We ran two hours up the featureless shore. The steady hammering of waves precluded conversation. An occasional spray of seawater punctuated the journey. I wrapped my hood tightly around my SBA cap and gazed east toward the tundra, where the land was as flat as the sea. Except for the receding hills of Scammon Bay, we seemed to be traveling out of sight of the coast.

Glenn was the first to spot the orange Coast Guard light blinking at the mouth of the Black River. We started into the river, then Myron called out and looped the boat back to show us a beaver he'd seen paddling along the water's edge.

The Black River was several hundred feet wide at its mouth, smooth-running as it left the tundra, silty brown rather than black, though presumably clear inland beyond the tide, which ran stripes up the center of the channel. Steep banks of loam rose several feet on either side, so the surrounding country lay on a separate plane, invisible above our heads. About a mile upstream a line of driftwood fish racks and a few tents appeared along the right shore. Myron pointed the skiff at the first racks and killed the engine.

The boat's anchor was almost as tall as our apprentice seaman. Glenn flung it mightily onto the crumbling black sod, catching himself as he fell forward after it. We climbed the bank and found ourselves on a silent, twilit prairie. The only sound was a faraway rabble of clucking voices. Myron tilted his head. "Do you hear the swans?" he asked.

For years Francis had camped here in a tent, but now he had built a one-room plywood cabin back from the crumbling bank. The cabin was surrounded by driftwood, sleds, and rusting piles of tin cans. Inside, Francis had a small sheet-metal woodstove already pumping out a cozy warmth. There was a window in the rear where two cots were pushed together, and a mess of dirty sleeping bags and old boots covered the floor. In a white plastic bucket, a slab of seal fat was rendering slowly into oil, emitting a faint overripe odor.

We sat on stumps at a low table, snacking on fry bread and strips of smoked sheefish slickened with the seal oil. Myron made smoky tea in a coffeepot over a Coleman stove, adding to the loose-leaf Lipton's sprigs of Labrador tea gathered from high ground outside the cabin. Glenn tilted the sugar bowl so that it avalanched into his teacup.

Myron said it was good to be away from it all. "The thing about getting to fish camp is that you give a sigh of relief and you get a deep breath of fresh air at the same time." He smiled at the phrase he'd just coined. Francis sipped tea as if he hadn't noticed.

It was well after midnight, but in fish camp you went to bed only when you were tired. They decided to fire up the steam bath. Francis sent Glenn's brother Richard to start the woodstove in the steam bath while Myron and Glenn set to work stretching and nailing Myron's canvas tent over a nearby frame of two-by-fours. I wandered downriver, looking for a dry spot of tundra where I could pitch my tent.

When Richard came by later to tell us the steam bath was hot, Myron said he was going to skip it after all.

I've got work to do," he said, exaggerating the swings of the hammer. "You've got to work when you're camping, even if it's the middle of the night."

Glenn was lifting nails out of the mud and tapping them straight with a hammer for Myron to reuse. He gave his new boss a doleful look, then hardened himself.

"I'm not taking a steam either," Glenn said. "I changed my mind."

On a calm evening a few days later, when the air was cool and the river shone with a pink translucence, Glenn and his brothers and cousins stood along the cutbank, watching the water's surface for the sudden appearance of a V.

"Qavlunaq!" they cried, and ran to get long-handled dip nets.

Qavlunaq, the wake of the unseen object. Qavlunaq was the rippling of a salmon as it swam close to the pearly surface of the river. In Yup'ik they said the fish was "making eyebrows."

Too young to go out alone in the boats, the children waited on shore, their dip nets suspended in the water. They chattered in English, switching to Yup'ik when some aspect of their surroundings was recognized only by the indigenous language.

Richard cried, "The fish are qavlunaqing!" His insight was rewarded when an invisible king salmon entered his net. A cousin helped lever the twenty-pound fish to shore, where it would proceed to Theresa Charlie's smokehouse.

I tried saying the word, and had to reach deep to pluck the qs. The sounds were unfamiliar, and Yup'ik vocabulary had not come quickly. I was missing most of what passed at Black River in the old language. All I caught were a few expressive phrases, but sometimes these came as sudden revelations of what remained unseen. Qavlunaq. For the next few days I repeated the word out loud until people finally stopped laughing at my pronunciation.

Theresa Charlie had arrived in a relative's boat with the rest of the children. Camp was filling up. There had been no announcement from Fish and Game about when commercial fishing would open. The adults were anxious, but Glenn had time to be a kid again.

The tundra was sere and brown in early June, and the sun shone steadily. Packs of cousins moved along the worn path beside the river, stopping outside the doors of friendly tents. Small children tagged along behind me, singing out "kass'aq"—a tag for whites descended from the early Russian traders, the Cossacks. In some villages, in some tones, the word can have the ugly, resentful meaning of honky, but here everyone smiled like the expression was something cute. They did not get many kass'aqs at Black River. The smaller children gathered outside my tent, fascinated by my strangeness, giggling as I clowned with my eyebrows, until Theresa called for them to keep away. I appreciated her thoughtfulness, but it hardly seemed fair, considering how many doorways I had peered into myself.

I joined the older children in their chores. In some ways their society was easier to approach than the world of adults—certainly their rudimentary chores were more appropriate to my level of skill. The children hauled in willows to feed the smokehouse fires, hung salmon on racks for drying, and hiked onto the tundra to gather eggs from nests. If they were old enough they carried .22s, and they took skiffs up sloughs beyond the tide, where they filled plastic jugs with drinking water. Later in the summer they would grub through grassy hummocks for little stores of edible cotton-grass roots assembled by rodents for winter— mouse food, they called it.

When they had energy to burn, they sought out a relatively dry patch of grass to play a local amalgam of baseball and dodgeball called Lapp game, probably a version of a sport brought to the Bering Sea coast by reindeer herders from Lapland.

One evening the Charlie children brought me out back of their cabin to show me the game. The essential piece of equipment was a spongy pink rubber ball dug out from under the house where its disappearance had brought a previous game to a close. They selected a splintered one-by-four for a bat, narrow enough at one end to get their hands around, and a second plank was set out in the tundra to mark a safe zone.

One of Glenn's sisters was the first pitcher. She stood immediately next to Richard, the first batter. After flipping the ball in the air, she leaped out of the path of the swinging one-by-four. Richard whacked the ball into the tundra and everyone on his team started to run back and forth between home and the safe zone. The fielders chased the ball and threw it at the runners; most often they missed and had to chase the ball again. Wiggles, their father's little white lead dog, barked furiously from a sled.

The tangled roughs and water hazards of the tundra added handicaps for the outfielder. In pursuit of an overthrown ball, I made a show-off broad jump and discovered that a narrow slough was wider than I'd estimated.

After about twenty minutes, everyone stopped to watch a flock of a dozen swans rise from a nearby pond, gather noisily in the air, and move away down the delta. Then play resumed until everyone was breathless from running and laughter and the ball was lost in a pile of rusting soda cans.

When the game ended it was time to eat. Though I slept apart in my tent to lighten the burden of my presence, I shared meals with the Charlie family.

Francis sat quietly at the low table as we ate and winced with pain whenever he shifted his weight on his driftwood stool. I had to ask why he was limping. He said he'd been hunting seal two months earlier, riding on a sled behind a snowmachine, and went over a ridge on the pack ice and fell. He'd been too busy to fly to the hospital in Bethel to see if the knee was broken.

"Maybe when commercial fishing is done," he said.

I asked why he spent so much time at Black River. "I like a quiet place," he said. He obliged my questions with short, specific answers. When I asked how long it takes to dry a king salmon, he replied, "Until it's dry."

He was not being droll. Nor was it that he lacked the words to say more. Speaking Yup'ik with Myron and other adults, Francis seemed hardly more talkative. Myron was the one who could hold forth on the importance to Yup'ik self-respect of remembering the old ways, on the challenge of living in two cultures. Francis was different, more old-fashioned. He moved quietly, passing on knowledge by gestures, by example, as I imagined his grandparents had done for him. During meals I watched and waited.

"Eskimo food," they called the fare: dried whitefish, boiled half-dried salmon, unleavened Pilot Bread crackers. Francis Charlie said that if he did not eat Eskimo food he would get sick. Eskimo food was a measure of his well-being. Its consumption was only part of a larger cycle of gathering, and you couldn't have the food without the whole cycle. Each day a Yup'ik father was expected to go out and work, just as my father went off every day on a train to New York City—except that with the Yup'ik provider, the food came directly. If you bought seal ribs with a paycheck, it would not be the same. Myron said boys were still initiated into the role of provider when they caught their first fish or brought home their first seal. One's first kill had to be shared with elders and other families, for that was the proper way to show respect to the animal. Even if other rituals of propitiation were no longer carried out, the importance of sharing was well understood. The idea of "Eskimo food" seemed to open onto all aspects of Yup'ik life. For Francis Charlie, each meal was an act of communion with the land and the past, with the life of the grandparents who raised him and the promise of a future for his children.

I was learning to eat Eskimo food with gusto myself, as if I might ingest understanding along with it. I even got used to dipping my fish in seal oil, though I touched the oil gingerly—hot vapors blew through my nostrils and ears as I chewed, and through another embrasure about twenty minutes later. I shared the oranges and salami I'd brought, glad to have something to add to the table but fearful for the fate of Yup'ik culture when the younger boys neglected the strips of salmon and begged for more sausage.

One evening Francis invited me to join him for a steam bath. The original Yup'ik sweat house, the qasgiq (the word is similar to the Inupiaq qalgi), had been home most of the year to the men of a village. It was a place for serious male conversation and also the ceremonial center of the community. During qasgiq ceremonies honoring the dead, when women and children might be invited to take part, pieces of food were thrust through the floorboards. It was a responsibility to one's name-sake, whose spirit was thought to rise up beneath the floor. Skins or grass mats kept children from dropping through to the underworld, as the veil between the two worlds during these ceremonies was usually thin, and the children's souls were newly arrived from the other side.

Today Yup'ik people sometimes call the steam bath a qasgiq, though Francis Charlie's fish camp qasgiq was certainly a modest structure, built of scrap plywood and only four feet high. We crouched to un-dress under a shredded plastic tarp and then crawled through a door to the prickling heat. Thirteen-year-old Richard was already inside. A glass pane behind the stove admitted soft light into the box, and Richard pointed to the head of a nail in the wall, which would leave a bright tat-too if I leaned against it. He was paler than others in his family, freckle-faced and more high-strung. Fiendishly, he splashed water on the hot rocks. Francis tucked a soft knitted-wool hat over his own ears like a shower cap and held out a hat to me. He murmured something in Yup'ik.

"He says your hair will get thirsty," Richard said.

When Richard had crawled out to cool off, Francis explained that he had been adopted, a nephew joined to the family in the Native fashion as one of their own. They were about to adopt another child, a baby from a relative in Sheldon's Point. Francis mentioned the baby with one of the first big happy smiles I'd seen from him.

Of all his children, Francis was especially close to Glenn, who had been sickly with pneumonia as a boy. At one point they'd considered sending Glenn to Bethel to be raised by relations, but now he was grow-ing strong. On winter weekends, when he was off from school, Glenn liked to go out hunting and trapping with his father. On one trip he had watched his father dust snow off blackfish traps; next time out he dusted them himself without having to be told. "He likes work," Francis said.

By now we were both running with sweat. I shifted my legs and felt my blood pound. Francis's carefully measured words were coming just slowly enough for me to take them in. There was little serious male conversation during our twenty minutes in the steam bath, and we undertook no sacred ceremonies, but the rite was having its effect: I began to feel less a visitor, more a grunting participant in a life that had gone on long before my world knew it existed. Francis ladled water on the rocks and blinked at the steam.

He said that Glenn's Yup'ik name, the name handed down when its possessor had passed on, was Ayagina'ar. It had been the name of Francis's own mother. Sometimes, Francis said, he called his son Aanaq, Yup'ik slang for Mom.

This year the fishermen from Scammon Bay had received an unhappy surprise when they reached their camps at Black River. Someone had come by during the winter and broken into the storage caches. The intruders had gone at the nets with knives, slashing cork lines off the gear. Nearly every net left in camp had been cut that way.

I heard a lot of talk about how the vandals must have come from the Yukon, though there wasn't great bitterness. People figured this was the act of a crazy person. Nobody had bothered reporting the incident to the state troopers. What were the troopers going to do about it—patrol the tundra coast in the middle of winter? The only time the troopers cared about this place, one fisherman grumbled, was when they wanted to catch Eskimos breaking the fishing laws.

Francis Charlie worked alone at his end of camp, calmly threading his net back together. He had cousins on the Yukon and was reluctant to fix blame.

"Maybe it was mice," he said.

"They don't like that you've been taking mouse food," I said. Francis grinned.

State troopers were on Myron's mind that afternoon when he took Glenn and me in his skiff to the Amukon store. In a state-sanctioned rite of passage, Glenn had to buy his first official crew member's license.

The store was one of the farthest sites upriver. We approached a ply-wood house surrounded by wooden-slat barrels, old outboard motors, stacks of nets, drift logs for firewood, fish racks set atop oil drums, a child's swing, and the hoses and tubs of the salting operation that had helped to launch the Black River fishery.

A fierce little woman in the yard wore a dirty flower-print qaspeq dress over pants and salt-crusted rubber boots. Angelina Amukon was angry because the Black River fishermen were no longer going to sell them kings just because cannery tenders paid more money. "My husband gave them boats, gave them their nets," she said.

The Amukons still packed king salmon fillets in barrels of salt for specialty export to Japan, but now they counted on relatives to catch the kings. Other fishermen said the Amukons had been tough bargainers, hard people to get receipts from. They relied on the Amukons mostly for their little store. From a wall of shelves in the front room of their cabin, the Amukons sold breakfast cereal, work gloves, rubber fishing boots.

Angelina sat at a table and was filling out a state license for Glenn when a floatplane roared low overhead, buzzed the camp, and landed on the river. It was the first plane I'd heard land at Black River all week. The population had grown steadily but strictly from boat traffic.

Angelina Amukon was loading the arms of a young customer with soda pop when two large white men stooped through the door and straightened up.

I sank into a shadowy corner. They came from my world, but I had been at Black River long enough to feel the strangeness of their presence.

The state Fish and Wildlife Protection officers were tall, big-shouldered men, suntanned and sandy-haired, wearing brown uniforms and hip boots and guns strapped to their sides. They towered over the Eskimos seated around the low table. Angelina shooed a boy away from a chair, and the bigger of the two wardens took a seat. Elderly John Amukon rose from a bed in the back room and shuffled out in his slippers.

The big warden got right to the point. There would be a commercial opening tomorrow, he said. Twelve hours, chum gear only. He'd appreciate it if they would pass the word. He looked from John Amukon to Angelina. This was bad news for the saltry, bad news for the fishermen of Black River. The kings, being so much larger than chums, wouldn't be trapped by the smaller mesh of the chum gear. They'd swim on by and head up the Yukon.

"I don't know anything about a king opening," the warden said peremptorily.

Several boys along the wall gazed up at the belt buckle of the second warden, who stood with his arms folded, blocking the light from the door.

"Maybe I put one king net in," Angelina said, peering over her glasses at the seated warden.

"Better not do that," he said.

"I only teasing you," she said. She broke into a big grin.

Everybody smiled, and then the game wardens started out the door.

"Thank you for coming," Angelina called after them.

That evening during supper Francis was back and forth to the CB radio, talking in Yup'ik with a cousin about where they should go for the next day's opening. Some fishermen planned to stay and fish off the mouth of Black River, others thought more salmon would have gathered farther north, nearer the mouth of the Yukon.

The AM radio was on as well, crackling with oldies drifting across Norton Sound from Nome. Then the local news: a distant report from Congress, something about offshore oil development in Norton Sound. I came to with the jolt of science-fiction travel and looked about at my gracious hosts tearing at strips of dried whitefish with their teeth, then went back to work on my own dryfish. I was getting to quite like the dense, oily taste and stringy texture, though if I dipped the meat, I carried the fumes of seal oil in my beard for hours afterward.

The door of the cabin stood open, the river outside, the tundra beyond. During the day Richard had pointed out three small figures, a mother and two children, holding hands as they walked far from camp. I'd imagined them to be engaged in some timeless gathering activity. Perhaps they were looking for eggs. The larger birds' nests were off-limits now—part of a cooperative agreement with federal authorities to protect declining goose populations—but smaller eggs were still part of the fish camp diet.

"What are they looking for?" I asked Richard.

"Shoes."

"Shoes?"

"One of their dogs took some."

I realized that I had yet to leave camp on the riverbank and see the tundra myself, so after supper I pulled on my rubber boots. The golden evening hours were beginning. I picked a winding course along the edge of ponds and clear streams, doubling back off dead-end peninsulas. Black earth bubbled beneath my boots. It was a country without wood or stone. The grass was short and chaffy, still brown from winter, but fresh blushes of green followed the watercourse, where small swimming birds skittered and splashed away from my advance.

A circus clatter of birdlife was all around. Five geese flew low to the ground in a V, making eyebrows for the coast and intent on getting there in the next few seconds. I was heading vaguely east, toward the mountains. Far ahead, two sandhill cranes danced noisily on stilt legs, lunging, broad wings outspread. I picked them as a destination.

After a while I stopped and looked back. With the river dropped out of sight, the camp looked like a prairie boomtown in a Western movie: a line of wall tents out in the treeless plains, with a few frame buildings adding a tentative permanence. I counted thirty tents and half a dozen plywood shacks. Usually the Black River camp is seen from the water. This was an unusual perspective, perhaps known only to gatherers of eggs and shoes.

I spotted Glenn in the distance, following my trail. The family's golden dog ran in excited circles beside him. Myron had said that if they decided to leave tonight, they'd send Glenn for me.

I started back. By the time I drew near to their messenger, he was wading thigh-deep across a pond, exploring in the shallow muck and in no apparent hurry to catch up. Glenn was studying the sucking sensation produced by a pair of hip waders his mother had brought from the store in Scammon Bay, a present for his first commercial fishing trip. A shrewd investment, since every night Glenn returned to camp wet and muddy to his knees.

"Dogs are better than people, you know why?" Glenn said as he splashed out of the pond and caught his breath. "Dogs find more little birds' eggs than we do."

He held out his hand. In his palm were three small eggs the size of macadamia nuts, outfitted in a camouflage pattern of green and brown.

"Did you see any nests?" Glenn asked. "Did you see any birds flying funny?"

I took the eggs and we started for the river. The eggs felt warm. Was it the warmth of his hand, or had they been warm like this in the grass where he found them? I felt I was walking home with something tugging at my fist—the heart of the tundra, a living thing. Qavlunaq.

Acknowledgments

"Soundings," by Carolyn Servid, first appeared in the *North Dakota Quarterly* 59 (Spring 1991). Reprinted by permission of Carolyn Servid.

"Entering the Ice Age," by John Dos Passos, originally appeared in *Holiday Travel*, April 1966. Reprinted by permission of the estate of John Dos Passos.

"Welcome Speech," by Jennie Thlunaut, is reprinted from *Haa Tuwunaagu Yis, For Healing Our Spirit: Tlingit Oratory*, edited by Nora Marks Dauenhauer and Richard Dauenhauer. Copyright © 1990 by the Sealaska Heritage Foundation.

Selections from "Narrative of the Expedition," by John Burroughs, are reprinted by permission from *Alaska: The Harriman Expedition, 1899*. Copyright © by Dover Publications, Inc.

"No Road," by John Keeble, first appeared in a somewhat different form in *Out of the Channel: The Exxon Valdez Oil Spill in Prince William Sound*, by John Keeble, and is reprinted here by permission. Copyright © 1991 by John Keeble. Published by HarperCollins.

Selections by Peter Kalifornsky appeared in a somewhat different form in *K'tl'egh'i Sukdu / A Dena'ina Legacy: The Collected Writings of Peter Kalifornsky*, edited by James Kari and Alan Boreas, and are reprinted by permission. Copyright © 1991 by the Alaskan Native Language Center, College of Liberal Arts, University of Alaska — Fairbanks, and by Peter Kalifornsky.

Selections from *Notes on the Islands of the Unalashka District*, by Ivan Veniaminov, are reprinted by permission. Copyright © by the Limestone Press, Fairbanks, Alaska, 1984.

Selections from *Libby: The Alaskan Diaries of Libby Beaman, 1879–1880*, by Betty John, are reprinted by permission of Council Oak Publishing, Tulsa, Oklahoma. Copyright © 1987 by Betty John.

"We Are All Paddling a Kayak Through Open Tundra, Not a River," by Carolyn Kremers, is forthcoming in *Manoa: A Pacific Journal of International Writing* 6 (Winter 1994).

Selections from *A Place for Winter*, by Paul Tiulana and Vivian Senungetuk, are reprinted by permission. Copyright © 1987 by the CIRI Foundation, Anchorage, Alaska.

"Villages of the Dead," by John Muir, is reprinted from *The Wilderness World of John Muir*, edited by Edwin Way Teale. Copyright © 1954 by Houghton Mifflin Co.

"Outwitting the Arctic," by Sally Carrighar, is reprinted by permission from *Moonlight at Midday*, published by Alfred A. Knopf, Inc. Copyright © 1965 by Sally Carrighar.

"The Embrace of Names," by Richard Nelson, first appeared in a somewhat different form in *Northern Lights* 8 (Summer 1992). Reprinted by permission of Richard Nelson.

Selections from *Arctic Wild*, by Lois Crisler, are reprinted by permission, published by Harper and Row, Publishers. Copyright © 1973 by the estate of Lois Crisler.

Selections from *Shandaa: In My Lifetime*, by Belle Herbert, are reprinted by permission. Copyright © 1982 by the Alaskan Native Language Center, University of Alaska, and William Pfisterer.

"Up the Black to Chalkyitsik," by Edward Hoagland, first appeared in a somewhat different form in *The Guardian* (London). The longer version reproduced here appeared in *Balancing Acts: Essays by Edward Hoagland* (New York: Simon & Schuster, 1992). Copyright © 1992 by Edward Hoagland. Reprinted by permission of Simon and Schuster.

"Leaving Alaska," by John Haines, originally appeared in *Alaska*, December 1992. Reprinted by permission of John Haines.

Selections from I *Married Wyatt Earp: The Recollections of Josephine Sarah Marcus Earp*, edited by Glenn G. Boyer, are reprinted by permission. Copyright © 1976 by the University of Arizona Press.

"The Wake of the Unseen Object," by Tom Kizzia, is reprinted by permission from *The Wake of the Unseen Object*, published by Holt and Co., Inc. Copyright © 1991 by Tom Kizzia.

The editors would like to thank the University of Colorado at Boulder for providing funds that helped make this book possible and Deirdre Perry for her generous help in the preparation of the manuscript.

About the Editors

Robert Hedin was born and raised in Minnesota and holds degrees from Luther College and the University of Alaska. His books include *Snow Country, At the Home-Altar, County O,* and *Tornadoes.* He also edited *In the Dreamlight: Twenty-one Alaskan Writers* with David Stark and *Alaska: Reflections on Land and Spirit* (University of Arizona Press, 1989) with Gary Holthaus. He has taught at Sheldon Jackson College, the Anchorage and Fairbanks campuses of the University of Alaska, and was Poet-in-Residence at Wake Forest University in Winston-Salem, North Carolina, from 1980 to 1982. He presently lives in Frontenac, Minnesota.

Gary Holthaus was born in Dubuque, Iowa, and holds degrees from Cornell College, Boston University, and Western Montana University. His books include *Unexpected Manna, Circling Back,* and *A Society to Match the Scenery: Personal Visions of the Future of the American West,* which he edited. He taught school in Naknek, Alaska, and later at Alaska Methodist University in Anchorage. From 1972 to 1991 he was Executive Director of the Alaska Humanities Forum, a statewide program of the National Endowment for the Humanities. Currently he is Director of the Center of the American West and teaches at the University of Colorado in Boulder.